THE JOURNEY OF SELF-DISCOVERY

Books by His Divine Grace A. C. Bhaktivedanta Swami Prabhupāda

Bhagavad-gītā As It Is
Śrīmad-Bhāgavatam (completed by disciples)
Śrī Caitanya-caritāmṛta
Kṛṣṇa, the Supreme Personality of Godhead
Teachings of Lord Caitanya
The Nectar of Devotion
The Nectar of Instruction
Śrī Īśopaniṣad
Light of the Bhāgavata
Easy Journey to Other Planets
Teachings of Lord Kapila, the Son of Devahūti
Teachings of Queen Kuntī
Message of Godhead
The Science of Self-Realization
The Perfection of Yoga
Beyond Birth and Death
On the Way to Kṛṣṇa
Rāja-vidyā: The King of Knowledge
Elevation to Kṛṣṇa Consciousness
Kṛṣṇa Consciousness: The Matchless Gift
Kṛṣṇa Consciousness: The Topmost Yoga System
Perfect Questions, Perfect Answers
Life Comes from Life
The Nārada-bhakti-sūtra (completed by disciples)
The Mukunda-mālā-stotra (completed by disciples)
Geetār-gān (Bengali)
Vairāgya-vidyā (Bengali)
Buddhi-yoga (Bengali)
Bhakti-ratna-boli (Bengali)
Back to Godhead magazine (founder)

Books compiled from the teachings of Śrīla Prabhupāda after his lifetime

The Journey of Self-Discovery
Civilization and Transcendence
The Laws of Nature
Renunciation Through Wisdom
Beyond Illusion and Doubt

Available from www.krishna.com and www.blservices.com

THE JOURNEY OF SELF-DISCOVERY

Articles from
Back to Godhead
magazine

His Divine Grace
A. C. Bhaktivedanta Swami Prabhupāda
Founder-*Ācārya* of the International Society for Krishna Consciousness

THE BHAKTIVEDANTA BOOK TRUST

Readers interested in the subject matter of this book are invited to contact the International Society for Krishna Consciousness (see address list in back of book) or any of the following information centers.

Karuna Bhavan
Bankhouse Rd, Lesmahagow
Lanarkshire, ML11 0ES, Scotland
Tel: +44 (0)1555 894790
Fax: +44 (0)1555 894526
karunabhavan@aol.com
www.iskcon.org.uk/scotland

ISKCON
83 Middle Abbey Street
Dublin 1, Republic of Ireland
Tel: +353 (0)1 8729775
mail@krishna.ie
www.krishna.ie

ISKCON Reader Services
P. O. Box 730, Watford
WD25 8ZE, United Kingdom
Tel: +44 (0)1923 857244
readerservices@pamho.net
www.iskcon.org.uk

Cover: Lord Śrī Kṛṣṇa invites all conditioned souls suffering in the desert of the material world to enter upon the path of self-discovery – the path of *bhakti-yoga,* or Kṛṣṇa consciousness. Ultimately this path leads one to His eternal, blissful, spiritual abode, where Kṛṣṇa and His intimate friends enjoy endless pastimes of love.

The Journey of Self-Discovery consists of articles published in *Back to Godhead* magazine between September 1975 and February 1985. The editors were Śrīla Prabhupāda's disciples Hayagrīva Dāsa, Jayādvaita Swami, and Draviḍa Dāsa.

www.krishna.com

ISBN 978-1-84599-062-6

Printed in 2007

Contents

Introduction

Are you in any way dissatisfied with your life as it now stands? Has the pursuit, or even the achievement, of the goals you have set for yourself become somewhat frustrating? If so, read on.

For one acquainted with the spiritual wisdom of India, the ideal life is not a fast-paced competitive run through a self-serve consumer paradise. There is a higher measure of success and happiness than the number of high-gloss gadgets, baubles, and thrills one can zoom through the checkout counter with – before Time runs out.

An awakened person will try to learn something worthwhile along the way, to gradually accumulate assets of permanent value. In the final analysis, the supreme accomplishment is to improve significantly the one possession that is really ours to keep – our consciousness, our sense of identity, our inner self. All else eventually slips away.

Seen in this way, life becomes a journey of self-discovery, and that is the theme of this book. *The Journey of Self-Discovery* is your guide to a new way of looking at life, a way proven to lead you to higher levels of awareness and satisfaction.

Thousands of people like yourself are already experiencing these results. All it takes is some expert guidance, the kind available from a person who has already completed the journey, who knows the ways and means by which you can arrive safely at your destination.

In *The Journey of Self-Discovery* you will become intimately acquainted with a spiritual master about whom Harvey Cox, of Harvard's School of Divinity, said, "Śrīla Prabhupāda is, of course, only one of thousands of teachers. But in another sense, he is one in a thousand, maybe one in a million." According to Dr. Cox, one of America's leading Christian theologians, Śrīla Prabhupāda's life was "pointed proof that one can be a transmitter of truth and still be a vital and singular person."

Śrīla Prabhupāda, the founding spiritual master of the International Society for Krishna Consciousness, translated over forty volumes of the most essential works of Vedic literature. Complete sets of these books, with original Sanskrit and Bengali texts, have been purchased by thousands of university libraries around the world, and dozens of scholars have praised them.

But that is not what you will find in *The Journey of Self-Discovery.* In these pages you will see Śrīla Prabhupāda taking the essential truths of the timeless Vedic wisdom of India and communicating them live to persons like yourself – in talks, conversations, and interviews. With gravity and wit, roses and thunderbolts, Śrīla Prabhupāda delivers transcendental knowledge with maximum impact and precision.

All the selections printed in *The Journey of Self-Discovery* originally appeared in *Back to Godhead,* the magazine Śrīla Prabhupāda founded in India in 1944. When he came to America and started the Hare Kṛṣṇa movement in 1966, he requested his new followers to take up the task of publishing the magazine. Ever since, *Back to Godhead* has served the vital function of bringing the Vedic knowledge to the contemporary world, addressing the spiritual needs of people confronting the frustrations of modern life.

Authoritative and informative, *The Journey of Self-Discovery* is also easy to read. The anthology format allows you to approach the book in a variety of ways. You can read *The Journey of Self-Discovery* from start to finish, proceeding through the systematically arranged selections. Or you can glance over the table of contents and find a selection of particular interest. Because each selection is short and complete in itself, you can easily explore topics that attract your attention without having to go through the entire book.

The principal lesson of *The Journey of Self-Discovery* is that our conscious selfhood is not an accidental cosmic side-effect, a fleeting electromagnetic discharge generated by a temporary configuration of subatomic particles at some point in space and time. Rather, each center of consciousness is itself an absolute, irreducible unit of reality. As Śrīla Prabhupāda tells physicist Gregory Benford, "We don't say that scientific knowledge is useless. Mechanics, electronics – this is also knowledge. . . . But the central point is *ātma-jñāna* – self-knowledge, knowledge of the soul."

And after we understand the soul, the quest for knowledge continues. Śrīla Prabhupāda tells a press conference in Los Angeles: "In the background of this body you can find the soul, whose presence is perceivable by consciousness. Similarly, in the universal body of the cosmic manifestation, one can perceive the presence of the Supreme Lord, or the Absolute Truth, by virtue of the presence of . . . Superconsciousness."

Just as we are individual and personal, the Superconsciousness is also individual and personal. In the Vedic scriptures, the identity of the Superconscious Self is revealed to be Kṛṣṇa, the Supreme Personality of Godhead. Śrīla Prabhupāda describes Kṛṣṇa as "the greatest artist," the source of all beauty and attraction.

The real key to happiness and satisfaction, Śrīla Prabhupāda explains, is discovering the eternal personal link between ourselves and the Superconsciousness. This state is called Kṛṣṇa consciousness, and in *The Journey of Self-Discovery* you will learn how to achieve this, the highest and most pleasurable consciousness, in your own life.

Kṛṣṇa consciousness is loving consciousness. In the selection "Absolute Love," Śrīla Prabhupāda says to his audience, "Everyone is frustrated – husbands, wives, boys, girls. Everywhere there is frustration, because our loving propensity is not being utilized properly." Śrīla Prabhupāda then goes on to explain how love is most fully experienced when directed toward the Supreme Person, Kṛṣṇa, who can perfectly and completely reciprocate with everyone.

This is the secret of lasting happiness. In "Kṛṣṇa, Enchanter of the Soul," Śrīla Prabhupāda advises, "A man is attracted by a woman, a woman is attracted by a man, and when they are united in sex, their attachment for this material world increases more and more. . . . But our business is not to be attracted by the glimmer of this material world; our business is to be attracted by Kṛṣṇa. And when we become attracted by the beauty of Kṛṣṇa, we will lose our attraction for the false beauty of this material world."

Here Śrīla Prabhupāda stands in contrast to the many so-called spiritual teachers who promise their followers they can have it all – unrestricted material enjoyment as well as spiritual profit. In "Show-Bottle Spiritualists Exposed," Śrīla Prabhupāda gives an unsparing critique of deceptive *gurus* and spiritualists who mislead their followers.

Śrīla Prabhupāda did not manufacture his own spiritual process, with a view to personal profit. Rather, he freely taught the specific meditation technique recommended in the *Vedas* for this age. In "Meditation Through Transcendental Sound," Śrīla Prabhupāda tells students at Boston's Northeastern University, "If you take up this simple process – chanting Hare Kṛṣṇa, Hare Kṛṣṇa, Kṛṣṇa Kṛṣṇa, Hare Hare/ Hare Rāma, Hare Rāma, Rāma Rāma, Hare Hare – you are immediately elevated to the transcendental platform."

Those who progress on the journey of self-discovery are better able to understand and solve the world's problems. In "Material Problems, Spiritual Solutions," we learn from Śrīla Prabhupāda how we can practically apply Kṛṣṇa consciousness to relieve the widespread suffering brought on by violence and food shortages.

In the early 1970s, Śrīla Prabhupāda gave a remarkably foresighted analysis of the failure of the communist system of government to provide happiness for its people. You will find this striking conversation in section seven, "Perspectives on Science and Philosophy."

In "Evolution in Fact and Fantasy" Śrīla Prabhupāda says, "We accept evolution, but not that the forms of the species are changing. The bodies are already there, but the soul is evolving by changing bodies and by transmigrating from one body to another. . . . The defect of the evolutionists is that they have no information of the soul."

Ultimately, the journey of self-discovery leads from this material world to the spiritual world. In "Entering the Spiritual World," Śrīla Prabhupāda tells his listeners, "Everything in the spiritual world is substantial and original. This material world is only an imitation. . . . It is just like a cinematographic picture, in which we see only the shadow of the real thing."

So for those who suspect that the real thing is something more than a soft drink, *The Journey of Self-Discovery* will illuminate the path that leads to life's ultimate, most perfect destination.

And for those who may not regard themselves as seekers but are nevertheless curious about the philosophy of the Hare Kṛṣṇa movement, *The Journey of Self-Discovery* provides a thorough yet compact introduction.

The Publishers

1

The Journey of Self-Discovery

The Physics of the Self

In October 1973, Dr. Gregory Benford, an associate professor of physics at the University of California at Irvine, visits Śrīla Prabhupāda in the garden of the Los Angeles Kṛṣṇa center. In the course of their intriguing discussion about the possibility of scientific understanding of the soul, Śrīla Prabhupāda declares, "We don't say that this scientific knowledge is useless. Mechanics, electronics – this is also knowledge . . . but the central point is ātma-jñāna *– self-knowledge, knowledge of the soul."*

Śrīla Prabhupāda: What is the current scientific knowledge about the spirit soul?
Dr. Benford: We have virtually no scientific knowledge about the soul.
Śrīla Prabhupāda: Therefore you have actually made no advancement in scientific knowledge.
Dr. Benford: Well, scientific knowledge is a different class of knowledge.
Śrīla Prabhupāda: Perhaps. There are so many departments of knowledge: the medical study of the body, the psychological study of the mind, and ultimately spiritual, transcendental knowledge. The body and mind are simply the coverings of the spirit soul, just as this shirt and coat are coverings for your body. If you simply take care of the shirt and coat and neglect the person who is covered by this shirt and coat, do you think that this is advancement of knowledge?
Dr. Benford: I think that there is no category of knowledge that is useless.
Śrīla Prabhupāda: We don't say that this scientific knowledge is useless. Mechanics, electronics – this is also knowledge. But different departments of knowledge differ in their comparative importance. For example, if someone wants to cook nicely, this is also a science. There

are many different departments of knowledge, but the central point is *ātma-jñāna* – self-knowledge, the knowledge of the soul.

Dr. Benford: The only form of knowledge that is verifiable – that is, verifiable in the sense of getting everybody to agree with it – is that which can be proved logically or experimentally.

Śrīla Prabhupāda: The science of the self can be verified logically.

Dr. Benford: How so?

Śrīla Prabhupāda: Just consider your body. You once had the body of a child, but now you don't have that body anymore; you have a different body. Yet anyone can understand that you once had the body of a child. So your body has changed, but you are still remaining.

Dr. Benford: I am not so sure it is the same "I."

Śrīla Prabhupāda: Yes, you are the same "I." Just as the parents of a child will say, after he has grown up, "Oh, just see how our son has grown!" He is the same person; his parents say so, his friends say so, his family says so – everyone says so. This is the evidence. You have to accept this point, because there is so much evidence. Your mother will deny that you are a different person, even though you have a different body.

Dr. Benford: But I may not be the same being that I was.

Śrīla Prabhupāda: Correct. "Not the same" means, for example, that a young child may talk nonsense now, but when he gets an adult body he does not speak foolishly. Although he is the same person, along with his change in body he has developed different consciousness. But the spirit soul, the person, is the same. He acts according to his body, that's all – according to his circumstances. A dog, for example, is also a spirit soul, but because he has a dog's body he lives and acts like a dog. Similarly, when the spirit soul has a child's body, he acts like a child. When he has a different body, the same soul acts like a man. According to circumstances his activities are changing, but he is the same. For example, now you are a scientist. In your childhood you were not a scientist, so your dealings at that time were not those of a scientist. One's dealings may change according to circumstances, but the person is the same.

Therefore, the conclusion is *tathā dehāntara-prāptir dhīras tatra na muhyati:* "When this body is finished, the soul gives it up and accepts another body." [*Bhagavad-gītā* 2.13] *Tathā dehāntara. Dehāntara* means "another body." This is our Sanskrit knowledge from the *Bhagavad-gītā*. When the spirit soul is injected into the womb of a woman, it forms a little body. Gradually, through the emulsification of secretions, the body develops to the size of a pea because of the presence of the spirit soul. Gradually the body develops nine holes – eyes, ears, mouth, nostrils, genitals, and rectum. In this way the body is developed to completion in seven months. Then consciousness comes.

Dr. Benford: At seven months?

Śrīla Prabhupāda: Yes. The child wants to come out. He feels uncomfortable; therefore he prays to God to kindly release him from the bondage. He promises that when he gets out he will become a devotee of God. So after nine months he comes out of the womb. But unless his parents are devotees, due to circumstances he forgets God. Only if the father and mother are devotees does he continue his God consciousness. Therefore, it is a great fortune to take birth in a family of Vaiṣṇavas, those who are God conscious. This God consciousness is real scientific knowledge.

Dr. Benford: Is it true that the children of all such parents are somewhat spiritually superior to the children of other parents?

Śrīla Prabhupāda: Generally, yes. They get the opportunity of being trained by the mother and father. Fortunately, my father was a great devotee, so I received this training from the very beginning. Somehow or other I had this spark of Kṛṣṇa consciousness, and my father detected it. Then I accepted my spiritual master. In this way I have come to this stage of *sannyāsa* [the renounced monastic order]. I am very much indebted to my father, for he took care of me in such a way that I became perfectly Kṛṣṇa conscious. My father used to receive many saintly persons at our home, and to every one of them he used to say, "Kindly bless my son so that he may become a servant of Rādhārāṇī [Lord Kṛṣṇa's eternal consort]." That was his only ambition. He taught me how to play the *mṛdaṅga* drum, although sometimes my mother was not very satisfied. She would say, "Why are you teaching him to play *mṛdaṅga*?" But my father would say, "No, no, he must learn a little *mṛdaṅga*." My father was very affectionate to me. Therefore, if due to past pious activities one gets a good father and mother, that is a great chance for advancing in Kṛṣṇa consciousness.

Dr. Benford: What will happen to you and your students next?
Śrīla Prabhupāda: We are going back to Kṛṣṇa. We have got everything: Kṛṣṇa's name, Kṛṣṇa's address, Kṛṣṇa's form, Kṛṣṇa's activities. We know everything, and we are going there. Kṛṣṇa promises this in the *Bhagavad-gītā* [4.9]:

janma karma ca me divyam
evaṁ yo vetti tattvataḥ
tyaktvā dehaṁ punar janma
naiti mām eti so 'rjuna

"One who knows Me in truth, scientifically," Kṛṣṇa says, "is eligible to enter into the kingdom of God. Upon leaving the body, he does not take his birth again in this material world, but attains My eternal abode."
Dr. Benford: How do you know that people return in some other form?
Śrīla Prabhupāda: We see that there are so many forms. Where do these different forms come from – the form of the dog, the form of the cat, the form of the tree, the form of the reptile, the forms of the insects, the forms of the fish? What is your explanation for all these different forms? That you do not know.
Dr. Benford: Evolution.
Śrīla Prabhupāda: Not exactly. The different species are already existing. "Fish," "tiger," "man" – all of these are already existing. It is just like the different types of apartments here in Los Angeles. You may occupy one of them according to your ability to pay rent, but all types of apartments are nevertheless existing at the same time. Similarly, the living entity, according to his *karma,* is given facility to occupy one of these bodily forms. But there is evolution, also – spiritual evolution. From the fish, the soul evolves to plant life. From plant forms the living entity enters an insect body. From the insect body the next stage is bird, then beast, and finally the spirit soul may evolve to the human form of life. And from the human form, if one becomes qualified, he may evolve further. Otherwise, he must again enter the evolutionary cycle. Therefore, this human form of life is an important juncture in the evolutionary development of the living entity.

In the *Bhagavad-gītā* [9.25] Kṛṣṇa says,

yānti deva-vratā devān
pitṝn yānti pitṛ-vratāḥ
bhūtāni yānti bhūtejyā
yānti mad-yājino 'pi mām

In other words, whatever you like you can achieve. There are different *lokas,* or planetary systems, and you can go to the higher planetary systems where the demigods live and take a body there, or you can go where the Pitās, or ancestors, live. You can take a body here in Bhūloka, the earthly planetary system; or you can go to the planet of God, Kṛṣṇaloka. This method of transferring oneself at the time of death to whatever planet one chooses is called *yoga.* There is a physical process of *yoga,* a philosophical process of *yoga,* and a devotional process of *yoga.* The devotees can go directly to the planet where Kṛṣṇa is.

Dr. Benford: Undoubtedly you are aware that there are a few people, both in Eastern and Western society, who feel it a bit more intellectually justifiable to be completely agnostic about matters of theology. They feel, more or less, that if God had wanted us to know something more about Him, then He would have made it more easily apprehendable.

Śrīla Prabhupāda: Then you don't believe in God?

Dr. Benford: I don't *not* believe in God; I'm just not forming an opinion until I have some evidence.

Śrīla Prabhupāda: But do you think that there is a God or not?

Dr. Benford: I have a suspicion that there may be, but it is unverified.

Śrīla Prabhupāda: But you think sometimes that there may be God, do you not?

Dr. Benford: Yes.

Śrīla Prabhupāda: So you are in doubt, suspicion – you are not certain – but your inclination is that you think there is a God, is it not? Your knowledge being imperfect, you are in doubt, that's all. Otherwise you are inclined to think of God. But because you are a scientific man, unless you perceive it scientifically, you do not accept. That is your position. But from your side, you believe in God.

Dr. Benford: Sometimes.

Śrīla Prabhupāda: Yes. Sometimes or at all times – it doesn't matter. That is the position of everyone. As long as one is in the human form of life, he has a dormant consciousness of God. It simply has to be developed by proper training. It is just like anything else in life. For example, you have become a scientist by proper training, proper education. Similarly, the dormant consciousness of God, or Kṛṣṇa, is there in everyone. It simply requires proper education to awaken it. However, this education is not given in the universities. That is the defect in modern education. Although the inclination to be Kṛṣṇa conscious is there, the authorities are unfortunately not giving any education about God. Therefore people are becoming godless, and they are feeling baffled in obtaining the true joy and satisfaction of life.

In San Diego, some priestly orders are going to hold a meeting to investigate the reasons why people are becoming averse to religion and not coming to church. But the cause is simple: Because your government does not know that life, especially human life, is meant for understanding God, they are supporting all the departments of knowledge very nicely – except the principal department, God consciousness.

Dr. Benford: So, of course, the reason is separation of Church and State.

Śrīla Prabhupāda: Reasons there may be many, but the principal reason is that this age is the Kali-yuga [the age of quarrel and hypocrisy]. People are not very intelligent; therefore they are trying to avoid this department of knowledge, the most important department of knowledge. And they are simply busy in the departments of knowledge in which the animals are also busy. Your advancement of knowledge is comprised of four things – eating, sleeping, mating, and defending. For example, you are discovering so many lethal weapons, and the politicians are taking advantage of it for defending. You are discovering so many chemicals to check pregnancy, and people are using them to increase sex life.

Dr. Benford: What do you think about the moon mission?

Śrīla Prabhupāda: That is also sleeping. You have spent so much money to go there and sleep, that's all. Otherwise, what can you do there?

Dr. Benford: You can go there and learn.

Śrīla Prabhupāda: You go there and sleep, that's all. Sleeping. You are spending billions and getting nothing in return.

Dr. Benford: It's worth more than that.

Śrīla Prabhupāda: No, nothing more, because these four principles –

eating, sleeping, mating, and defending – are the background. If you have no knowledge beyond this body, you cannot go beyond this bodily jurisdiction. You may have very gorgeous, polished bodily knowledge, but your whole range of activities is within these four principles of eating, sleeping, mating, and defending. This knowledge is prevalent among the lower animals, also. They know how to eat, how to sleep, how to have sexual intercourse, and how to defend.

Dr. Benford: But they don't know anything about nuclear physics!

Śrīla Prabhupāda: That does not mean that you are improved over the animals. It is the same thing – only polished. You are improving from the bullock cart to the car, that's all – simply a transformation of material knowledge.

Dr. Benford: There is knowledge about the structure of the physical world.

Śrīla Prabhupāda: But it is a waste of energy, because in your activities you cannot go beyond this bodily jurisdiction of eating, sleeping, mating, and defending. The dog may sleep on the ground, and you may sleep in a very nice apartment, but when you sleep your enjoyment and the dog's enjoyment are the same. You may have so many electrical appliances and other material conveniences, but when you sleep you forget everything. Therefore this gorgeous sleeping accommodation is simply a waste of time.

Dr. Benford: You seem to place emphasis on what knowledge does for you. What about the sheer joy of discovering how nature works? For example, now we think that we understand matter like this [*pointing to the grass*]. We think that we know from experiments, theory, and analysis that it is made up of particles that we cannot see, and we can analyze the properties of it through experiment. We know that it is made up of molecules. We understand some of the forces that hold it together, and this is the first time we knew this. We didn't know it before.

Śrīla Prabhupāda: But what is the benefit? Even if you knew every particle of this grass, what would be the benefit? The grass is growing. It will grow with or without your knowledge. You may know it or not know it, but it will not make any difference. Anything you like you may study from a material, analytical point of view. Any nonsense thing you take you can study and study and compile a voluminous book. But what will be the use of it?

Dr. Benford: I seem to view the world as the sum of its component parts.

Śrīla Prabhupāda: Suppose I take this grass. I can write volumes of books – when it came into existence, when it died, what the fibers are, what the molecules are. In so many ways I can describe this insignificant foliage. But what is the use of it?

Dr. Benford: If it has no use, why did God put it there? Isn't it worthwhile studying?

Śrīla Prabhupāda: Our point is that you would rather study the insignificant grass than the God who has created everything. If you could understand Him, then automatically you would understand the grass. But you want to separate His grass from Him, to study it separately. In this way you can compile volumes and volumes on the subject; but why waste your intelligence in that way? The branch of a tree is beautiful as long as it is attached to the main trunk, but as soon as you cut it off it will dry up. Therefore, what is the use of studying the dried-up branch? It is a waste of intelligence.

Dr. Benford: But why is it a waste?

Śrīla Prabhupāda: Certainly it is a waste, because the result is not useful.

Dr. Benford: Well, what is "useful"?

Śrīla Prabhupāda: It is useful to know yourself – what you are.

Dr. Benford: Why is knowledge of myself better than knowledge of a plant?

Śrīla Prabhupāda: If you understand what you are, then you understand other things. That is called *ātma-tattva, ātma-jñāna,* self-knowledge. *That* is important. I am a spirit soul, and I am passing through so many species of life. But what is my position? I don't wish to die, because I am afraid to change bodies. Therefore, I am afraid of death. This question should be raised first: I don't want unhappiness, but unhappiness comes. I don't want death, but death comes. I don't want disease, but disease comes. I don't want to become an old man, but old age comes anyway. What is the reason that these things are coming by force? Who is enforcing these things? I do not know, but these are the real problems. I don't want excessive heat, but there is excessive heat. Why? Who is enforcing these things? Why are they being enforced? I don't want this heat; what have I done? These are real questions, not just studying foliage and writing volumes of books. That is a waste of energy. *Study yourself.*

Understanding the Living Force

In a statement delivered at a press conference in Los Angeles in December of 1968, Śrīla Prabhupāda challenges the world's intellectual leaders to review their definition of what constitutes life. "In the background of this body you can find the soul, whose presence is perceivable by dint of consciousness. Similarly, in the universal body of the cosmic manifestation, one can perceive the presence of the Supreme Lord, or the Absolute Truth, by virtue of the presence of . . . Superconsciousness."

The International Society for Krishna Consciousness is a movement aiming at the spiritual reorientation of mankind through the simple process of chanting the holy names of God. The human life is meant for ending the miseries of material existence. Our present-day society is trying to end these miseries by material progress. However, it is visible to all that in spite of extensive material progress, human society is not peaceful.

The reason is that the human being is essentially a spirit soul. It is the spirit soul which is the background of the development of the material body. However the materialistic scientists may deny the spiritual existence in the background of the living force, there is no better understanding than accepting this living force as ultimately the spirit soul within the body.

The body is changing – from one form to another – but the spirit soul is existing eternally, without changes. This fact we can experience even in our own life. Since the beginning of our material body in the womb of our mother, our body has been changing from one shape to another at every second and at every minute. This process is generally known as "growth," but actually it is a change of body.

On this earth we see change of day and night and change of season.

The more primitive mentality attributes this phenomenon to changes occurring in the sun. For example, in the winter primitive people think the sun is getting weaker, and at night they presume, sometimes, that the sun is dead. With more advanced knowledge we see that the sun is not changing at all in this way. Seasonal and diurnal changes are attributed to the change of the relative positions of the earth and the sun.

Similarly, we experience bodily changes: from embryo to child to youth to maturity to old age to death. The less intelligent mentality presumes that after death the spirit soul's existence is forever finished, just as primitive tribes believe that the sun dies at sunset. Actually, however, the sun is rising in another part of the world. Similarly, the soul is accepting another type of body. When the body gets old like an old garment and is no longer usable, the soul accepts another body, just as we accept a new suit of clothes. Modern civilization is practically unaware of this truth.

People do not care about the constitutional position of the soul. There are different departments of knowledge in different universities and many technological institutions, all to study and understand the subtle laws of material nature, and there are medical research laboratories to study the physiological condition of the material body, but there is no institution to study the constitutional position of the soul. This is the greatest drawback of materialistic civilization, which is simply an external manifestation of the soul.

People are enamored of the glittering manifestation of the cosmic body or the individual body, but they do not try to understand the basic principle of this glittering situation. The body looks very beautiful, working with full energy and exhibiting great traits of talent and wonderful brainwork. But as soon as the soul is away from the body, this entire glittering situation of the body becomes useless. Even the great scientists who have offered many wonderful scientific contributions have been unable to trace out the personal self, which is the cause of such wonderful discoveries.

The Kṛṣṇa consciousness movement, therefore, is basically trying to teach this science of the soul, not in any dogmatic way, but through complete scientific and philosophical understanding. In the background of this body you can find the soul, whose presence is perceivable by dint of consciousness. Similarly, in the universal body of the cosmic manifestation, one can perceive the presence of the Supreme Lord, or the Absolute Truth, by virtue of the presence of the Supersoul and superconsciousness.

The Absolute Truth is systematically explained in the *Vedānta-sūtra* (generally known as the Vedānta philosophy), which in turn is elaborately explained by the *Śrīmad-Bhāgavatam,* a commentary by the same author. The *Bhagavad-gītā* is the preliminary study of the *Śrīmad-Bhāgavatam* for understanding the constitutional position of the Supreme Lord, or the Absolute Truth.

An individual soul is understood in three aspects: first as the consciousness pervading the entire body, then as the spirit soul within the heart, and ultimately as a person. Similarly, the Absolute Truth is first realized as impersonal Brahman, then as localized Supersoul (Paramātmā), and at the end as the Supreme Personality of Godhead, Kṛṣṇa. Kṛṣṇa is all-inclusive. Or in other words, Kṛṣṇa is simultaneously Brahman, Paramātmā, and the Personality of Godhead, just as every one of us is simultaneously consciousness, soul, and person.

The individual person and the Supreme Person are qualitatively one but quantitatively different. Just like the drop of seawater and the vast mass of seawater – both are qualitatively one. The chemical composition of the drop of seawater and that of the mass of seawater are one and the same. But the quantity of salt and other minerals in the whole sea is many, many times greater than the quantity of salt and other minerals contained in the drop of seawater.

The Kṛṣṇa consciousness movement upholds the individuality of the soul and the Supreme Soul. From the Vedic *Upaniṣads* we can understand that both the Supreme Person, or God, and the individual person are eternal living entities. The difference is that the supreme living entity, or Supreme Person, maintains all the innumerable other living entities. In the Christian way of understanding, the same principle is admitted, because in the Bible it is taught that the contingent entities should pray to the Supreme Father so that He may supply means of maintenance and give pardon for their sinful activities.

So it is understood from every source of scriptural injunction that the Supreme Lord, or Kṛṣṇa, is the maintainer of the contingent living entity and that it is the duty of the contingent entity to feel obliged to the Supreme Lord. This is the whole background of religious principles. Without these acknowledgments there is chaos, as we find in our daily experience at the present moment.

Everyone is trying to become the Supreme Lord, either socially, politically, or individually. Therefore there is competition for this false lordship, and there is chaos all over the world – individually, nationally, socially, collectively. The Kṛṣṇa consciousness movement is trying to establish the supremacy of the Absolute Personality of Godhead. One who has attained a human body and intelligence is meant for this understanding, because this consciousness makes his life successful.

This Kṛṣṇa consciousness movement is not a new introduction by mental speculators. Actually, this movement was started by Kṛṣṇa Himself. On the Battlefield of Kurukṣetra, at least five thousand years ago, the movement was presented by Kṛṣṇa in the *Bhagavad-gītā*. From *Bhagavad-gītā* we can also understand that He had spoken this system of consciousness long, long before – at least forty million years ago – when He had imparted it to the sun-god, Vivasvān.

So this movement is not at all new. It is coming down in disciplic succession and from all the great leaders of India's Vedic civilization, including Śaṅkarācārya, Rāmānujācārya, Madhvācārya, Viṣṇu Svāmī, Nimbārka, and lately, about 480 years ago, Lord Caitanya. The disciplic system is still being followed today. This *Bhagavad-gītā* is also very widely used in all parts of the world by great scholars, philosophers, and religionists. But in most cases the principles are not followed as they are. The Kṛṣṇa consciousness movement presents the principles of the *Bhagavad-gītā* as they are – without any misinterpretation.

From the *Bhagavad-gītā* we can understand five main principles, namely God, the living entity, the material and spiritual nature, time, and activities. Out of these five items, God, the living entity, nature (material or spiritual), and time are eternal. But activities are not eternal.

Activities in the material nature are different from activities in the spiritual nature. Though the spirit soul is eternal (as we have explained), activities performed under the influence of the material nature are temporary. The Kṛṣṇa consciousness movement aims at placing the spirit soul in his eternal activities. We can practice eternal activities even when we are materially engaged. To act spiritually simply requires direction, but it is possible, under the prescribed rules and regulations.

The Kṛṣṇa consciousness movement teaches these spiritual activities, and if one is trained in such spiritual activities, one is transferred to the spiritual world, of which we get ample evidence from the Vedic literatures, including the *Bhagavad-gītā.* The spiritually trained person can be transferred to the spiritual world easily – by change of consciousness.

Consciousness is always present, because it is the symptom of the living spirit soul, but at the present moment our consciousness is materially contaminated. For instance, water pouring down from a cloud is pure, but as soon as the water comes in touch with the earth it becomes muddy – immediately. Yet if we filter the same water, the original clearness can be regained. Similarly, Kṛṣṇa consciousness is the process of clearing our consciousness. And as soon as our consciousness is clear and pure, we are eligible to be transferred to the spiritual world for our eternal life of knowledge and bliss. This is what we are hankering for in this material world, but we are being frustrated at every step on account of material contamination. Therefore, this Kṛṣṇa consciousness movement should be taken very seriously by the leaders of human society.

The Science of Spiritual Life

What happens to the conscious self at the time of death? On October 10, 1975, in Westville, South Africa, Śrīla Prabhupāda explains the science of reincarnation to Dr. S.P. Oliver, Rector of the University of Durban.

Dr. Oliver: We are left in this twentieth century, this last part of the century, with a new global search for the truth about the spiritual. We, of course, in the Western world, are not familiar with the *Bhagavad-gītā*. Our problem is basically, I think, the one that you raised in your lecture: How do we make the spiritual a scientific reality? And I think you were quite right. I think really few people get the point that you were trying to make – that this is a scientific matter.
Śrīla Prabhupāda: That is the beginning of the *Bhagavad-gītā* – scientifically presenting spiritual knowledge. Therefore I raised the question, What is transmigration of the soul? Nobody could reply properly. We are changing bodies. There are so many varieties of bodies, and we may enter into any one of them after death. This is the real problem of life. *Prakṛteḥ kriyamāṇāni guṇaiḥ karmāṇi sarvaśaḥ:* Nature is working, providing us with material bodies. This body is a machine. This machine, just like a car, has been offered to us by material nature, by the order of God, Kṛṣṇa. So the real purpose of life is to stop this perpetual transmigration from one body to another, one body to another, and revive our original, spiritual position, so that we can live an eternal, blissful life of knowledge. That is the aim of life.
Dr. Oliver: The conception of transmigration is not, of course, in the Christian religion.
Śrīla Prabhupāda: It's not a question of religion. Religion is a kind of faith that develops according to time and circumstances. The reality is

that we are spirit souls. By the laws of material nature, we are carried from one body to another. Sometimes we are happy, sometimes distressed; sometimes in the heavenly planets, sometimes in lower planets. And human life is meant for stopping this process of transmigration and reviving our original consciousness. We have to go back home, back to Godhead, and live eternally. This is the whole scheme of Vedic literature.

The *Bhagavad-gītā* gives the synopsis of how to act in this life. Therefore, through the teachings of the *Bhagavad-gītā* we can begin to understand the constitutional position of the soul.

First of all we have to understand what we are. Am I this body or something else? This is the first question. I was trying to answer this, but some people in my audience thought it was a kind of Hindu culture. It is not Hindu culture. It is a scientific conception. You are a child for some time. Then you become a boy. Then you become a young man, and then you become an old man. In this way you are always changing bodies. This is a fact. It is not a Hindu conception of religion. It applies to everyone.

dehino 'smin yathā dehe
kaumāraṁ yauvanaṁ jarā
tathā dehāntara-prāptir
dhīras tatra na muhyati

[*To a devotee:*] Find this verse.

Devotee: [*reads*] "As the embodied soul continuously passes, in this body, from boyhood to youth to old age, the soul similarly passes into another body at death. A sober person is not bewildered by such a change." [*Bhagavad-gītā* 2.13]

Śrīla Prabhupāda: In the *Bhagavad-gītā* everything is explained very logically, very scientifically. It is not a sentimental explanation.

Dr. Oliver: The problem, as I see it, is how to get modern man to make an in-depth study of what is contained or outlined in this book, especially when he's caught up in an educational system that denies a place for this very concept or even the philosophy of it. There is either complete neutrality or just a simple rejection of these truths.

Śrīla Prabhupāda: They do not accept the soul?
Dr. Oliver: They accept the soul. I think so. But they do not care to analyze what it means.
Śrīla Prabhupāda: Without analyzing this, what is their situation? First of all, they should analyze the distinction between a dead body and a living body. The body is always dead, just like a motorcar without a driver. The car is always a lump of matter. Similarly, this body, with or without the soul, is a lump of matter.
Dr. Oliver: It isn't worth very much. I think around fifty-six cents.
Śrīla Prabhupāda: But if one cannot distinguish between the car and the driver of the car, then he is just like a child. A child thinks the car is running automatically. But that is his foolishness. There is a driver. The child may not know, but when he is a grown-up and has been educated and *still* he does not know, then what is the meaning of his education?
Dr. Oliver: In the Western world the whole range of education covers only primary, secondary, and tertiary education. There is no place for an in-depth study of the soul.
Śrīla Prabhupāda: I talked with one professor in Moscow. Maybe you know him – Professor Kotovsky. He teaches at the Soviet Academy of Sciences. I had a talk with him for about an hour. He said, "After this body is annihilated, everything is finished." I was surprised that he told me this. He is known to be a very good scholar, yet still he does not know about the soul.
Dr. Oliver: We have an Indology course here, given by a scholar from Vienna. But what he teaches, what kind of basic philosophy, I wouldn't know. There are about forty students. In essence they ought to start by making a detailed study of the *Bhagavad-gītā* and use that as a basis for their whole philosophy.
Śrīla Prabhupāda: So why not appoint someone to teach *Bhagavad-gītā As It Is*? That is essential.
Dr. Oliver: Our university almost has an obligation to make a study of these points in depth.
Śrīla Prabhupāda: By thoroughly studying *Bhagavad-gītā,* one begins his spiritual education.
Dr. Oliver: Well, this is apparently what one needs. Our Hindu community here in South Africa seems to lack any fixed idea of what

constitutes Hinduism. The young people especially are living in a complete vacuum. For various reasons, they do not want to accept religion, because this is what they see around them. They cannot identify with the Christian religion, the Islamic religion, or the Hindu religion. They are largely ignorant.

Śrīla Prabhupāda: They should be shown the right path. This is the original, authentic path.

Dr. Oliver: There were not very many great scholars in South Africa amongst our Indian community. The Indian people came, by and large, as workers on the sugar plantations – field workers. A few were jewelers and tailors and so on. Then for the last hundred years there was a political struggle, resisting transportation back to India. They were fighting to make a living and to find their own place in this country. As I see it, they must give meaning to the essence of their own beliefs and faith. I've been telling them that we are privileged to have them here in this country, with their background, and that they mustn't cut themselves away from it and drift into a vacuum. But they don't know to whom they should turn. So basically, they and myself and others want to know how we get this spirit into our own hearts, and how does this then issue out into everyday living?

Śrīla Prabhupāda: That is all explained in the *Bhagavad-gītā:* how to live peacefully in this world and how to go back home, back to Godhead.

Dr. Oliver: But how does one get modern man to voluntarily make this experiment? The real tragedy is we have wandered so far away from the spirit that we do not know where to start. And we can't get a few dozen honest believers to sit down and try to find out how much God wants to give of His mind to our minds.

Śrīla Prabhupāda: God is giving Himself. We just have to accept Him. That requires a little advancement. Otherwise, everything is there. God says that the soul is eternal and the body is changing. It is a very simple example. A boy becomes a young man, and a young man becomes an old man. There is no denying this fact. I can understand it, and you can understand it. It is very simple. I remember that as a boy I was jumping, and I cannot do that now because I have a different body. So I am conscious that I possessed a body like that. Now I do not possess it. The body is changing, but I am the same person eternally. It requires a little intelligence to see this, that's all. I am the owner of the body, and I am an eternal soul. The body is changing.

Dr. Oliver: Now, having accepted that, a further problem then arises: What are the implications?

Śrīla Prabhupāda: Yes. If I understand that I am not this body, yet at the present moment I am engaged only to keep my body comfortable, without taking care of my *self*, that is wrong. For example, if I am cleansing this shirt and coat thrice daily, but I am hungry – that would be impractical. Similarly, this civilization is wrong in this basic way. If I take care of your shirt and coat, but I don't give you anything to eat, then how long will you be satisfied? That is my point. That is the basic mistake. Material civilization means taking care of the body and bodily comforts. But the owner of the body, the spirit soul, gets no care. Therefore everyone is restless. They are changing the "ism" from capitalism to communism, but they do not know what the mistake is.

Dr. Oliver: There is very little difference. They are both material.

Śrīla Prabhupāda: The communists think that if we take control of the government, everything will be adjusted. But the mistake is there – both the communists and the capitalists are taking care of the external body, not the eternal identity, the soul. The soul must be peaceful. Then everything will be peaceful.

bhoktāraṁ yajña-tapasāṁ
sarva-loka-maheśvaram
suhṛdaṁ sarva-bhūtānāṁ
jñātvā māṁ śāntim ṛcchati

[*To a devotee:*] Read that verse.

Devotee: "A person in full consciousness of Me, knowing Me to be the ultimate beneficiary of all sacrifices and austerities, the Supreme Lord of all planets and demigods, and the benefactor and well-wisher of all living entities, attains peace from the pangs of material miseries." [*Bhagavad-gītā* 5.29]

Śrīla Prabhupāda: This means that one must know what God is. Because you are part and parcel of God, you already have a very intimate relationship with Him. Our business is knowing God. So at the present moment, there is no information. People have no complete idea.

Dr. Oliver: Well, I believe that if a satellite in the sky can reveal what is happening from one pole to the other pole, then surely God can reveal His spirit and His mind to anyone who wants to obey Him, who wants to know Him, and who sincerely wants to follow Him.
Śrīla Prabhupāda: Yes, yes. So here in the *Bhagavad-gītā* God is explaining Himself. We have to take it by logic and reason. Then it will be a clear understanding of God.
Dr. Oliver: Yes, but how to get this across?
Śrīla Prabhupāda: The teaching is there. We have to understand it by authoritative discussion.
Dr. Oliver: I think so. This is probably where one has to start. We have to sit down and discuss this, much the same as some professors would discuss any scientific experiment.
Śrīla Prabhupāda: The process for understanding is described here:

tad viddhi praṇipātena
paripraśnena sevayā
upadekṣyanti te jñānaṁ
jñāninas tattva-darśinaḥ

[*To a devotee:*] Find out that verse.
Devotee: "Just try to learn the truth by approaching a spiritual master. Inquire from him submissively and render service unto him. The self-realized souls can impart knowledge unto you because they have seen the truth." [*Bhagavad-gītā* 4.34]
Śrīla Prabhupāda: Read the purport.
Devotee: "The path of spiritual realization is undoubtedly difficult. The Lord therefore advises us to approach a bona fide spiritual master in the line of disciplic succession from the Lord Himself. No one can be a bona fide spiritual master without following this principle of disciplic succession. The Lord is the original spiritual master, and a person in the disciplic succession can convey the message of the Lord as it is to his disciple.

"No one can be spiritually realized by manufacturing his own process, as is the fashion of the foolish pretenders. The *Śrīmad-Bhāgavatam* (6.3.19) says, *dharmaṁ tu sākṣād bhagavat-praṇītam:* the path of religion is directly enunciated by the Lord. Therefore, mental speculation or dry arguments cannot help lead one to the right path. Nor by independent study of books of knowledge can one progress in spiritual life.

"One has to approach a bona fide spiritual master to receive the knowledge. Such a spiritual master should be accepted in full surrender, and one should serve the spiritual master like a menial servant, without false prestige. Satisfaction of the self-realized spiritual master is the secret of advancement in spiritual life. Inquiries and submission constitute the proper combination for spiritual understanding. Unless there is submission and service, inquiries from the learned spiritual master will not be effective. One must be able to pass the test of the spiritual master, and when he sees the genuine desire of the disciple, he automatically blesses the disciple with genuine spiritual understanding.

"In this verse, both blind following and absurd inquiries are condemned. Not only should one hear submissively from the spiritual master, but one must also get a clear understanding from him, in submission and service and inquiries. A bona fide spiritual master is by nature very kind toward the disciple. Therefore when the student is submissive and is always ready to render service, the reciprocation of knowledge and inquiries becomes perfect."

Śrīla Prabhupāda: The practical example is here. These European and American boys are coming from well-to-do families. Why are they serving me? I am Indian, coming from a poor country. I cannot pay them. When I came to the West, I had no money. I brought only forty rupees. That was only an hour's expenditure in America. So their soul is to carry out my instruction. And therefore they are making progress. *Praṇipātena paripraśnena* – they are asking questions. I am trying to reply to them, and they have all got full faith. They are serving like menial servants. This is the process.

If the spiritual master is bona fide and the disciple is very sincere, then the knowledge will be there. This is the secret. *Yasya deve parā bhaktir yathā deve tathā gurau* – Vedic knowledge is revealed unto those who have faith in both the Lord and the spiritual master. Therefore in Vedic society, the students are automatically sent to the *gurukula* [the place of the spiritual master], regardless of whether one is a king's son or from some other background. Even Kṛṣṇa had to go to *gurukula*.

There is a story that once Kṛṣṇa went with a classmate to the forest to collect dry wood for His spiritual master. Suddenly there was a heavy rainstorm, and they could not get out of the forest. The whole night they remained in the forest with great difficulty. The next morning, the *guru*, their teacher, along with other students, came to the forest and found them. So even Kṛṣṇa, whom we accept as the Supreme Lord, had to go to *gurukula* and serve the spiritual master as a menial servant.

So all of the students at the *gurukula* learn how to be very submissive and how to live only for the benefit of the *guru*. They are trained from the very beginning to be first-class submissive students. Then the *guru*, out of affection and with an open heart, teaches the boys all he knows. There is no question of money. It is all done on the basis of love and education.

Dr. Oliver: I might have difficulty accepting parts of what you've indicated here, simply because I don't know. But basically I accept that God lives in us and that when we leave things to Him, He knows how to direct these things. The challenge is living life so that He will be satisfied. This is where the difficulty comes in: you need the inspiration to be disciplined. This will only become a reality in one's life if one practices it, and practices it with others who share this commitment.

Śrīla Prabhupāda: Therefore we have this International Society for Krishna Consciousness – showing how to live a life of dedication to God. That is required. Without practical life in God consciousness, it remains simply theoretical. That may help, but it takes longer. My students are being trained up in practical spiritual life, and they are established.

Dr. Oliver: I want to thank you very much, and I pray that God will bless your visit to our country and our people here.

Śrīla Prabhupāda: Hare Kṛṣṇa.

Reincarnation Explained

Remembrances of past lives can be fascinating, but the real goal of understanding reincarnation is to become free from the painful cycle of birth and death. In a lecture delivered in London in August of 1973, Śrīla Prabhupāda warns, "This is not a very good business – to die and take birth again. We know that when we die we'll have to enter again into the womb of a mother – and nowadays mothers are killing the children within the womb."

dehino 'smin yathā dehe
kaumāraṁ yauvanaṁ jarā
tathā dehāntara-prāptir
dhīras tatra na muhyati

"As the embodied soul continuously passes, in this body, from boyhood to youth, and then to old age, the soul similarly passes into another body at death. A sober person is not bewildered by such a change." [*Bhagavad-gītā* 2.13]

Generally, people cannot understand this simple verse. Therefore, Kṛṣṇa says, *dhīras tatra na muhyati:* "Only a sober man can understand." But what is the difficulty? How plainly Kṛṣṇa has explained things! There are three stages of life. The first, *kaumāram,* lasts until one is fifteen years old. Then, from the sixteenth year, one begins youthful life, *yauvanam.* Then, after the fortieth or fiftieth year, one becomes an old man, *jarā.* So those who are *dhīra* – sober-headed, cool-headed – they can understand: "I have changed my body. I remember how I was playing and jumping when I was a boy. Then I became a young man, and

I was enjoying my life with friends and family. Now I am an old man, and when this body dies I shall again enter a new body."

In the previous verse Kṛṣṇa said to Arjuna, "All of us – you, Me, and all the soldiers and kings who are present here – we existed in the past, we are existing now, and we shall continue to exist in the future." This is Kṛṣṇa's statement. But rascals will say, "How was I existing in the past? I was born only in such-and-such a year. Before that I was not existing. At the present time I am existing. That's all right. But as soon as I die, I'll not exist." But Kṛṣṇa says, "You, I, all of us – we were existing, we are still existing, and we shall continue to exist." Is that wrong? No, it is a *fact*. Before our birth we were existing in a different body; and after our death we shall continue to exist in a different body. This is to be understood.

For example, seventy years ago I was a boy, then I became a young man, and now I have become an old man. My body has changed, but I, the proprietor of the body, am existing unchanged. So where is the difficulty in understanding? *Dehino 'smin yathā dehe. Dehinaḥ* means "the proprietor of the body," and *dehe* means "in the body." The body is changing, but the soul, the proprietor of the body, remains unchanged.

Anyone can understand that his body has changed. So in the next life the body will also change. But we may not remember; that is another thing. In my last life, what was my body? I do not remember. So forgetfulness is our nature, but our forgetting something does not mean that it did not take place. No. In my childhood I did so many things I do not remember, but my father and mother remember. So, forgetting does not mean that things did not take place.

Similarly, death simply means I have forgotten what I was in my past life. That is death. Otherwise I, as spirit soul, have no death. Suppose I change my clothes. In my boyhood I wore certain clothes, in my youth I wore different clothes. Now, in my old age, as a *sannyāsī* [a renunciant], I am wearing different clothes. The clothes may change, but that does not mean that the *owner* of the clothes is dead and gone. No.

This is a simple explanation of transmigration of the soul.

Also, all of us are individuals. There is no question of merging together. Every one of us is an individual. God is an individual, and we are also individuals. *Nityo nityānāṁ cetanaś cetanānām:* "Of all the eternal, conscious, individual persons, one is supreme." The difference is that God never changes His body, but we change our bodies in the material world. When we go to the spiritual world, there is no more change of body. Just as Kṛṣṇa has His *sac-cid-ānanda-vigraha,* an eternal form of bliss and knowledge, so when you go back home, back to Godhead, you will also get a similar body. The difference is that even when Kṛṣṇa comes to the material world, He does not change His body. Therefore one of His names is Acyuta, "He who never falls."

Kṛṣṇa never changes. He never falls down, because He is the controller of *māyā,* the material energy. We are controlled by the material energy, and Kṛṣṇa is the controller of the material energy. That is the difference between Kṛṣṇa and us. And not only does He control the material energy, but He controls the spiritual energy also – all energies. Everything that we see, everything manifested – that is Kṛṣṇa's energy. Just as heat and light are the energies of the sun, everything manifested is made up of the energies of Kṛṣṇa.

There are many energies, but they have been divided into three principal ones: the external energy, the internal energy, and the marginal energy. We living entities are the marginal energy. *Marginal* means that we may remain under the influence of the external energy or we may remain under the influence of the internal energy, as we like. The independence is there. After speaking *Bhagavad-gītā* Kṛṣṇa says to Arjuna, *yathecchasi tathā kuru:* "Whatever you like, you can do." Kṛṣṇa gives this independence to Arjuna. He does not force one to surrender. That is not good. Something forced will not stand. For example, we advise our students, "Rise early in the morning." This is our advice. We do not force anyone. Of course, we may force someone once or twice, but if he does not practice it, force will be useless.

Similarly, Kṛṣṇa does not force anyone to leave this material world. All conditioned souls are under the influence of the external, or material, energy. Kṛṣṇa comes here to deliver us from the clutches of the material energy. Because we are part and parcel of Kṛṣṇa, we are all directly Kṛṣṇa's sons. And if a son is in difficulty, the father suffers also, indirectly. Suppose the son has become a madman – or, nowadays, a hippy. The father is very sorry: "Oh, my son is living like a wretch." So, the father is not happy. Similarly, the conditioned souls in this material world are suffering so much, living like wretches and rascals. So Kṛṣṇa is not happy. Therefore He comes personally to teach us how to return to Him. (*Yadā yadā hi dharmasya glānir bhavati . . . tadātmānaṁ sṛjāmy aham.*)

When Kṛṣṇa comes, He comes in His original form. But unfortunately we understand Kṛṣṇa to be one of us. In one sense He is one of us, since He is the father and we are His sons. But He's the chief: *nityo nityānāṁ cetanaś cetanānām.* He's more powerful than us. He's the most powerful, the supreme powerful. We have a little power, but Kṛṣṇa has infinite power. That is the difference between Kṛṣṇa and us. We cannot be equal to God. Nobody can be equal to Kṛṣṇa or greater than Him. Everyone is under Kṛṣṇa. *Ekale īśvara kṛṣṇa, āra saba bhṛtya:* Everyone is the servant of Kṛṣṇa; Kṛṣṇa is the only master. *Bhoktāraṁ yajña-tapasāṁ sarva-loka-maheśvaram:* "I am the only enjoyer; I am the proprietor," Kṛṣṇa says. And that is a fact.

So, we are changing our body, but Kṛṣṇa does not change His. We should understand this. The proof is that Kṛṣṇa remembers past, present, and future. In the fourth chapter of *Bhagavad-gītā* you'll find that Kṛṣṇa says He spoke the philosophy of *Bhagavad-gītā* to the sun-god some 120,000,000 years ago. How does Kṛṣṇa remember? Because He does not change His body. We forget things because we are changing our body at every moment. That is a medical fact. The corpuscles of our blood are changing at every second. But the body is changing imperceptibly. That is why the father and mother of a growing child do not notice how his body is changing. A third person, if he comes after some time and sees that the child has grown, says, "Oh, the child has grown so big." But the father and mother have not noticed that he has grown so big, because they are always seeing him and the changes are taking place imperceptibly, at every moment. So our body is always changing, but *I*, the soul, the proprietor of the body, am not changing. This is to be understood.

We are all individual souls, and we are eternal, but because our body is changing we are suffering birth, death, old age, and disease. The Kṛṣṇa consciousness movement is meant to get us out of this changing condition. "Since I am eternal, how can I come to the permanent position?" That should be our question. Everyone wants to live eternally; nobody wants to die. If I come before you with a revolver and say, "I am going to kill you," you will immediately cry out, because you do not want to die. This is not a very good business – to die and take birth again. It is very troublesome. This we all know subconsciously. We know that when we die we'll have to enter again into the womb of a mother – and nowadays mothers are killing the children within the womb. Then again another mother . . . The process of accepting another body again and again is very long and very troublesome. In our subconscious we remember all this trouble, and therefore we do not want to die.

So our question should be this: "I am eternal, so why have I been put into this temporary life?" This is an intelligent question. And this is our real problem. But rascals set aside this real problem. They are thinking of how to eat, how to sleep, how to have sex, how to defend. Even if you eat nicely and sleep nicely, ultimately you have to die. The problem of death is there. But they don't care about this real problem. They are very much alert to solve the temporary problems, which are not actually problems at all. The birds and beasts also eat, sleep, have sexual intercourse, and defend themselves. They know how to do all these things, even without the human beings' education and so-called civilization. So these things are not our real problems. The real problem is that we do not want to die but death takes place. This is our real problem.

But the rascals do not know it. They are always busy with temporary problems. For example, suppose there is severe cold. This is a problem. We have to search out a nice coat or a fireplace, and if these are not available we are in distress. So severe cold is a problem. But it is a temporary problem. Severe cold, winter, has come, and it will go. It is not a permanent problem. My permanent problem is that because of ignorance I am taking birth, I am accepting disease, I am accepting old age, and I am accepting death. These are my real problems. Therefore Kṛṣṇa says, *janma-mṛtyu-jarā-vyādhi-duḥkha-doṣānudarśanam:* Those who are actually in knowledge see these four problems – birth, death, old age, and disease.

Now, Kṛṣṇa says, *dhīras tatra na muhyati:* "A sober man is not perplexed at the time of death." If you prepare yourself for death, why should you be perplexed? For example, if in your childhood and boyhood you prepare yourself nicely, if you become educated, then you will get a nice job, a nice situation, and be happy. Similarly, if you prepare yourself in this life for going back home, back to Godhead, then where is your perplexity at the time of death? There is no perplexity. You'll know, "I am going to Kṛṣṇa. I am going back home, back to Godhead. Now I'll not have to change material bodies; I'll have my spiritual body. Now I shall play with Kṛṣṇa and dance with Kṛṣṇa and eat with Kṛṣṇa." This is Kṛṣṇa consciousness – to prepare yourself for the next life.

Sometimes a dying man cries out, because according to *karma* those who are very, very sinful see horrible scenes at the time of death. The sinful man knows he is going to accept some abominable type of body. But those who are pious, the devotees, die without any anxiety. Foolish people say, "You devotees are dying, and the nondevotees are also dying, so what is the difference?" There is a difference. A cat catches her kitten in its mouth, and it also catches the mouse in its mouth. Superficially we may see that the cat has caught both the mouse and the kitten in the same way. But there are differences of catching. The kitten is feeling pleasure: "Oh, my mother is carrying me." And the mouse is feeling death: "Oh, now I'm going to die." This is the difference. So, although both devotees and nondevotees die, there is a difference of feeling at the time of death – just like the kitten and the mouse. Don't think that both of them are dying in the same way. The bodily process may be the same, but the mental situation is different.

In *Bhagavad-gītā* [4.11] Kṛṣṇa says,

janma karma ca me divyam
evaṁ yo vetti tattvataḥ
tyaktvā dehaṁ punar janma
naiti mām eti so 'rjuna

If you simply try to understand Kṛṣṇa, you can go to Him at the time of death. Everything about Kṛṣṇa is divine, transcendental. Kṛṣṇa's activities, Kṛṣṇa's appearance, Kṛṣṇa's worship, Kṛṣṇa's temple, Kṛṣṇa's glories – everything is transcendental. So if one understands these things, or even *tries* to understand, then one becomes liberated from the process of birth and death. This is what Kṛṣṇa says. So become very serious to understand Kṛṣṇa, and remain in Kṛṣṇa consciousness. Then these problems – birth, death, old age, and disease – will be solved automatically, very easily.

A *dhīra*, a sober man, will think, "I want to live eternally. Why does death take place? I want to live a very healthy life. Why does disease come? I don't want to become an old man. Why does old age come?" *Janma-mṛtyu-jarā-vyādhi*. These are real problems. One can solve these problems simply by taking to Kṛṣṇa consciousness, simply by understanding Kṛṣṇa. And for understanding Kṛṣṇa, the *Bhagavad-gītā* is there, very nicely explained. So make your life successful. Understand that you are not the body. You are embodied *within* the body, but you are not the body. For example, a bird may be within a cage, but the cage is not the bird. Foolish persons take care of the cage, not the bird, and the bird suffers starvation. So we are suffering spiritual starvation. Therefore nobody is happy in the material world. Spiritual starvation. That is why you see that in an opulent country like America – enough food, enough residences, enough material enjoyment – still they are becoming hippies. The young people are not satisfied, because of spiritual starvation. Materially you may be very opulent, but if you starve spiritually you cannot be happy.

A spiritual rejuvenation is required. You must realize, *ahaṁ brahmāsmi:* "I am not this body; I am *brahman,* spiritual soul." Then you'll be happy. *Brahma-bhūtaḥ prasannātmā na śocati na kāṅkṣati samaḥ sarveṣu bhūteṣu*. Then there will be equality, fraternity, brotherhood. Otherwise it is all bogus – simply high-sounding words. There cannot be equality, fraternity, and so on without Kṛṣṇa consciousness. Come to the spiritual platform; then you will see everyone equally. Otherwise you will think, "I am a human being with hands and legs, and the cow has no hands and legs. So let me kill the cow and eat it." Why? What right do you have to kill an animal? You have no vision of equality, for want of Kṛṣṇa consciousness. Therefore, in this material world, so-called education, culture, fraternity – all these are bogus. Kṛṣṇa consciousness is the right subject matter to be studied. Then society will be happy. Otherwise not. Thank you very much.

The Self and Its Bodies

"You are suffering because in your past life you indulged in sense gratification and got a body according to karma,*" Śrīla Prabhupāda tells listeners at a lecture delivered at the Hare Kṛṣṇa center in Detroit, Michigan, in June 1976. He then goes on to explain the secret of how to become free from* karma *and enjoy perfect happiness.*

yathājñas tamasā yukta
upāste vyaktam eva hi
na veda pūrvam aparaṁ
naṣṭa-janma-smṛtis tathā

"As a sleeping person acts according to the body manifested in his dreams and accepts it to be himself, so one identifies with his present body, which he acquired because of his past religious or irreligious actions, and is unable to know his past or future lives." [*Śrīmad-Bhāgavatam* 6.1.49]

Here is a very good example of the ignorance that covers the living entity in the material world. When we dream, we forget everything about ourselves – that we are Mr. Such-and-such, an inhabitant of such-and-such a place, with such-and-such bank balance. Everything is forgotten. And when we awaken, we forget about the dream. But whether we are in the wakened state or the dreaming state, we are seeing our own activities. In the dream we are the seer, and in the so-called awake condition we are also the seer. So we, the spirit soul, who is experiencing, remain the same, but the circumstances change, and we forget.

Similarly, we cannot remember what we were in our previous life.

Nor do we know what we are going to become in our next life. But it is a fact that, as spirit souls, we are eternal. We existed in the past, we exist at the present time, and we shall continue to exist in the future. Kṛṣṇa explains this in the *Bhagavad-gītā* [2.12]: "O Arjuna, you, I, and all these persons who have assembled on this battlefield have existed before, and we shall continue to exist in the future." This is the preliminary understanding in spiritual life – knowing "I am eternal."

As spirit souls, we do not take birth, nor do we die (*na jāyate mriyate vā kadācit*). We are not finished with the destruction of the material body (*na hanyate hanyamāne śarīre*). The destruction of the body is going on already. Our childhood body is now destroyed; you cannot find that body. Our youthful body is also destroyed; we cannot find it anymore. And in the same way, our present body will also be destroyed, and we shall get another body (*tathā dehāntara-prāptiḥ*).

When the soul transmigrates, the gross body is lost. The gross body is made of matter, and anything material will eventually be finished. That is the nature of matter. But the spirit soul is never finished.

So we are changing bodies, one after another. Why are there different types of bodies? Because the living entity, the spirit soul, is contacting various modes of material nature. And according to what modes are influencing him, the living entity develops a gross body.

So we have acquired our present body because of our past activities. *Karmaṇā daiva-netreṇa jantur dehopapattaye:* One gets a particular type of body according to his past *karma,* or material activities. Nature acts automatically, according to our *karma*. Suppose you contract some disease. Nature will act: you will have to develop that disease and undergo some suffering. Similarly, when we come under the influence of the modes of material nature and perform karmic activities, we must transmigrate from body to body. Nature's law works so perfectly.

Now, when we come to the civilized human life, we should ask, "Why am I suffering?" The problem is that because we are under the spell of *māyā,* illusion, we take suffering to be enjoyment. *Māyā* means "that which is not." We are thinking we are enjoying, but actually we are suffering. In this material body we *have* to suffer. We suffer on account of the body. Pinching cold, scorching heat – we feel these things on account of the body. Under certain circumstances we feel pleasure. But in the *Bhagavad-gītā* [2.14] Kṛṣṇa advises,

mātrā-sparśās tu kaunteya
śītoṣṇa-sukha-duḥkha-dāḥ
āgamāpāyino 'nityās
tāṁs titikṣasva bhārata

"Material happiness and distress are caused by the body. They come and go just like seasonal changes. So do not be disturbed; try to tolerate them."

As long as we are in this material world, happiness and distress will come and go. So we should not be disturbed by them. Our real business is trying for self-realization. That must go on; it must not stop. Self-realization is the goal of human life. Suffering and so-called happiness will go on as long as we have a material body, but we must come to the knowledge that "I am not the body; I am a spirit soul. I have gotten this body because of my past activities." That is knowledge.

Now, a sensible man should consider, "Since I am a spirit soul and my body is simply a covering, is it not possible to end this process of transmigration from body to body?" This is human life – inquiring how to stop the contamination of the material body.

Unfortunately, people in the modern so-called civilization do not ask this question. They are mad after gratifying the senses of the body, so they act irresponsibly. As explained in the *Śrīmad-Bhāgavatam* [5.5.4],

nūnaṁ pramattaḥ kurute vikarma
yad indriya-prītaya āpṛṇoti
na sādhu manye yata ātmano 'yam
asann api kleśada āsa dehaḥ

"People who act only for sense gratification are certainly mad, and they perform all kinds of abominable activities. In this way they insure their transmigration from body to body perpetually and thus experience all kinds of miseries."

We do not understand that the body is always *kleśada* – it always gives us pain. For the time being we may feel some pleasure, but actually the body is a reservoir of pain. Here is a good analogy in this connection: Formerly, when the government officers would want to punish a criminal, they would tie his hands, take him into the middle of a river, and push him down into the water. When he was almost drowned, they would draw him up from the water by his hair and give him a little rest. And then again they would push him down into the water. That was one system of punishment.

Similarly, whatever little pleasure we are experiencing in this material world is exactly like the pleasure the criminal would feel when he was drawn up from the water. Severe suffering with a few moments of relief – this is what life in the material world is like.

That is why Sanātana Gosvāmī, who had been a wealthy minister in the Muslim government in India, presented himself to Śrī Caitanya Mahāprabhu and asked, *ke āmi, kene āmāya jāre tāpa-traya:* "Who am I? And why am I suffering the threefold miseries?" This is intelligence. We are constantly undergoing some sort of distress, whether caused by the body and mind, inflicted by other living entities, or brought about by natural disturbances. We don't want all these miseries, but they are forced upon us. So when one accepts a spiritual master, the first question should be, "Why am I suffering?"

But we have become so dull, like the animals, that we never ask this question. The animals are suffering (everyone knows this), but they cannot ask why. When an animal is being taken to the slaughterhouse, he cannot ask, "Why am I being taken by force to the slaughterhouse?" But if you take a human being to be killed, he'll make a great noise: "This man is taking me to be killed! Why am I being killed?" So one important distinction between human life and animal life is that only the human being can ask, "Why am I suffering?"

Whether you are President Nixon or a man in the street, you are suffering. That's a fact. You are suffering on account of your body, and you are doing something that will cause you to accept another material body. You are suffering because in your past life you indulged in sense gratification and got a body according to *karma,* and if you engage in sense gratification in this life and do not try to elevate yourself, you'll again get a body and suffer. By nature's way you'll get another body according to the mentality you have at the time of death. And as soon as you get another body, your suffering will begin again. Even in the womb of the mother you will suffer. To remain in that compact bag for so many months, hands and legs all tied up, unable to move – this is suffering. And nowadays there is also a risk of being killed in the womb. And when you come out, more suffering. So we should be intelligent enough to ask, "Why am I suffering? And how can I stop this suffering?" And until we ask "Why am I suffering?" our human life has not begun. We remain animals.

Asking about the ultimate cause of our suffering is called *brahma-jijñāsā,* inquiry into the Absolute Truth. As it is said in the beginning of the *Vedānta-sūtra, athāto brahma-jijñāsā:* "Having gotten the human form of life, one should inquire into Brahman, the Absolute Truth." So we should take advantage of the human form of life. We should not live like animals, without any inquiry into the Absolute Truth, without trying to find out how to stop our miserable material life.

Of course, we *are* actually trying to stop our own miseries by working so hard in the struggle for existence. Why do we try to get money? Because we think, "If I get money, my distress will be mitigated." So the struggle for existence is going on, and everyone is trying to become happy by getting sense gratification. But sense gratification is not real happiness. Real happiness is spiritual happiness, which comes from serving Kṛṣṇa. That is happiness. Material happiness is simply perverted happiness.

Material happiness is like the mirage of water in the desert. In the desert there is no water, but when a thirsty animal sees the mirage of water in the desert, he runs after it – and dies. We know that there is no water in the desert – that the "water" is just a reflection of the sunshine – but animals do not know this. Similarly, human life means to give up looking for happiness through sense gratification, which is just like a mirage in the desert, and to try for spiritual happiness.

We can awaken to this higher happiness simply by chanting the Hare Kṛṣṇa *mahā-mantra:* Hare Kṛṣṇa, Hare Kṛṣṇa, Kṛṣṇa Kṛṣṇa, Hare Hare/ Hare Rāma, Hare Rāma, Rāma Rāma, Hare Hare. Chanting Hare Kṛṣṇa is such a simple thing, yet it can relieve all our suffering in the material world.

Our suffering is caused by the many dirty things within our heart.

We are just like a criminal who has dirty things within his heart. He thinks, "If I get such-and-such thing, I'll be happy." And at the risk of his life he commits a crime. A burglar, a thief, knows that if he is captured by the police he'll be punished, but still he goes and steals. Why? *Nūnaṁ pramattaḥ:* He has become mad after sense gratification. That's all.

So we have to purify our hearts of our dirty desires, which are forcing us to act for sense gratification and suffer. And in this age the purification is very, very easy: Just chant Hare Kṛṣṇa. That's all. This is Caitanya Mahāprabhu's contribution. *Ceto-darpaṇa-mārjanaṁ bhava-mahā-dāvāgni-nirvāpaṇam.* If you chant the Hare Kṛṣṇa *mantra,* you will be relieved of the suffering caused by transmigrating perpetually from body to body. Chanting is such a simple thing. There is no question of caste, creed, nationality, color, social position. No. By the grace of God, everyone has a tongue and ears. So everyone can chant Hare Kṛṣṇa, Hare Kṛṣṇa, Kṛṣṇa Kṛṣṇa, Hare Hare/ Hare Rāma, Hare Rāma, Rāma Rāma, Hare Hare. Just chant Hare Kṛṣṇa and be happy.

Thank you very much.

2

Superconsciousness

Everyone Can See God

The Vedic literature is unique among all the world's scriptures because it details a practical process by which anyone can purify his or her consciousness and see God face to face. In this lecture, delivered in Los Angeles on August 15, 1972, Śrīla Prabhupāda explains, "One must actually be very eager to see God. . . . One must be very serious and think, 'Yes, I have been informed about God. So if there is a God, I must see Him.'"

tac chraddadhānā munayo
jñāna-vairāgya-yuktayā
paśyanty ātmani cātmānaṁ
bhaktyā śruta-gṛhītayā

"The seriously inquisitive student or sage, well equipped with knowledge and detachment, realizes the Absolute Truth by rendering devotional service in terms of what he has heard from the Vedic literature, *Vedānta-śruti*." [*Śrīmad-Bhāgavatam* 1.2.12]

People sometimes ask, "Have you seen God?" or "Can you show me God?" Sometimes we meet these questions. So the answer is "Yes, I am seeing God. You can also see God; everyone can see God. But you must have the qualification." Suppose something is wrong with a motorcar; it is not running. Everyone is seeing it, but a mechanic sees it differently. He's qualified to see it with greater understanding. So he replaces some missing part, and immediately the car runs. But although for seeing a machine we require so much qualification, we want to see God without any qualification. Just see the folly! People are such rascals, they are such fools, that they want to see God with their imagined qualifications.

Kṛṣṇa says in the *Bhagavad-gītā, nāhaṁ prakāśaḥ sarvasya yoga-māyā-*

samāvṛtaḥ: "I am not exposed to everyone. My energy, *yogamāyā,* is covering Me from their vision." So how can you see God? But this rascaldom is going on – this "Can you show me God?" "Have you seen God?" God has become just like a plaything, so that cheaters advertise some ordinary man by saying, "Here is God. Here is an incarnation of God."

Na māṁ duṣkṛtino mūḍhāḥ prapadyante narādhamāḥ. Sinful rascals, fools, the lowest of mankind – they inquire like that: "Can you show me God?" What qualification have you acquired by which you can see God? Here is the qualification: *tac chraddadhānā munayaḥ.* One must first of all be faithful (*śraddadhāna*). One must actually be very much eager to see God. Not that one takes it as a frivolous thing – "Can you show me God?" – or as some magic. They think God is magic. No. One must be very serious and think, "Yes, I have been informed about God. So if there is a God, I must see Him."

There is a story in this connection. It is very instructive, so try to hear. One professional reciter was publicly reciting the *Śrīmad-Bhāgavatam,* and he was describing that Kṛṣṇa is very highly decorated with all kinds of jewels when He goes to tend the cows in the forest. So, there was a thief in that meeting, and he thought, "Why not go to Vṛndāvana and plunder this boy? He's in the forest with so many valuable jewels. I can go there and catch the child and take all the jewels." This was his intention. So he was serious. "I must find that boy," he thought. "Then in one night I shall become a millionaire."

The thief's qualification was his feeling: "I *must* see Kṛṣṇa! I *must* see Kṛṣṇa!" That anxiety, that eagerness, made it possible for him to actually see Kṛṣṇa in Vṛndāvana. He saw Kṛṣṇa in just the same way as the *Bhāgavatam* reader had described. Then the thief said, "Oh, You are such a nice boy, Kṛṣṇa." He began to flatter Him; he thought that by flattering Him he would easily take all the jewels. Then he proposed his real business: "May I take some of these ornaments? You are so rich."

"No, no, no," said Kṛṣṇa. "My mother will be angry! I cannot give them away." Kṛṣṇa was playing just like a child.

So the thief became more and more eager for Kṛṣṇa to give Him the jewels, but by Kṛṣṇa's association he was becoming purified. Then at last Kṛṣṇa said, "All right, you can take them." Then the thief became a devotee immediately, because by Kṛṣṇa's association he had been completely purified. So somehow or other you should come in contact with Kṛṣṇa. Then you'll be purified.

The *gopīs* are another example of great eagerness to see Kṛṣṇa. The *gopīs* came to Kṛṣṇa, being captivated by His beautiful features. They were young girls, and Kṛṣṇa was *so* beautiful. Actually they were lusty when they came to Kṛṣṇa, but Kṛṣṇa is so pure that they became first-class devotees. There is no comparison to the *gopīs'* devotion, because they loved Kṛṣṇa with heart and soul. That is the qualification. They loved Kṛṣṇa so much that they didn't care for family or reputation when they went out in the dead of night. Kṛṣṇa's flute was sounding, and they were all fleeing their homes. Their fathers, their brothers, their husbands all said, "Where are you going? Where are you going in this dead of night?" But the *gopīs* didn't care. They neglected their children, their family, everything. Their only thought was, "We must go to Kṛṣṇa."

This eagerness is required. We must be very, very eager to see Kṛṣṇa. Many *gopīs* who were forcibly stopped from going to Kṛṣṇa lost their lives because of their great feelings of separation. So this eagerness is wanted; then you can see God. Whether you are lusty or a thief or a murderer or whatever it may be – somehow or other you must develop this eagerness, this desire: "I *must* see Kṛṣṇa." Then Kṛṣṇa will be seen.

The first thing Kṛṣṇa is looking for is how eager you are to see Him. Kṛṣṇa will respond. If you are actually eager to see Kṛṣṇa – whether you are lusty, or you want to steal His ornaments, or some way or other you have become attracted to Kṛṣṇa – then it is sure your efforts will be successful.

But you must desire Kṛṣṇa *only*. In this connection, Rūpa Gosvāmī has written a verse:

smerāṁ bhaṅgī-traya-paricitāṁ sāci-vistīrṇa-dṛṣṭiṁ
vaṁśī-nyastādhara-kiśalayām ujjvalāṁ candrakeṇa
govindākhyāṁ hari-tanum itaḥ keśi-tīrthopakaṇṭhe
mā prekṣiṣṭhās tava yadi sakhe bandhu-saṅge 'sti raṅgaḥ

The idea is that one *gopī* is advising another *gopī*, "My dear friend, there is one boy – His name is Govinda. He is standing on the bank of the Yamunā near the Keśī-ghāṭa, and He is playing on His flute. He is so beautiful, especially during this full-moon night. If you have any intentions to enjoy in this material world with your children, husband, or other family members, then please do not go there." *Bhaṅgī-traya:* Kṛṣṇa always stands in a three-curved way with His flute. That is Kṛṣṇa's *tribhaṅga* form, bending in three places. So the one *gopī* says to the other, "If you think that you'll enjoy your life more in this material world, then do not go to see Kṛṣṇa. Do not go there." The idea is that if you once see Kṛṣṇa, then you'll forget all this nonsensical materialistic enjoyment. That is seeing Kṛṣṇa.

When Dhruva Mahārāja saw Kṛṣṇa, he said, *svāmin kṛtārtho 'smi varaṁ na yāce:* "My dear Lord, I don't want anything else." Dhruva Mahārāja went to see Kṛṣṇa to get the kingdom of his father, and when he saw Kṛṣṇa, Kṛṣṇa offered, "Now, whatever benediction you want, you take." Dhruva said, "My dear Lord, I no longer have any desire." That is seeing Kṛṣṇa.

So, if you're eager to see Kṛṣṇa, regardless of whatever motive you have, somehow or other, due to your eagerness, you'll see Kṛṣṇa. That is the only qualification.

In another verse, Rūpa Gosvāmī says, *kṛṣṇa-bhakti-rasa-bhāvitā matiḥ krīyatāṁ yadi kuto 'pi labhyate.* (I have translated the words *Kṛṣṇa consciousness* from *kṛṣṇa-bhakti-rasa-bhāvitā.*) So here Rūpa Gosvāmī advises, "If Kṛṣṇa consciousness is available, please purchase it immediately. Don't delay. It is a very nice thing."

Yes, Kṛṣṇa consciousness is available. You can purchase it from this Kṛṣṇa consciousness movement. But what is the price? It is such a nice thing, but you have to pay the price. What is that? *Tatra laulyam api mūlyam ekalam:* Simply your eagerness. That is the price. You have to pay this price. Then you get Kṛṣṇa, immediately. Kṛṣṇa is not poor, and the Kṛṣṇa-seller – the Kṛṣṇa devotee – he's also not poor. He can distribute Kṛṣṇa free. And he's doing that. You simply have to purchase Him by your eagerness.

Someone may say, "Oh, eagerness? I have eagerness." Ah-h-h . . . but it is not so easy. *Janma-koṭi-sukṛtair na labhyate:* This eagerness cannot be achieved even by executing pious activities for millions of births. If you simply go on performing pious activities, still this eagerness is not available.

So, this eagerness is a very important thing, but it can be awakened only by the association of devotees. Therefore we are giving everyone a chance to invoke that eagerness; then you'll see God, face to face.

This life is meant for seeing Kṛṣṇa. It is not meant for becoming dogs and hogs. Unfortunately, the whole modern civilization is training people to become dogs and hogs. It is only this institution – this Kṛṣṇa consciousness movement – that is teaching people how to see Kṛṣṇa. It is so important.

Tac chraddadhānā munayo jñāna-vairāgya-yuktayā. By eagerness, you'll automatically be enriched with knowledge and detachment. Knowledge does not mean "Now we have discovered this atomic bomb." That is not knowledge. What knowledge is that? People are already dying, and you have discovered something that will accelerate death. But we are giving knowledge to *stop* death. That is Kṛṣṇa consciousness; that is knowledge. *Jñāna-vairāgya-yuktayā.* And as soon as you get this knowledge, automatically you become detached from all this nonsensical materialistic happiness.

Thank you very much.

Beyond Religion

In June 1976, Śrīla Prabhupāda fields questions sent to him from the editors of Bhavan's Journal, *one of Bombay's leading cultural and religious periodicals.*

Devotee: Here is the first question: "It is said that the greatest strength of Hinduism is its catholicity, or breadth of outlook, but that this is also its greatest weakness in that there are very few religious observances that are obligatory for all, as in other religions. Is it necessary and possible to outline certain basic minimum observances for all Hindus?"
Śrīla Prabhupāda: As far as Vedic religion is concerned, it is not for the Hindus; it is for all living entities. That is the first thing to be understood. Vedic religion is called *sanātana-dharma,* "the eternal occupation of the living entity." The living entity is *sanātana* [eternal], God is *sanātana,* and there is *sanātana-dharma. Sanātana-dharma* is meant for all living entities, not just the so-called Hindus. Hinduism, this "ism," that "ism" – these are all misconception. Historically, *sanātana-dharma* was followed regularly in India, and Indians were called "Hindus" by the Muslims. The Muslims saw that the Indians lived on the other side of the River Sind, and the Muslims pronounced *Sind* as *Hind.* Therefore they called India "Hindustan" and the people who lived there "Hindus." But the word *Hindu* has no reference in the Vedic literature, nor does so-called Hindu *dharma.* Now that *sanātana-dharma,* or Vedic *dharma,* is being distorted, not being obeyed, not being carried out properly, it has come to be known as Hinduism. But that is a freak understanding; that is not a real understanding. We have to study *sanātana-dharma* as it is described in the *Bhagavad-gītā* and other Vedic literatures; then we'll understand what Vedic religion is. [*To a devotee:*] Read from the eleventh chapter of *Bhagavad-gītā,* eighteenth verse.

Devotee [*reads*]:

tvam akṣaraṁ paramaṁ veditavyaṁ
tvam asya viśvasya paraṁ nidhānam
tvam avyayaḥ śāśvata-dharma-goptā
sanātanas tvaṁ puruṣo mato me

"O Lord Kṛṣṇa, You are the supreme primal objective. You are the ultimate resting place of all this universe. You are inexhaustible, and You are the oldest. You are the maintainer of the eternal religion, the Personality of Godhead. This is my opinion."

Śrīla Prabhupāda: This understanding is wanted. Kṛṣṇa is eternal, we are eternal, and the place where we can live and exchange our feelings with Kṛṣṇa – that is eternal. And the system that teaches this eternal process of reciprocation – that is *sanātana-dharma,* which is meant for everyone.

Devotee: So what would be the daily prescribed religious observances followed by one who is aspiring for this *sanātana-dharma*? What would he do? The complaint is that within Hinduism – or, let's say, *sanātana-dharma* – there is such a breadth, there is so much variegatedness in different types—

Śrīla Prabhupāda: Why do you go to variegatedness? Why don't you take the real purpose of religion from Kṛṣṇa? Kṛṣṇa says [*Bhagavad-gītā* 18.66], *sarva-dharmān parityajya mām ekaṁ śaraṇaṁ vraja:* "Give up all other so-called *dharmas* and just surrender to Me." Why don't you take that? Why are you taking up variegated practices under the name of so-called Hinduism? Why don't you take the advice of the *sanātana,* Kṛṣṇa? You refuse to accept *sanātana-dharma* – what the *sanātana,* God, says – but you say, "How can we avoid so many varieties and come to the right point?" Why accept varieties? Take to this one consciousness: *sarva-dharmān parityajya mām ekaṁ śaraṇaṁ vraja.* Why don't you do that?

Devotee: How can people do this practically, on a daily basis?

Śrīla Prabhupāda: How are *we* doing it? Is what we are doing not practical? People will manufacture their own impractical way of religion, but they won't take our practical system. What is that? *Man-manā bhava mad-bhakto mad-yājī māṁ namaskuru:* Simply think of Kṛṣṇa, become His devotee, worship Him, and offer obeisances to Him. Where is the difficulty? Where is the impracticality? Kṛṣṇa says, "This is your duty. If you do this you will come to Me without any doubt." Why don't you do that? Why remain Hindu? Why remain Muslim? Why remain Christian? Give up all this nonsense. Just surrender to Kṛṣṇa and understand, "I am a devotee of Kṛṣṇa, a servant of Kṛṣṇa." Then everything will immediately be resolved.

Devotee: But the Hindus would say, "There are so many other aspects to Hindu *dharma.*"

Śrīla Prabhupāda: Real *dharma* is defined in *Śrīmad-Bhāgavatam: dharmaṁ tu sākṣād bhagavat-praṇītam.* "What God says – *that* is *dharma.*" Now, God says, "Give up all other *dharmas* and just surrender unto Me." So take *that dharma.* Why do you want to remain a Hindu? And besides, what Hindu does not accept the authority of Kṛṣṇa? Even today, if any Hindu says, "I don't care for Kṛṣṇa and *Bhagavad-gītā,*" he will immediately be rejected as a madman. Why don't you take Kṛṣṇa's instruction? Why go elsewhere? Your trouble is that you do not know what religion is, and you do not know what *sanātana-dharma* is. In our Kṛṣṇa consciousness society there are many who were formerly so-called Hindus, so-called Muslims, and so-called Christians, but now they don't care for "Hindu" or "Muslim" or "Christian." They care only for Kṛṣṇa. That's all. If you follow a false religious system, you suffer; but if you follow a real religious system, you'll be happy.

Unfortunately, the Indian people gave up the real religious system – *sanātana-dharma,* or *varṇāśrama-dharma* – and accepted a hodgepodge thing called "Hinduism." Therefore there is trouble. Vedic religion means *varṇāśrama-dharma,* the division of society into four social classes and four spiritual orders of life. The four social classes are the *brāhmaṇas* [priests and intellectuals], the *kṣatriyas* [political leaders and military men], the *vaiśyas* [merchants and farmers], and the *śūdras* [manual laborers]. The four spiritual orders are the *brahmacārīs* [celibate students], the *gṛhasthas* [householders], the *vānaprasthas* [retired persons], and the *sannyāsīs* [renunciants]. When all these classes and orders work harmoniously to satisfy the Lord, that is real religion, or *dharma.*

Devotee: The next question is this: "In the Kali-yuga, the present age of quarrel, *bhakti* [devotional service to God] has been described as the most suitable path for God realization. Yet how is it that Vedāntic teachings, which stress *jñāna* [knowledge, or intellectual speculation], are emphasized by noted savants?"

Śrīla Prabhupāda: The so-called Vedāntists are cheaters; they do not know what *vedānta* is. But people want to be cheated, and the cheaters are taking advantage of them. The word *veda* means "knowledge," and *anta* means "end." So the meaning of *vedānta* is "the ultimate knowledge," and the *Vedānta-sūtra* teaches this. (A *sūtra* is an aphorism: in a few words, a big philosophy is given.) The first aphorism in the *Vedānta-sūtra* is *athāto brahma-jijñāsā:* "Now, in the human form of life, one should inquire about Brahman, the Absolute Truth." So the study of the *Vedānta-sūtra* begins when one is inquisitive about the Absolute Truth. And what is that Absolute Truth? That is answered in a nutshell in the second aphorism. *Janmādy asya yataḥ:* "Brahman is the origin of everything." So Brahman is God, the origin of everything. And all *veda,* or knowledge, culminates in Him. This is confirmed by Kṛṣṇa in *Bhagavad-gītā* [15.15]: *vedaiś ca sarvair aham eva vedyah.* "The purpose of all the *Vedas,* all books of knowledge, is to search out Me."

So the whole *Vedānta-sūtra* is a description of the Supreme Personality of Godhead. But because in this Kali-yuga people will not be able to study *Vedānta-sūtra* nicely on account of a lack of education, Śrīla Vyāsadeva personally wrote a commentary on the *Vedānta-sūtra.* That commentary is *Śrīmad-Bhāgavatam (bhāṣyāṁ brahma-sūtrāṇām). Śrīmad-Bhāgavatam* is the real commentary on the *Vedānta-sūtra,* written by the same author, Vyāsadeva, under the instruction of Nārada, his spiritual master. *Śrīmad-Bhāgavatam* begins with the same aphorism as the *Vedānta-sūtra, janmādy asya yataḥ,* and then continues, *anvayād itarataś cārtheṣv abhijñaḥ svarāṭ.*

So, actually, in the *Śrīmad-Bhāgavatam* the *Vedānta-sūtra* is explained by the author of the *Vedānta-sūtra.* But some rascals, without understanding the *Vedānta-sūtra,* without reading the natural commentary on the *Vedānta-sūtra,* are posing themselves as Vedāntists and misguiding people. And because people are not educated, they're accepting these rascals as Vedāntists. Actually, the so-called Vedāntists are bluffers; they are not Vedāntists. They do not know anything of the *vedānta.* The *Vedānta-sūtra* is explained in *Śrīmad-Bhāgavatam,* and if we take *Śrīmad-Bhāgavatam* as the real explanation of the *Vedānta-sūtra* we can understand what *vedānta* is. But if we take shelter of the bluffers, then we will not learn *vedānta*. People do not know anything, so they can be bluffed and cheated by anyone. But now they should learn from the Kṛṣṇa consciousness movement what *vedānta* is and what the explanation of *vedānta* is. Then they will be benefited.

Devotee: Generally, those who follow the impersonalistic commentary on the *Vedānta-sūtra* are concerned with liberation from the miseries of the material world. Does *Śrīmad-Bhāgavatam* also describe liberation?

Śrīla Prabhupāda: Yes. Since *Śrīmad-Bhāgavatam* is the real commentary on the *Vedānta-sūtra,* we find this verse describing liberation in this age:

kaler doṣa-nidhe rājann
asti hy eko mahān guṇaḥ
kīrtanād eva kṛṣṇasya
mukta-saṅgaḥ paraṁ vrajet

In this Kali-yuga, which is an ocean full of faults, there is one benediction. What is that? One can become liberated simply by chanting the Hare Kṛṣṇa *mantra.* This is real *vedānta,* and actually it is happening.

Devotee: Are you saying that the conclusion of the *Vedānta-sūtra* and the conclusion of *Śrīmad-Bhāgavatam* are one and the same – *bhakti*?

Śrīla Prabhupāda: Yes.

Devotee: But how does *bhakti* tie in to the conclusion of Vedāntic knowledge or wisdom? Here it says that *bhakti* is the most suitable and easiest path of God realization, but it also says that the Vedāntic teachings stress *jñāna,* or knowledge. Is that a fact?

Śrīla Prabhupāda: What is *jñāna*? That is explained by Lord Kṛṣṇa in *Bhagavad-gītā* [7.19]: *bahūnāṁ janmanām ante jñānavān māṁ prapadyate.* "After many, many births, he who is actually in knowledge surrenders unto Me." So unless one surrenders to Kṛṣṇa, there is no *jñāna.* This impersonalistic *"jñāna"* is all nonsense. The impersonalists are passing themselves off as *jñānīs,* but they have no knowledge at all. *Vedānta* means "the ultimate knowledge." So the subject matter of ultimate knowledge is Kṛṣṇa, God. If one does not know who God is, who Kṛṣṇa is, then where is one's knowledge? But if a rascal claims, "I am a man of knowledge," then what can be done?

In the same verse we just mentioned, Kṛṣṇa concludes, *vāsudevaḥ sarvam iti sa mahātmā su-durlabhaḥ:* "When one understands that Vāsudeva, Kṛṣṇa, is everything, one is in knowledge." Before that, there is no knowledge. It is simply misunderstanding. *Brahmeti paramātmeti bhagavān iti śabdyate.* One may begin by searching out impersonal Brahman by the speculative method, and then one may progress to realization of Paramātmā, the localized aspect of the Supreme. That is the secondary stage of realization. But the final stage is understanding the Supreme Personality of Godhead, Kṛṣṇa. So if you do not understand Kṛṣṇa, where is your knowledge? Halfway knowledge is no knowledge. We want complete knowledge, and that complete knowledge is possible by the grace of Kṛṣṇa, through *Bhagavad-gītā.*

Devotee: Can I ask the next question, Śrīla Prabhupāda? "Is a *guru* essential for one to enter the spiritual path and attain the goal? And how does one recognize one's *guru*?"

Śrīla Prabhupāda: Yes, a *guru* is necessary. That is explained in the *Bhagavad-gītā.* When Kṛṣṇa and Arjuna were talking as friends, there was no conclusion. Therefore Arjuna decided to accept Kṛṣṇa as his *guru.* [*To a devotee:*] find out this verse: *kārpaṇya-doṣopahata-svabhāvaḥ—*

Devotee [*reads*]:

kārpaṇya-doṣopahata-svabhāvaḥ
pṛcchāmi tvāṁ dharma-sammūḍha-cetāḥ
yac chreyaḥ syān niścitaṁ brūhi tan me
śiṣyas te 'haṁ śādhi māṁ tvāṁ prapannam

"Now I am confused about my duty and have lost all composure because of miserly weakness. In this condition I am asking You to tell me for certain what is best for me. Now I am Your disciple, and a soul surrendered unto You. Please instruct me." [*Bhagavad-gītā* 2.7]

Śrīla Prabhupāda: Not only Arjuna but everyone is perplexed about his duty. Nobody can decide for himself. When a physician is seriously sick, he does not prescribe his own treatment. He knows his brain is not in order, so he calls for another physician. Similarly, when we are perplexed, bewildered, when we cannot reach any solution – at that time the right person to search out is the *guru.* It is essential; you cannot avoid it.

So, in our present state of existence we are all perplexed. And under the circumstances, a *guru* is required to give us real direction. Arjuna represents the perplexed materialistic person who surrenders to a *guru.* And to set the example Arjuna decided on Kṛṣṇa as his *guru.* He did not go to anyone else. So the real *guru* is Kṛṣṇa. Kṛṣṇa is *guru* not only for Arjuna but for everyone. If we take instruction from Kṛṣṇa and abide by that instruction, our life is successful. The mission of the Kṛṣṇa consciousness movement is to get everyone to accept Kṛṣṇa as *guru.* That is our mission. We don't say, "I am Kṛṣṇa." We never say that. We simply ask people, "Please abide by the orders of Kṛṣṇa."

Devotee: Some of these so-called *gurus* will say some things that Kṛṣṇa says, but they'll give other instructions also. What is the position of such persons?

Śrīla Prabhupāda: They are most dangerous. Most dangerous. They are opportunists. According to the customer, they give some teachings so he will be pleased. Such a person is not a *guru;* he's a servant. He wants to serve his so-called disciples so that they may be satisfied and pay him something. A real *guru* is not a servant of his disciples; he is their master. If one becomes a servant, if he wants to please the disciples by flattering them to get their money, then he is not a *guru.* A *guru* should also be a servant, yes – but a servant of the Supreme. The literal meaning of the word *guru* is "heavy" – heavy with knowledge and authority, because his knowledge and authority come from Kṛṣṇa. You cannot utilize the *guru* for satisfying your whims.

Kṛṣṇa says, *sarva-dharmān parityajya mām ekaṁ śaraṇaṁ vraja:* "Abandon all varieties of religion and just surrender unto Me." And we say the same thing: "Surrender to Kṛṣṇa. Give up all other ideas of so-called *dharma,* or religiosity." We don't say, "I am the authority." No. We say, "Kṛṣṇa is the authority, and you should try to understand Kṛṣṇa." This is the Kṛṣṇa consciousness movement.

The Unseen Controller

"Even the most complicated computers need trained men to handle them. Similarly, we should know that this great machine, which is known as the cosmic manifestation, is manipulated by a supreme spirit. That is Krsna." In an excerpt from his book Kṛṣṇa Consciousness: The Matchless Gift, *Śrīla Prabhupāda offers intriguing insights into how God creates and controls the universe.*

The purpose of this Hare Kṛṣṇa movement is to bring man back to his original consciousness, which is Kṛṣṇa consciousness, clear consciousness. When water falls from the clouds, it is uncontaminated, like distilled water, but as soon as it touches the ground it becomes muddy and discolored. Similarly, we are originally pure spirit soul, part and parcel of Kṛṣṇa, and therefore our original, constitutional position is as pure as God's. In *Bhagavad-gītā* [15.7] Śrī Kṛṣṇa says:

mamaivāṁśo jīva-loke
jīva-bhūtaḥ sanātanaḥ
manaḥ ṣaṣṭhānīndriyāṇi
prakṛti-sthāni karṣati

"The living entities in this conditioned world are My eternal fragmental parts. Due to conditioned life, they are struggling very hard with the six senses, which include the mind."

Thus all living entities are part and parcel of Kṛṣṇa. It should always be remembered that when we speak of Kṛṣṇa we are speaking of God, because the name *Kṛṣṇa* denotes the all-attractive Supreme Personality of Godhead. As a fragment of gold is qualitatively the same as a gold reservoir, so the minute particles of Kṛṣṇa's body are therefore qualitatively as good as Kṛṣṇa. The chemical composition of God's body and the eternal spiritual body of the living entity is the same – spiritual. Thus originally, in our uncontaminated condition, we possessed a form as good as God's, but just as rain falls to the ground, so we come in contact with this material world, which is manipulated by the external energy, or material nature.

When we speak of external energy or material nature, the questions may be raised, "Whose energy? Whose nature?" Material energy or nature is not active independently. Such a concept is foolish. In the *Bhagavad-gītā* it is clearly stated that material nature does not work independently. When a foolish man sees a machine he may think that it is working automatically, but actually it is not – there is a driver, someone in control, although we sometimes cannot see the controller behind the machine due to our defective vision. There are many electronic mechanisms which work very wonderfully, but behind these intricate systems is a scientist who pushes the button. This is very simple to understand: since a machine is matter, it cannot work on its own accord but must work under spiritual direction. A tape recorder works, but it works according to the plans and under the direction of a living entity, a human being. The machine is complete, but unless it is manipulated by a spirit soul, it cannot work. Similarly, we should understand that this cosmic manifestation which we call nature is a great machine, and that behind this machine there is God, Kṛṣṇa. This is also affirmed in *Bhagavad-gītā*, where Kṛṣṇa says,

mayādhyakṣeṇa prakṛtiḥ
sūyate sa-carācaram
hetunānena kaunteya
jagad viparivartate

"This material nature, which is one of My energies, is working under My direction, O son of Kuntī, producing all the moving and nonmoving beings. Under its rule this manifestation is created and annihilated again and again." [*Bhagavad-gītā* 9.10]

So Kṛṣṇa says that material nature is acting under His direction.

Thus behind everything there is a supreme controller. Modern civilization does not understand this due to lack of knowledge. It is the purpose of this Society for Krishna Consciousness, therefore, to enlighten all people who have been maddened by the influence of the three modes of material nature. In other words, our aim is to awaken mankind to its normal condition.

There are many universities, especially in the United States, and many departments of knowledge, but they are not discussing these points. Where is the department for this knowledge that we find given by Śrī Kṛṣṇa in the *Bhagavad-gītā*? When I spoke before some students and faculty members at the Massachusetts Institute of Technology, the first question I raised was: "Where is the technological department which is investigating the difference between a dead man and a living man?" When a man dies, something is lost. Where is the technology to replace it? Why don't scientists try to solve this problem? Because this is a very difficult subject matter, they set it aside and busily engage in the technology of eating, sleeping, mating, and defending. However, the Vedic literatures inform us that this is animal technology. Animals are also trying their best to eat well, to have an enjoyable sex life, to sleep peacefully, and to defend themselves. What, then, is the difference between man's knowledge and the animals' knowledge? The fact is that man's knowledge should be developed to explore that difference between a living body and a dead body.

That spiritual knowledge was imparted by Kṛṣṇa to Arjuna in the beginning of the *Bhagavad-gītā*. Being a friend of Kṛṣṇa's, Arjuna was a very intelligent man, but his knowledge, as all men's, was limited. Kṛṣṇa spoke, however, of subject matters which were beyond Arjuna's finite knowledge. These subjects are called *adhokṣaja* because our direct perception, by which we acquire material knowledge, fails to approach them. For example, we have many powerful microscopes to see what we cannot see with our limited vision, but there is no microscope that can show us the soul within the body. Nevertheless, the soul is there.

The *Bhagavad-gītā* informs us that in this body there is a proprietor – the spirit soul. I am the proprietor of my body, and other souls are the proprietors of their bodies. I say "my hand," but not "I hand." Since it is "my hand," I am different from the hand, being its owner. Similarly, we speak of "my eye," "my leg," "my" this, "my" that. In the midst of all these objects which belong to me, where am I? The search for the answer to this question is the process of meditation. In real meditation, we ask, "Where am I? What am I?" We cannot find the answers to these questions by any material effort, and because of this all the universities are setting these questions aside. They say, "It is too difficult a subject." Or they brush it aside: "It is irrelevant."

Thus engineers direct their attention to creating and attempting to perfect the horseless carriage and the wingless bird. Formerly, horses were drawing carriages, and there was no air pollution, but now there are cars and airplanes, and the scientists are very proud. "We have invented horseless carriages and wingless birds," they boast. Although they invent imitation wings for the airplane, they cannot invent a soulless body. When they are able to do this, they will deserve credit. But such an attempt would necessarily be frustrated, for we know that there is no machine that can work without a spirit soul behind it. Even the most complicated computers need trained men to handle them. Similarly, we should know that this great machine known as the cosmic manifestation is manipulated by a supreme spirit. That is Kṛṣṇa.

Scientists are searching for the ultimate cause or the ultimate controller of this material universe and are postulating different theories and proposals, but the real means for knowledge is very easy and perfect: we need only hear from the perfect person, Kṛṣṇa. By accepting the knowledge imparted in *Bhagavad-gītā*, anyone can immediately know that this great cosmic machine, of which the earth is a part, is working so wonderfully because there is a driver behind it – Kṛṣṇa.

Our process of knowledge is very easy. Kṛṣṇa's instruction, *Bhagavad-gītā,* is the principal book of knowledge given by the *ādi-puruṣa* Himself, the Supreme Primeval Person, the Supreme Personality of Godhead. He is indeed the perfect person. It may be argued that although we have accepted Him as a perfect person, there are many others who do not. But one should not think that this acceptance is whimsical: He is accepted as the perfect person on the evidence of many authorities. We do not accept Kṛṣṇa as perfect simply on the basis of our whims or sentiments. No – Kṛṣṇa is accepted as God by many Vedic authorities like Vyāsadeva, the author of all Vedic literatures. The treasure house of knowledge is contained in the *Vedas,* and their author, Vyāsadeva, accepts Kṛṣṇa as the Supreme Personality of Godhead, and Vyāsadeva's spiritual master, Nārada, also accepts Kṛṣṇa as such. Nārada's spiritual master, Brahmā, accepts Kṛṣṇa not only as the Supreme Person but the supreme controller as well – *īśvaraḥ paramaḥ kṛṣṇaḥ:* "The supreme controller is Kṛṣṇa."

There is no one in the creation who can claim that he is not controlled. Everyone, regardless of how important or powerful, has a controller over his head. Kṛṣṇa, however, has no controller; therefore He is God. He is the controller of everyone, but there is no one superior to Him, no one to control Him; nor is there anyone equal to Him, no one to share His platform of absolute control. This may sound very strange, for there are many so-called Gods nowadays. Indeed, Gods have become very cheap, being especially imported from India. People in other countries are fortunate that Gods are not manufactured there, but in India Gods are manufactured practically every day. We often hear that God is coming to Los Angeles or New York and that people are gathering to receive Him, etc. But Kṛṣṇa is not the type of God who is created in a mystic factory. No. He was not *made* God: He *is* God.

We should know, then, on the basis of authority, that behind this gigantic material nature, the cosmic manifestation, there is God – Kṛṣṇa – and that He is accepted by all Vedic authorities. Acceptance of authority is not new for us; everyone accepts authority – in some form or another. For education we go to a teacher or to a school or simply learn from our father and mother. They are all authorities, and our nature is to learn from them. In our childhood we asked, "Father, what is this?" and Father would say, "This is a pen," "These are spectacles," or "This is a table." In this way, from the very beginning of life a child learns from his father and mother. A good father and mother never cheat when their son inquires from them; they give exact and correct information. Similarly, if we get spiritual information from an authority, and if the authority is not a cheater, then our knowledge is perfect. However, if we attempt to reach conclusions by dint of our own speculative powers, we are subject to fall into error. The process of induction, by which one reasons from particular facts or individual cases and arrives at a general conclusion, is never a perfect process. Because we are limited and our experience is limited, the inductive process of acquiring knowledge will always remain imperfect.

But if we receive information from the perfect source, Kṛṣṇa, and if we repeat that information, then what we are speaking can also be accepted as perfect and authoritative. This process of *paramparā,* or disciplic succession, means hearing from Kṛṣṇa, or from authorities who have accepted Kṛṣṇa, and repeating exactly what they have said. In *Bhagavad-gītā* Kṛṣṇa recommends this process of knowledge: *evaṁ paramparā-prāptam imaṁ rājarṣayo viduḥ.* "This supreme science was thus received through the chain of disciplic succession, and the saintly kings understood it in that way." [*Bhagavad-gītā* 4.2]

Formerly, knowledge was passed down by great saintly kings, who were the authorities. In previous ages, however, these kings were *ṛṣis* – great learned scholars and devotees – and because they were not ordinary men, the government which they headed worked very nicely. There are many instances in Vedic civilization of kings who attained perfection as devotees of God. For example, Dhruva Mahārāja went to the forest to search out God, and by practice of severe penance and austerity he found God within six months.

The Kṛṣṇa consciousness process is also based on austerity, but it is not very difficult. There are restrictions governing eating and sex life (only *prasādam,* food first offered to Kṛṣṇa, is taken, and sex is restricted to married life), and there are other regulations which facilitate and foster spiritual realization. It is not possible in these days to imitate Dhruva Mahārāja, but by following certain basic Vedic principles, we can make advancement in spiritual consciousness, Kṛṣṇa consciousness. As we advance, we become perfect in knowledge. What is the use of becoming a scientist or a philosopher if we cannot say what our next life will be? A realized student of Kṛṣṇa consciousness can very easily say what his next life is, what God is, what the living entity is, and what his relationship with God is. His knowledge is perfect because it is coming from perfect books of knowledge, such as the *Bhagavad-gītā* and the *Śrīmad-Bhāgavatam.*

This, then, is the process of Kṛṣṇa consciousness. It is very easy, and anyone can adopt it and make his life perfect. If someone says, "I'm not educated at all, and I cannot read books," he is still not disqualified.

He can still perfect his life by simply chanting the *mahā-mantra:* Hare Kṛṣṇa, Hare Kṛṣṇa, Kṛṣṇa Kṛṣṇa, Hare Hare/ Hare Rāma, Hare Rāma, Rāma Rāma, Hare Hare. Kṛṣṇa has given us a tongue and two ears, and we may be surprised to know that Kṛṣṇa is realized through the ears and tongue, not through the eyes. By hearing His message, we learn to control the tongue, and after the tongue is controlled, the other senses follow. Of all the senses, the tongue is the most voracious and difficult to control, but it can be controlled simply by chanting Hare Kṛṣṇa and tasting *kṛṣṇa-prasādam,* food offered to Kṛṣṇa.

We cannot understand Kṛṣṇa by sensual perception or by speculation. It is not possible, for Kṛṣṇa is so great that He is beyond our sensual range. But He can be understood by surrender. Kṛṣṇa therefore recommends this process:

sarva-dharmān parityajya
mām ekaṁ śaraṇaṁ vraja
ahaṁ tvāṁ sarva-pāpebhyo
mokṣayiṣyāmi mā śucaḥ

"Give up all varieties of religiousness and just surrender unto Me; and in return I shall protect you from all sinful reactions. Therefore you have nothing to fear." [*Bhagavad-gītā* 18.66]

Unfortunately, our disease is that we are rebellious – we automatically resist authority. Yet although we say that we don't want authority, nature is so strong that it forces authority upon us. We are forced to accept the authority of nature. What can be more pathetic than a man who claims to answer to no authority but who follows his senses blindly wherever they lead him? Our false claim to independence is simply foolishness. We are all under authority, yet we say that we don't want authority. This is called *māyā,* illusion. We do, however, have a certain independence – we can choose to be under the authority of our senses or the authority of Kṛṣṇa. The best and ultimate authority is Kṛṣṇa, for He is our eternal well-wisher, and He always speaks for our benefit. Since we have to accept some authority, why not accept His? Simply by hearing of His glories from the *Bhagavad-gītā* and the *Śrīmad-Bhāgavatam* and by chanting His names – Hare Kṛṣṇa – we can swiftly perfect our lives.

Who Is Kṛṣṇa?

August 1973, at Bhaktivedanta Manor, in the countryside near London. Several thousand guests (including the Indian High Commissioner) listen to Śrīla Prabhupāda speak about the confidential identity of the Supreme Personality of Godhead, who is revealed in India's timeless Vedic scriptures to be not an old man with a long white beard but a sublimely attractive and eternal youth.

Your Excellency the High Commissioner, ladies, and gentlemen, I thank you very much for your coming here and participating in this ceremony – Janmāṣṭamī, the advent of Lord Kṛṣṇa. In the *Bhagavad-gītā* [4.9] Kṛṣṇa says,

janma karma ca me divyam
evaṁ yo vetti tattvataḥ
tyaktvā dehaṁ punar janma
naiti mām eti so 'rjuna

"One who knows the transcendental nature of My appearance and activities does not, upon leaving the body, take his birth again in this material world, but attains My eternal abode, O Arjuna."

It is a fact that we can stop our repeated births and deaths and achieve the state of immortality. But the modern civilization – our great philosophers, great politicians, and great scientists – they have no idea that it is possible to attain the stage of *amṛtatvam*, immortality. We are all *amṛta*, deathless, immortal. In the *Bhagavad-gītā* [2.20] it is said, *na jāyate mriyate vā kadācit:* We living entities – we never die and never take birth. *Ajo nityaḥ śāśvato 'yaṁ purāṇo na hanyate hanyamāne śarīre.* Every one of us – we are primeval and eternal, without beginning and without end. And after the annihilation of this body, we do not die. But when the body is finished, we will have to accept another body:

dehino 'smin yathā dehe
kaumāraṁ yauvanaṁ jarā
tathā dehāntara-prāptir
dhīras tatra na muhyati

"As the embodied soul continuously passes, in this body, from boyhood to youth to old age, the soul similarly passes into another body at death. A sober person is not bewildered by such a change." [*Bhagavad-gītā* 2.13]

At the present moment, all over the world people are lacking knowledge of this simple thing: that all of us living entities are part and parcel of Lord Kṛṣṇa – that like Kṛṣṇa, we are eternal, we are blissful, and we are cognizant. Kṛṣṇa is described in the Vedic literatures:

īśvaraḥ paramaḥ kṛṣṇaḥ
sac-cid-ānanda-vigrahaḥ
anādir ādir govindaḥ
sarva-kāraṇa-kāraṇam

"Kṛṣṇa, who is known as Govinda, is the Supreme Personality of Godhead. He has an eternal, blissful, spiritual body. He is the origin of all, but He has no origin, for He is the prime cause of all causes." [*Brahma-saṁhitā* 5.1]

When I say *Kṛṣṇa,* that means "God." It is sometimes said, "God has no name." That's a fact. But God's name is given by His activities. For instance, Kṛṣṇa accepted sonship to Mahārāja Nanda and Yaśodāmāyī and also to Vasudeva and Devakī. Of course, no one is actually the father or mother of Kṛṣṇa, because Kṛṣṇa is the original father of everyone. But when Kṛṣṇa comes here, when He makes His advent, He accepts certain exalted devotees as His father, as His mother.

Still, Kṛṣṇa is *ādi-puruṣam,* the original person. Then must Kṛṣṇa be very old? No. *Nava-yauvanaṁ ca:* Always a fresh youth. That is Kṛṣṇa. When Kṛṣṇa was on the Battlefield of Kurukṣetra, He was just like a boy of twenty years or, at most, twenty-four years. But at that time

He had great-grandchildren. So Kṛṣṇa is always a youth. These are the statements of the Vedic literatures.

But if we simply read the Vedic literatures as a formality, it will be very difficult to understand what Kṛṣṇa is – although all the *Vedas* are meant for understanding Kṛṣṇa. In the *Bhagavad-gītā* [15.15] Kṛṣṇa says, *vedaiś ca sarvair aham eva vedyaḥ:* "By all the *Vedas* it is I who am to be known." What is the use of studying the *Vedas* if you do not understand Kṛṣṇa? The ultimate goal of education is to understand the Supreme Lord, the supreme father, the supreme cause. As it is said in the *Vedānta-sūtra, athāto brahma-jijñāsā:* "Now – in the human form of life – is the time to discuss the Supreme Absolute Truth, Brahman."

And what is this Brahman? *Janmādy asya yataḥ.* Brahman is the one from whom everything emanates. So science and philosophy mean finding out the ultimate cause of everything. And this we are getting from the Vedic literature – that Kṛṣṇa is *sarva-kāraṇa-kāraṇam,* the cause of all causes.

Just try to understand. For instance, I am caused by my father; my father is caused by his father; *he* is caused by *his* father, who is caused by *his* father . . . In this way, if you go on searching, then you'll ultimately come to someone who is the cause that has no cause. *Anādir ādir govindaḥ:* The cause that has no cause is Govinda – Kṛṣṇa. I may be the cause of my son, but at the same time I am the result of another cause (my father). But the Vedic literatures say that Kṛṣṇa is the original person; He has no cause. That is Kṛṣṇa.

Therefore Kṛṣṇa says, "Just try to learn about the transcendental nature of My advent and activities." The advent of Kṛṣṇa – it is a very important thing. We should try to understand Kṛṣṇa, why He makes His advent, why He comes down to this material world, what His business is, what His activities are. If we simply try to understand Kṛṣṇa, then what will be the result? The result will be *tyaktvā dehaṁ punar janma naiti mām eti so 'rjuna:* we will get immortality.

The aim of life is *amṛtatvāya kalpate,* to achieve immortality. So today, on the advent of Kṛṣṇa, we shall try to understand the philosophy of Kṛṣṇa.

His Excellency was speaking of peace. The peace formula is there in the *Bhagavad-gītā* – spoken by Kṛṣṇa. What is that?

bhoktāraṁ yajña-tapasāṁ
sarva-loka-maheśvaram
suhṛdaṁ sarva-bhūtānāṁ
jñātvā māṁ śāntim ṛcchati

"A person in full consciousness of Me, knowing Me to be the ultimate beneficiary of all sacrifices and austerities, the Supreme Lord of all planets and demigods, and the benefactor and well-wisher of all living entities, attains peace from the pangs of material miseries." [*Bhagavad-gītā* 5.29] The politicians and diplomats are trying to establish peace in the world. We have the United Nations and many other organizations. They are working to establish real peace and tranquillity, to eliminate misunderstanding between man and man and nation and nation. But that is not happening. The defect is that the root is wrong. Everyone is thinking, "It is my country," "It is my family," "It is my society," "It is my property." This "my" is illusion. In the Vedic literatures it is said, *janasya moho 'yam ahaṁ mameti:* This "I-and-my" philosophy is *māyā* – illusion.

So if you want to get out of this *māyā,* this illusion, then you have to accept Kṛṣṇa's formula. *Mām eva ye prapadyante māyām etāṁ taranti te:* Whoever surrenders to Kṛṣṇa can easily cross beyond all illusion. Everything is there in the *Bhagavad-gītā,* for our guidance. If we accept the philosophy of the *Bhagavad-gītā* – as it is – everything is there. Peace is there, prosperity is there.

Unfortunately, we do not accept it, or we misinterpret it. This is our misfortune. In the *Bhagavad-gītā* [9.34] Kṛṣṇa says, *man-manā bhava mad-bhakto mad-yājī māṁ namaskuru:* "Always think of Me, become My devotee, worship Me, and offer obeisances unto Me." Is it a very difficult task? Here is Kṛṣṇa's Deity. If you think of this Deity, is it very difficult? You come into the temple, and just as a devotee would do, you offer your respect to the Deity. As far as possible, try to worship the Deity.

Kṛṣṇa does not want your property. Kṛṣṇa is open to the poorest man for being worshiped. What is He asking? He says, *patraṁ puṣpaṁ phalaṁ toyaṁ yo me bhaktyā prayacchati:* "With devotion, if a person offers Me a little leaf, a little fruit, a little water, I accept it." [*Bhagavad-gītā* 9.26] Kṛṣṇa is not hungry, but Kṛṣṇa wants to make you a devotee. That is the main point. *Yo me bhaktyā prayacchati:* "Offer something to Me – with devotion." That is the main principle. Offer Kṛṣṇa some little thing. Kṛṣṇa is not hungry; Kṛṣṇa is providing food for everyone. But Kṛṣṇa wants your love, your devotion. Therefore He is begging a little water or fruit or a flower. In this way, *man-manā bhava mad-bhakta:* you can think of Kṛṣṇa and become His devotee.

There is no difficulty in understanding Kṛṣṇa and accepting Kṛṣṇa consciousness. But we'll not do it – that is our disease. Otherwise, it is not difficult at all. And as soon as we become a devotee of Kṛṣṇa, we understand the whole universal situation. Our *bhāgavata* philosophy, our God conscious philosophy, is also a kind of spiritual communism, because we regard Kṛṣṇa as the supreme father and all living entities as sons of Kṛṣṇa. And Kṛṣṇa says, *sarva-loka-maheśvaram:* He is the proprietor of all planets. Therefore whatever there is, either in the sky or in the water or on the land, it is all Kṛṣṇa's property. And because we are all sons of Kṛṣṇa, every one of us has the right to use our father's property. But we should not encroach upon others. This is the formula for peace. *Īśāvāsyam idaṁ sarvaṁ . . . mā gṛdhaḥ kasyasvid dhanam:* "Everything belongs to God, and since you are sons of God, you have the right to use your father's property. But do not take more than you need. This is punishable." [*Īśopaniṣad* 1] If anyone takes more than he needs, then he's a thief. *Yajñārthāt karmaṇo 'nyatra loko 'yaṁ karma-bandhanaḥ* [*Bhagavad-gītā* 3.9]: Whatever we do, we should do it for the satisfaction of Kṛṣṇa. We should act for Kṛṣṇa; we should do everything for Kṛṣṇa.

That is what we are teaching here. In this temple we are all residing happily – Americans, Indians, Englishmen, Canadians, Africans – people from all different parts of the world. You know that. It is like that not only in this temple, but wherever people are Kṛṣṇa conscious, throughout the world. Kṛṣṇa makes His advent to teach this lesson.

When we forget this philosophy – that Kṛṣṇa is the supreme father, Kṛṣṇa is the supreme proprietor, Kṛṣṇa is the supreme enjoyer, and Kṛṣṇa is the supreme friend of everyone – when we forget this, then we come into this material world and struggle for existence, fight with one another. This is material life.

Nor can we get any relief through our politicians, diplomats, philosophers. They have tried so much, but actually nothing they have tried has become fruitful. Take the United Nations. It was organized after the second great war, and they wanted, "We shall now settle everything peacefully." But there is no such thing. The fighting is going on, between Pakistan and India or between Vietnam and America or this and that. Mundane politics and diplomacy and philosophy – this is not the process. The process is Kṛṣṇa consciousness. Everyone has to understand this point, that we are not proprietors. The actual proprietor is Kṛṣṇa. That's a fact. Take America, for example. Say two hundred years ago, the European immigrants were not the proprietors. Somebody else was the proprietor, and before that somebody else was the proprietor, or it was vacant land. But the actual proprietor is Kṛṣṇa. Artificially we are claiming, "It is my property." This is called *māyā,* illusion. So Kṛṣṇa makes His advent to give us this lesson. Kṛṣṇa says, *yadā yadā hi dharmasya glānir bhavati bhārata:* "My dear Arjuna, I come when there are discrepancies in the process of religious life." [*Bhagavad-gītā* 4.7]

And what is real *dharma,* real religious life? The simple definition of *dharma* is *dharmaṁ tu sākṣād bhagavat-praṇītam:* "Real religious life is that which is enunciated directly by the Supreme Personality of Godhead." [*Śrīmad-Bhāgavatam* 6.3.19] For instance, what do you mean by "civil law"? Civil law means the word given by the state. You cannot make civil law at home. That is not possible. Whatever the government gives you – "You should act like this" – that is law. Similarly *dharma,* religious life, means the direction given by God. That is *dharma.* Simple definition. If you create some *dharma* or I create some *dharma* or another man creates another *dharma,* these are not *dharma.*

Therefore Kṛṣṇa ends the *Bhagavad-gītā* by saying, *sarva-dharmān parityajya mam ekaṁ śaraṇaṁ vraja:* "Just give up all your concocted ideas about *dharma* and surrender to Me." [*Bhagavad-gītā* 18.66] This is *dharma* – surrender to Kṛṣṇa. Any other *"dharma"* is not *dharma.* Otherwise why does Kṛṣṇa ask, *sarva-dharmān parityajya* – "Give it all up"? He has already said, "In every age I make My advent to establish the principles of religion." And at last He says that we should give up all the so-called religious principles that we have manufactured. All these man-made principles are not actually religious principles. Real *dharma,* real religious life, means what is given by God. But we have no understanding of what God is and what His word is. That is modern civilization's defect.

But the order is there, God is there – it is simply that we won't accept. So where is the possibility of peace? Everything is there, ready-made. But we won't accept. So what is the remedy for our disease? We are searching after peace, but we won't accept the very thing that will actually give us peace. This is our disease. Therefore, this Kṛṣṇa consciousness movement is trying to awaken the dormant Kṛṣṇa consciousness in everyone's heart. Just consider: four or five years ago, these Europeans and Americans had never even heard of Kṛṣṇa – so how are they now taking Kṛṣṇa consciousness so seriously? Kṛṣṇa consciousness is already there in everyone's heart. It simply has to be awakened. And this awakening process is described in the *Caitanya-caritāmṛta* [*Madhya* 22.107]:

nitya-siddha kṛṣṇa-prema 'sādhya' kabhu naya
śravaṇādi-śuddha-citte karaye udaya

Love for Kṛṣṇa, devotion for Kṛṣṇa, is within everyone's heart, but we have forgotten. So this Kṛṣṇa consciousness movement is simply meant for awakening that dormant love, by giving everyone the chance to hear about Kṛṣṇa. This is the process.

For instance, when you are sleeping, I have to call you loudly. "Mr. Such-and-such! Such-and-such! Get up! You have to tend to this business." No other senses will act when you are sleeping. But the ear will act. Therefore in this age, when people are so fallen that they will not listen to anything, if we chant this Hare Kṛṣṇa *mahā-mantra* they'll be awakened to Kṛṣṇa consciousness. This is practical. So if we are actually anxious for peace and tranquillity in society, then we must be very serious about understanding Kṛṣṇa. That is my request. Don't take the Kṛṣṇa consciousness movement lightly.

This movement can solve all the problems of life, all the problems in the world. Social, political, philosophical, religious, economic – everything can be solved by Kṛṣṇa consciousness. Therefore, we request those who are leaders – like His Excellency, who is present here – to try to understand this Kṛṣṇa consciousness movement. It is very scientific and authorized. It is not a mental concoction or a sentimental movement. It is a most scientific movement. So we are inviting all leaders from all countries to try to understand. If you are sober, if you are actually reasonable, you'll understand that this Kṛṣṇa consciousness movement is the most sublime movement for the welfare of the whole human society.

Anyone may come – we are prepared to discuss this subject matter. The ultimate goal of human life is to achieve immortality. *Tyaktvā dehaṁ punar janma naiti.* This is our mission, but we have forgotten this. We are simply leading the life of cats and dogs, without any knowledge that we can achieve that perfection of life where there will be no more birth, no more death. We do not even understand that there is the possibility of *amṛtatvam,* immortality. But it is totally possible. Nobody wants to die. Nobody wants to become an old man. Nobody wants to become diseased. This is our natural inclination. Why? Because originally, in our spiritual form, there is no birth, no death, no old age, no disease. So after moving through the evolutionary process, up through the aquatics, plants, trees, birds, when at last we come to this human form of body – then we should know what the goal of life is. The goal of life is *amṛtatvam,* to become immortal.

Immortal you *can* become, simply by becoming Kṛṣṇa conscious. Kṛṣṇa says it. It is a fact. We simply have to understand. *Janma karma ca me divyam evaṁ yo vetti tattvataḥ.* If you try to understand Kṛṣṇa in truth, then *tyaktvā dehaṁ punar janma naiti:* After giving up this body, you won't have to accept any more material bodies. And as soon as you don't accept any more material bodies, that means you have become immortal. The thing is, by nature we *are* immortal. And Kṛṣṇa comes here to teach us this lesson:

mamaivāṁśo jīva-loke
jīva-bhūtaḥ sanātanaḥ
manaḥ ṣaṣṭānīndriyāṇi
prakṛti-sthāni karṣati

"You are immortal by nature. As spirit soul, you are part and parcel of Me. I am immortal, and so you are also immortal. Unnecessarily, you are trying to be happy in this material world." [*Bhagavad-gītā* 15.7]

You have already tried and tried to find happiness in sensuous life, through so many bodies – as cats, as dogs, as demigods, as trees, as plants, as insects. So now that you have a human body, with its higher intelligence, don't be captivated by sensuous life. Just try to understand Kṛṣṇa. That is the verdict of the Vedic literatures. *Nāyaṁ deho deha-bhājāṁ nṛloke kaṣṭān kāmān arhate viḍ-bhujāṁ ye* [*Śrīmad-Bhāgavatam* 5.5.1]: To work very hard like dogs and hogs for sense gratification is not the proper ambition of human life; human life is meant for a little austerity. *Tapo divyaṁ putrakā yena sattvaṁ śuddhyet:* We have to purify our existence; that is the mission of human life. Why should we purify our existence? *Brahma-saukhyaṁ tv anantam:* Because then we will get spiritual realization, the unlimited, endless pleasure and happiness. That is real pleasure, real happiness:

ramante yogino 'nante
satyānande-cid-ātmani
iti rāma-padenāsau
paraṁ brahmābhidhīyate

"The mystics derive unlimited transcendental pleasures from the Absolute Truth, and therefore the Supreme Absolute Truth, the Personality of Godhead, is also known as Rāma." [*Padma Purāṇa*]

All the great saintly persons of India have cultivated this spiritual knowledge so nicely and fully. Formerly, people used to go to India to find out about spiritual life. Even Jesus Christ went there. And yet we are not taking advantage of it. It is not that these literatures and directions are meant only for the Indians or for the Hindus or for the *brāhmaṇas.* No. They are meant for everyone, because Kṛṣṇa claims, *ahaṁ bīja-pradaḥ pitā:* "I am everyone's father." Therefore, He is very anxious to make us peaceful and happy. Just as an ordinary father wants to see that his son is well situated and happy, similarly Kṛṣṇa wants to see every one of us well situated and happy. Therefore He comes sometimes. This is the purpose of Kṛṣṇa's advent. Thank you very much.

The Supreme Artist

In February 1973, Śrīla Prabhupāda was invited to speak at an art gallery in Auckland, New Zealand. There he invited his listeners to contemplate the works of the supreme artist – Lord Kṛṣṇa. "The rose is created out of the energies of the Supreme Lord, but these energies are so subtle and so artistic that a nice flower can bloom overnight. So, Krsna is the greatest artist."

Ladies and gentlemen, I thank you very much for coming here and giving us a chance to speak about the supreme artist. The *Vedas* describe how great an artist Kṛṣṇa is: *na tasya kāryaṁ karaṇaṁ ca vidyate na tat-samaś cābhyadhikaś ca dṛśyate.* Nobody can be found who is greater than the Supreme Personality of Godhead or equal to Him, and although He is the greatest artist, He doesn't have to do anything personally.

In this world everyone of us knows somebody lesser than us, somebody equal to us, and somebody greater than us. That is our experience. However great you may be, you will find somebody equal to you and somebody greater than you. But as far as the Supreme Personality of Godhead is concerned, great sages have concluded by research and experiment that nobody is equal to Him or greater than Him.

God is so great that He has nothing to do, no duties He must perform (*na tasya kāryaṁ karaṇaṁ ca vidyate*). Why? *Parāsya śaktir vividhaiva śrūyate:* His energies are multifarious, and they are working automatically, according to His desire (*svābhāvikī jñāna-bala-kriyā ca*). Suppose you are an artist. To paint a picture of a very nice rose, you have to take your brush, mix your colors on the palate, and tax your brain to make the picture beautiful. But in a garden you can see not only one rose but many thousands of roses blooming. They have been very artistically "painted" by nature.

But we should go deeper into the matter. What is nature? Nature is a working instrument, that's all – an energy. Without some energy working, how could the rose bloom so beautifully from the bud? There must be some energy working, and that energy is Kṛṣṇa's energy. But it acts so subtly and swiftly that we cannot understand how it is working.

The material energies seem to be working automatically, but actually there is a brain behind them. When you paint a picture, everyone can see that you are working. Similarly, the "painting" of the actual rose is also worked out by several energies. Don't think that the rose has been created automatically. No. Nothing is created automatically. The rose is created out of the energies of the Supreme Lord, but these energies are so subtle and so artistic that a nice flower can bloom overnight.

So, Kṛṣṇa is the greatest artist. Nowadays, in the electronic age, a scientist just pushes a button and his machine works so perfectly. Or an airplane pilot simply pushes a button and a huge machine just like a small city flies in the sky. So if it is possible for ordinary men of this world to work so wonderfully simply by pushing some buttons, how much greater must be God's ability to work. How much more fertile His brain must be than ordinary artists' or scientists' brains. Simply by His desire – "Let there be creation!" – everything is immediately manifest. So Kṛṣṇa is the greatest artist.

There is no limit to Kṛṣṇa's artistic ability, because Kṛṣṇa is the seed of all creation (*bījaṁ māṁ sarva-bhūtānām*). You have all seen a banyan tree. It grows from a small seed. This small seed has so much potency that if you sow it in a fertile place and water it, one day it will become a big banyan tree. Now, what are the potencies, what are the artistic and scientific arrangements, within that small seed that allow it to grow into a big banyan tree? Also, on that banyan tree there are many thousands of fruits, and within each fruit there are thousands of seeds, and each seed contains the potency of another tree. So where is the scientist who can create in that way? Where is the artist within this material world who can create a work of art as pleasing as a banyan tree? These inquiries should be made.

The first aphorism of the *Vedānta-sūtra* is *athāto brahma-jijñāsā:* "In the human form of life one should inquire about the Absolute Truth." So one should carefully study these questions. You cannot manufacture a machine that automatically grows into a big banyan tree. So don't you think there must be a big artistic brain, a great scientific brain, behind nature? If you simply say, "Nature is working," that is not a sufficient explanation.

The second aphorism of the *Vedānta-sūtra* is *janmādy asya yataḥ:* "The Absolute Truth is He from whom everything is generated." We have to expand our vision from the small things to the great things. Now we become amazed when we see a small sputnik flying in the sky. It is flying toward the moon, and we are giving all credit to the scientists, and the scientists are challenging, "What is God? Science is everything."

But if you are intelligent you will compare the sputnik to the millions and trillions of planets and stars. Just on this tiny earth planet there are so many oceans, so many mountains, so many skyscrapers. But if you go above this planet a few million miles, it will look just like a small spot. You will see it as just a spot in the sky. And there are millions of planets floating in the sky like swabs of cotton. So if we give so much credit to the scientists who have manufactured a sputnik, how much more credit we should give to the person who has manufactured this universal arrangement. This is Kṛṣṇa consciousness – appreciating the greatest artist, the greatest scientist.

We may appreciate so many artists, but unless we appreciate the greatest artist, Kṛṣṇa, our life is wasted. We find that appreciation in the *Brahma-saṁhitā*, the prayers of Lord Brahmā, the creator of this universe. In appreciation of Govinda, Kṛṣṇa, he sings,

yasya prabhā prabhavato jagad-aṇḍa-koṭi-
koṭiṣv aśeṣa-vasudhādi-vibhūti-bhinnam
tad brahma niṣkalam anantam aśeṣa-bhūtaṁ
govindam ādi-puruṣaṁ tam aham bhajāmi

Now we are trying to understand the planetary system by our scientific method. But we have not been able to finish studying even the nearest planet, the moon, what to speak of the millions and billions of other planets. But from the *Brahma-saṁhitā* we get this knowledge: *yasya prabhā prabhavato jagad-aṇḍa-koṭi-koṭiṣu.* By the glaring effulgence emanating from Kṛṣṇa's body, innumerable universes are created. We cannot study even one universe, but from the *Brahma-saṁhitā* we get information that there are innumerable universes and that in each and every universe there are innumerable planets (*jagad-aṇḍa-koṭi-koṭiṣu*). (*Jagad-aṇḍa* means "universes," and *koṭi-koṭiṣu* means "in innumerable.") So there are innumerable universes with innumerable suns, innumerable moons, and innumerable planets.

All of this is made possible by Kṛṣṇa's bodily effulgence, which is called the *brahma-jyotir*. The *jñānīs*, those who are trying to approach the Absolute Truth by mental speculation, by dint of their tiny brain power, can at most approach this *brahma-jyotir*. But that *brahma-jyotir* is only the illumination of Kṛṣṇa's body. The best analogy is the sunshine. The sunshine is coming from the sun globe. The sun is localized, and the effulgence of the sun, the sunshine, is distributed all over the universe. Just as the moon reflects the sunshine, the sun also reflects the *brahma-jyotir*. And the *brahma-jyotir* is the bodily effulgence of Kṛṣṇa.

So the greatest art is to understand Kṛṣṇa. That is the greatest art. If we actually want to be an artist, we should try to understand, or try to be intimately associated with, the greatest artist, Kṛṣṇa. For this purpose we have established the International Society for Krishna Consciousness. The members of this society are trained to see in everything the display of Kṛṣṇa's artistic sense. That is Kṛṣṇa consciousness – to see the artistic hand of Kṛṣṇa everywhere.

In the *Bhagavad-gītā* [10.8] Kṛṣṇa says, *ahaṁ sarvasya prabhavo mattaḥ sarvaṁ pravartate:* "Whatever you see is an emanation from Me. Everything is created out of My energy." One should understand this fact – that Kṛṣṇa is the origin of everything. Lord Brahmā confirms this in his *Brahma-saṁhitā* [5.1]: *īśvaraḥ paramaḥ kṛṣṇaḥ*. "Kṛṣṇa is the supreme controller." Here in this material world we have experience of many controllers. Every one of us is a controller. You are a controller; I am a controller. But above you there is another controller, and above him there is another controller, and so on. You may go on searching out controller after controller, and when you come to the supreme controller – He who is not controlled by anyone but who controls everyone else – that is Kṛṣṇa. This is our definition of God: the supreme controller.

Nowadays it has become a cheap business to see many "Gods." But you can test someone to see if he is God. If he is controlled by somebody else, he is not God. Only if he is the supreme controller should you accept him as God. That is the simple test for God.

Now, another quality of God is that He is full of pleasure (*ānanda-mayo 'bhyāsāt*). By nature the Supreme Absolute Person is *ānanda-maya*, full of pleasure. Suppose you are an artist. You engage in artistic work just to get some pleasure. By painting a picture you enjoy some *rasa*, some pleasurable mellow. Otherwise, why would you work so hard? There must be some pleasure in painting.

So, Kṛṣṇa is *raso vai saḥ*, the reservoir of all pleasurable mellows. He is *sac-cid-ānanda-vigrahaḥ*, full of eternity, knowledge, and pleasure. (*Ānanda* means "pleasure.") His pleasure potency is Śrīmatī Rādhārāṇī. You have seen pictures of Rādhā and Kṛṣṇa. So, Rādhārāṇī is the manifestation of Kṛṣṇa's pleasure potency. As I have already explained, Kṛṣṇa has innumerable energies, and one of these is His pleasure potency, Rādhārāṇī.

So those who have developed love of God are enjoying transcendental pleasure at every moment by seeing the artistic work of Kṛṣṇa everywhere. That is the position of a devotee. Therefore we request everyone to become a devotee, to become Kṛṣṇa conscious, so that you will see the artistic work of Kṛṣṇa everywhere.

Seeing Kṛṣṇa everywhere is not difficult. For example, suppose you are thirsty and you drink some water. When you drink you feel so much pleasure. And Kṛṣṇa is the reservoir of all pleasure (*raso vai saḥ*). So, that pleasure you feel by drinking water – that is Kṛṣṇa. Kṛṣṇa states this in *Bhagavad-gītā* [7.8]: *raso 'ham apsu kaunteya.* "I am the taste of water." For an ordinary person, who cannot fully appreciate Kṛṣṇa, Kṛṣṇa is giving the instruction that He is the taste of the water that quenches your thirst. If you simply try to understand that this taste is Kṛṣṇa, or God, you become God conscious.

So it is not very difficult to become Kṛṣṇa conscious. You simply require a little training. And if you read *Bhagavad-gītā As It Is* – understanding it the way it is stated by Kṛṣṇa Himself, without any rascaldom or false interpretation – you will become Kṛṣṇa conscious. And if you become Kṛṣṇa conscious, your life is successful. You will return to Kṛṣṇa (*tyaktvā dehaṁ punar janma naiti mām eti*).

There is no loss in becoming Kṛṣṇa conscious, but the gain is very great. Therefore we request all of you to try to become Kṛṣṇa conscious. Read *Bhagavad-gītā As It Is;* you will find all the information you need to become Kṛṣṇa conscious. Or, if you don't want to read *Bhagavad-gītā,* please chant Hare Kṛṣṇa, Hare Kṛṣṇa, Kṛṣṇa Kṛṣṇa, Hare Hare/ Hare Rāma, Hare Rāma, Rāma Rāma, Hare Hare. You will still become Kṛṣṇa conscious.

Thank you very much.

Absolute Love

"Everyone is frustrated – husbands, wives, boys, girls. Everywhere there is frustration, because our loving propensity is not being utilized properly." In this lecture given in Seattle, Washington, in October of 1968, Śrīla Prabhupāda reveals how we can achieve complete satisfaction by directing our love toward the Supreme Person.

oṁ ajñāna-timirāndhasya
jñānāñjana-śalākayā
cakṣur unmīlitaṁ yena
tasmai śrī-gurave namaḥ

"I offer my respectful obeisances unto my spiritual master, who has opened my eyes, which were blinded by the darkness of ignorance, with the torchlight of knowledge."

Everyone in this material world is born into ignorance, or darkness. Actually, the nature of this material world is that it is dark. It may be lighted with sunlight, moonlight, fire, or electricity, but its nature is dark. That is a scientific fact. So everyone born in this material world – from Brahmā, the chief personality in the topmost planet of this universe, down to the ant – is born into the darkness of ignorance.

Now, the Vedic injunction is, *tamasi mā jyotir gamaḥ:* "Don't remain in darkness; come to the light." And for this, a spiritual master is needed. It is the duty of the spiritual master to open the eyes of the person in darkness with the torch of knowledge, and one should offer one's respectful obeisances unto such a spiritual master.

People should not be kept in darkness; they should be brought into the light. Therefore, in every human society there is a religious institution of some sort. What is the purpose of Hinduism, Mohammedanism,

Christianity, or Buddhism? The purpose is to bring people to the light. That is the purpose of religion.

And what is that light? That light is the Supreme Personality of Godhead. The *Śrīmad-Bhāgavatam* states, *dharmaṁ tu sākṣād bhagavat-praṇītam:* "The codes of religion are directly given by the Supreme Personality of Godhead." In the state there are laws that you must follow. The head of the state gives some laws, and if you are a good citizen you obey those laws, and live peacefully. These laws may be different according to time, circumstances, or people – the state laws of India may not agree cent percent with the laws of the United States – but in every state there are laws that you must obey. One has to abide by the law. Otherwise one is considered the lowest in society, a criminal, and is subject to punishment. That is the general principle.

Similarly, religion means to obey the laws of God. That's all. And if a human being does not obey the laws of God, he is no better than an animal. All scriptures, all religious principles, are meant to elevate man from the animal platform to the human platform. Therefore, a person without religious principles, without God consciousness, is no better than an animal. That is the verdict of the Vedic literature:

āhāra-nidrā-bhaya-maithunaṁ ca
sāmānyam etat paśubhir narāṇām
dharmo hi teṣām adhiko viśeṣo
dharmeṇa hīnāḥ paśubhiḥ samānāḥ

Eating, sleeping, sex, and defense – these four principles are common to both human beings and animals. The distinction between human life and animal life is that a man can search after God but an animal cannot. That is the difference. Therefore a man without that urge for searching after God is no better than an animal.

Unfortunately, at the present moment in every state and every society people are trying to forget God. Some people publicly say there is no God; others say that if there is a God, He is dead; and so on. They have built such a so-called advanced civilization, with so many skyscraper buildings, but they are forgetting that all of their advancement is dependent on God, on Kṛṣṇa. This is a very precarious condition for the human society.

There is a very nice story that describes what happens to a society that forgets the Supreme Personality of Godhead.

Once a rat was being troubled by a cat. So the rat went to a saintly person who had mystic powers and said, "My dear sir, I am very much troubled."

"What is the difficulty?"

The rat said, "A cat always chases me, so I have no peace of mind."

"Then what do you want?"

"Please make me into a cat."

"All right, become a cat."

After a few days, the cat came to the saintly person and said, "My dear sir, again I am in trouble."

"What is that trouble?"

"The dogs are chasing me."

"Then what do you want?"

"Make me a dog."

"All right, become a dog."

Then after a few days the dog came and said, "Sir, again I am in trouble."

"What is the trouble?"

"The foxes are chasing me."

"Then what do you want?"

"To become a fox."

"All right, become a fox."

Then the fox came and said, "Oh, tigers are chasing me."

"Then what do you want?"

"I want to become a tiger."

"All right, become a tiger."

Now the tiger began to stare at the saintly person. "I shall eat you," the tiger said.

"Oh, you shall eat me? I have made you a tiger, and you want to eat me!"

"Yes, I am a tiger, and now I shall eat you."

Then the saintly person cursed him: "Again become a rat!"

And the tiger became a rat.

So, our human civilization is like this. The other day I was reading the *World Almanac.* It said that within the next hundred years people will be living underground – like rats. Scientific advancement has created the atomic bomb to kill men, and when it will be used people will have to go underground and become like rats. From tiger to rat. That is going to happen; it is nature's law.

If you defy the laws of your state, you will be put into difficulty. Similarly, if you continue to defy the authority of the Supreme Lord, you will suffer. Again you will become rats. As soon as the atomic bombs explode, all civilization on the surface of the globe will be finished. You may not like to think about these things – you may regard them as very unpalatable – but these are the facts.

Satyaṁ gṛhyāt priyaṁ gṛhyān mā priyāḥ satyam apriyam. It is a social convention that if you want to speak the truth you should speak it very palatably. But we are not meant for social convention. We are preachers, servants of God, and we must speak the real truth, whether you like it or not.

A godless civilization cannot be happy. That is a fact. So we have started the Kṛṣṇa consciousness movement to awaken this godless civilization. Just try to love God; this is our simple request. You have love within you – you want to love somebody. A young boy tries to love a young girl; a young girl tries to love a young boy. This is natural, because the loving propensity is within everybody. But we have created circumstances in which our love is being frustrated. Everyone is frustrated – husbands, wives, boys, girls. Everywhere there is frustration, because our loving propensity is not being utilized properly. Why? Because we have forgotten to love the Supreme Person. That is our disease.

So the purpose of religion is to train people how to love God. That is the purpose of all religion. Whether your religion is Christianity or Hinduism or Mohammedanism, the purpose of your religion is to train you how to love God, because that is your constitutional position.

In the *Śrīmad-Bhāgavatam* [1.2.6] it is said, *sa vai puṁsāṁ paro dharmo yato bhaktir adhokṣaje.* Now, in English dictionaries this word *dharma* is generally translated as "religion," a kind of faith, but the actual meaning of *dharma* is "essential characteristic." For example, sugar's *dharma,* or essential characteristic, is sweetness. If you are given some white powder and you find that it is not sweet, you will at once say, "Oh, this is not sugar; it is something else." So sweetness is the *dharma* of sugar. Similarly, a salty taste is the *dharma* of salt, and pungency is the *dharma* of chili.

Now, what is *your* essential characteristic? You are a living entity, and you have to understand your essential characteristic. That characteristic is your *dharma,* or religion – not the Christian religion, the Hindu religion, this religion, that religion. Your eternal, essential characteristic – that is your religion.

And what is that characteristic? Your essential characteristic is that you want to love somebody, and therefore you want to serve him. That is your essential characteristic. You love your family, you love your society, you love your community, you love your country. And because you love them, you want to serve them. That tendency to engage in loving service is your essential characteristic, your *dharma.* Whether you are a Christian, a Mohammedan, or a Hindu, this characteristic will remain. Suppose today you are a Christian. Tomorrow you may become a Hindu, but your serving mood, that loving spirit, will stay with you. Therefore, the tendency to love and serve others is your *dharma,* or your religion. This is the universal form of religion.

Now, you have to apply your loving service in such a way that you will be completely satisfied. Because your loving spirit is now misplaced, you are not happy. You are frustrated and confused. The *Śrīmad-Bhāgavatam* tells us how to apply our spirit of loving devotion perfectly:

sa vai puṁsāṁ paro dharmo
yato bhaktir adhokṣaje
ahaituky apratihatā
yayātmā suprasīdati

That religion is first class which trains you to love God. And by this religion you will become completely satisfied.

If you develop your love of God to the fullest extent, you will become a perfect person. You will feel perfection within yourself. You are hankering after satisfaction, full satisfaction, but that full satisfaction can be obtained only when you love God. Loving God is the natural function of every living entity. It doesn't matter whether you are a Christian or a Hindu or a Muhammadan. Just try to develop your love of God. Then your religion is very nice. Otherwise it is simply a waste of time (*śrama eva hi kevalam*). If after executing rituals in a particular type of religion throughout your whole life you have no love for God, then you have simply wasted your time.

The Kṛṣṇa consciousness movement is the postgraduate movement of all kinds of religion. We are inviting all Christians, Muslims, and Hindus – everyone – to please come associate with us and try to love God. And the method is very simple: Just chant His holy names – Hare Kṛṣṇa, Hare Kṛṣṇa, Kṛṣṇa Kṛṣṇa, Hare Hare/ Hare Rāma, Hare Rāma, Rāma Rāma, Hare Hare.

All my students are Americans, and they have come from either Christian or Jewish families. None of them have come from Hindu families. So the process I have given them – the process of chanting the Hare Kṛṣṇa *mantra* – is universal. It is not Hindu or Indian.

The Sanskrit word *mantra* is a combination of two syllables, *man* and *tra*. *Man* means "mind," and *tra* means "deliverance." Therefore a *mantra* is that which delivers you from mental concoction, from hovering on the mental plane. So if you chant this *mantra* – Hare Kṛṣṇa, Hare Kṛṣṇa, Kṛṣṇa Kṛṣṇa, Hare Hare/ Hare Rāma, Hare Rāma, Rāma Rāma, Hare Hare – very soon you'll find that you are coming from the darkness to the light.

I do not wish to take much of your time, but I simply want to impress upon you the importance of chanting Hare Kṛṣṇa. Try an experiment: Chant Hare Kṛṣṇa for one week, and see how much spiritual progress you make. We don't charge anything, so there is no loss. But there is great profit; that is guaranteed. Therefore please chant Hare Kṛṣṇa, Hare Kṛṣṇa, Kṛṣṇa Kṛṣṇa, Hare Hare/ Hare Rāma, Hare Rāma, Rāma Rāma, Hare Hare.

Thank you very much.

Entering the Spiritual World

"Everything in the spiritual world is substantial and original. This material world is only an imitation. . . . It is just like a cinematographic picture, in which we see only the shadow of the real thing." In this lecture, delivered in October 1966 in New York City, Śrīla Prabhupāda gives an amazing glimpse into the nature of the spiritual world and some positive instructions on how to arrive there at the end of life's perilous journey.

paras tasmāt tu bhāvo 'nyo
'vyakto 'vyaktāt sanātanaḥ
yaḥ sa sarveṣu bhūteṣu
naśyatsu na vinaśyati

"Yet there is another unmanifest nature, which is eternal and is transcendental to this manifested and unmanifested matter. It is supreme and is never annihilated. When all in this world is annihilated, that part remains as it is." [*Bhagavad-gītā* 8.20]

We cannot calculate the length and breadth of even this universe, yet there are millions and millions of universes like this one within the material sky. And above this material sky there is another sky, which is called the spiritual sky. In that sky all the planets are eternal, and life is eternal, also. We cannot know these things by our material calculations, so we must take this information from the *Bhagavad-gītā*.

This material manifestation is only one fourth of the whole manifestation, both spiritual and material. In other words, three fourths of the total manifestation is beyond the covered, material sky. The material covering is millions and millions of miles thick, and only after penetrating it can one enter the open, spiritual sky. Here Kṛṣṇa uses the words *bhāvaḥ anyaḥ*, which mean "another nature." In other words, there is another, spiritual nature besides the material one we ordinarily experience.

But even now we are experiencing the spiritual as well as the material nature. How is that? Because we ourselves are a combination of matter and spirit. We are spirit, and only as long as we are within the material body does it move. As soon as we are out of the body, it is as good as stone. So, since we can all personally perceive that there is spirit as well as matter, we should also know that there is a spiritual world as well.

In the seventh chapter of *Bhagavad-gītā* Kṛṣṇa discusses the spiritual and material natures. The spiritual nature is superior, and the material nature is inferior. In this material world the material and spiritual natures are mixed, but if we go beyond this material nature altogether – if we go to the spiritual world – we will find only the superior, spiritual nature. This is the information we get in the eighth chapter.

It is not possible to understand these things by experimental knowledge. The scientists can see millions and millions of stars through their telescopes, but they cannot approach them. Their means are insufficient. What to speak of other planets, they cannot approach even the moon planet, which is the nearest. Therefore, we should try to realize how incapable we are of understanding God and God's kingdom by experimental knowledge. And since getting understanding this way is not possible, it is foolishness to try. Rather, we have to understand God by hearing *Bhagavad-gītā*. There is no other way. No one can understand who his father is by experimental knowledge. One has to simply believe his mother when she says, "Here is your father." Similarly, one has to believe *Bhagavad-gītā;* then one can get all the information.

Nonetheless, while there is no possibility of experimental knowledge about God, if one becomes advanced in Kṛṣṇa consciousness he will realize God directly. For example, through realization I am firmly convinced of whatever I am saying here about Kṛṣṇa. I am not speaking blindly. Similarly, anyone can realize God. *Svayam eva sphuraty adaḥ:* Direct knowledge of God will be revealed to anyone who sticks to the process of Kṛṣṇa consciousness. Such a person will actually understand, "Yes, there is a spiritual kingdom, where God resides, and I have to go there. I must prepare to go there." Before going to another country, one may hear so much about it, but when he actually goes there he understands everything directly. Similarly, if one takes up the process of Kṛṣṇa consciousness, one day he'll understand God and the kingdom of God directly, and the whole problem of his life will be solved.

Here Kṛṣṇa uses the word *sanātanaḥ* to describe that spiritual kingdom. The material nature has a beginning and an end, but the spiritual nature has no beginning and no end. How is that? We can understand by a simple example: Sometimes, when there is a snowfall, we see that the whole sky is covered by a cloud. But actually that cloud is covering only an insignificant part of the whole sky. Because we are very minute, however, when a cloud covers a few hundred miles of the sky, to us the sky looks completely covered. Similarly, this entire material manifestation (called the *mahat-tattva*) is like a cloud covering an insignificant portion of the spiritual sky. And just as when the cloud clears we can see the bright, sunlit sky, so when we get clear of this covering of matter we can see the original, spiritual sky.

Furthermore, just as a cloud has a beginning and an end, the material nature also has a beginning and an end, and our material body also has a beginning and an end. Our body simply exists for some time. It takes birth, grows, stays for some time, gives off some by-products, dwindles, and then vanishes. These are the six transformations of the body. Similarly, every material manifestation undergoes these six transformations. Thus at the end this whole material world will be vanquished.

But Kṛṣṇa assures us, *paras tasmāt tu bhāvo 'nyo 'vyakto 'vyaktāt sanātanaḥ:* "Beyond this destructible, cloudlike material nature, there is another, superior nature, which is eternal. It has no beginning and no end." Then He says, *yaḥ sa sarveṣu bhūteṣu naśyatsu na vinaśyati:* "When this material manifestation is annihilated, that superior nature will remain." When a cloud in the sky is annihilated, the sky remains. Similarly, when the cloudlike material manifestation is annihilated, the spiritual sky remains. This is called *avyakto 'vyaktāt.*

There are many volumes of Vedic literature containing information about the material sky and the spiritual sky. In the Second Canto of *Śrīmad-Bhāgavatam* we find a description of the spiritual sky: what its nature is, what kind of people live there, what their features are –

everything. We even get information that in the spiritual sky there are spiritual airplanes. The living entities there are all liberated, and when they fly in their airplanes they look as beautiful as lightning.

So, everything in the spiritual world is substantial and original. This material world is only an imitation. Whatever we see in this material world is all imitation, shadow. It is just like a cinematographic picture, in which we see only the shadow of the real thing.

In *Śrīmad-Bhāgavatam* [1.1.1] it is said, *yatra tri-sargo 'mṛṣā:* "This material world is illusory." We have all seen a pretty mannequin of a girl in a shopkeeper's showcase. Every sane man knows that it is an imitation. But the so-called beautiful things in this material world are just like the beautiful "girl" in the shopkeeper's window. Indeed, whatever beautiful thing we see here in this material world is simply an imitation of the real beauty in the spiritual world. As Śrīdhara Svāmī says, *yat satyatayā mithyā sargo 'pi satyavat pratīyate:* "The spiritual world is real, and the unreal, material manifestation only appears real." Something is real only if it will exist eternally. Reality cannot be vanquished. Similarly, real pleasure must be eternal. Since material pleasure is temporary, it is not actual, and those who seek real pleasure don't take part in this shadow pleasure. They strive for the real, eternal pleasure of Kṛṣṇa consciousness.

Here Kṛṣṇa says, *yaḥ sa sarveṣu bhūteṣu naśyatsu na vinaśyati:* "When everything in the material world is annihilated, that spiritual nature will remain eternally." The aim of human life is to reach that spiritual sky. But people do not know the reality of the spiritual sky. The *Bhāgavatam* says, *na te viduḥ svārtha-gatiṁ hi viṣṇum:* "People do not know their self-interest. They do not know that human life is meant for understanding spiritual reality and preparing ourselves for being transferred to that reality. It is not meant for remaining here in the material world." The whole of Vedic literature instructs us like this. *Tamasi mā jyotir gamaḥ:* "Don't remain in the darkness; go to the light." This material world is darkness. We are artificially illuminating it with electric lights and fires and so many other things, but its nature is dark. The spiritual world, however, is not dark; it is full of light. Just as on the sun planet there is no possibility of darkness, so there is no possibility of darkness in the spiritual nature, because every planet there is self-illuminated.

It is clearly stated in *Bhagavad-gītā* that the supreme destination, from which there is no return, is the abode of Kṛṣṇa, the Supreme Person. The *Brahma-saṁhitā* describes this supreme abode as *ānanda-cinmaya-rasa,* a place where everything is full of spiritual bliss. Whatever variegatedness is manifest there is all of the quality of spiritual bliss – nothing there is material. That spiritual variegatedness is the spiritual expansion of the Supreme Godhead Himself, for the manifestation there is totally of the spiritual energy.

Although the Lord is always in His supreme abode, He is nonetheless all-pervading by His material energy. So by His spiritual and material energies, He is present everywhere – in both the material and the spiritual universes. In *Bhagavad-gītā,* the words *yasyāntaḥ-sthāni bhūtāni* indicate that everything is sustained by Him, whether it be spiritual or material energy.

It is clearly stated in *Bhagavad-gītā* that only by *bhakti,* or devotional service, can one enter into the Vaikuṇṭha (spiritual) planetary system. In all the Vaikuṇṭhas there is only one Supreme Godhead, Kṛṣṇa, who has expanded Himself into millions and millions of plenary portions. These plenary expansions are four-armed, and They preside over innumerable spiritual planets. They are known by a variety of names: Puruṣottama, Trivikrama, Keśava, Mādhava, Aniruddha, Hṛṣīkeśa, Saṅkarṣaṇa, Pradyumna, Śrīdhara, Vāsudeva, Dāmodara, Janārdana, Nārāyaṇa, Vāmana, Padmanābha, and so on. These plenary expansions are like the leaves of a tree, the main trunk of the tree being like Kṛṣṇa. Kṛṣṇa, dwelling in Goloka Vṛndāvana, His supreme abode, systematically and flawlessly conducts all affairs of both universes (material and spiritual) by the power of His all-pervasiveness.

Now, if we are at all interested in reaching Kṛṣṇa's supreme abode, then we must practice *bhakti-yoga.* The word *bhakti* means "devotional service," or, in other words, submission to the Supreme Lord. Kṛṣṇa clearly says, *puruṣaḥ sa paraḥ pārtha bhaktyā labhyas tv ananyayā.* The words *tv ananyayā* here mean "without any other engagement." So, to reach the spiritual abode of the Lord, we must engage in pure devotional service to Kṛṣṇa.

One definition of *bhakti* is given in the authoritative book *Nārada-pañcarātra:*

sarvopādhi-vinirmuktaṁ
tat-paratvena nirmalam
hṛṣīkena hṛṣīkeśa-
sevanaṁ bhaktir ucyate

"*Bhakti,* or devotional service, means engaging all our senses in the service of the Lord, the Supreme Personality of Godhead, who is the master of all the senses. When the spirit soul renders service unto the Supreme, there are two side effects. First, he is freed from all material designations, and second, his senses are purified simply by being employed in the service of the Lord."

Now we are encumbered by so many bodily designations. "Indian," "American," "African," "European" – these are all bodily designations. Our bodies are not we ourselves, yet we identify with these designations. Suppose one has received a university degree and identifies himself as an M.A. or a B.A. or a Ph.D. *He* is not that degree, but he has identified with that designation. So, *bhakti* means to free oneself from these designations (*sarvopādhi-vinirmuktam*). *Upādhi* means "designation." If someone gets the title "Sir," he becomes very happy: "Oh, I have this 'Sir' title." He forgets that this title is only his designation – that it will exist only as long as he has his body. But the body is sure to be vanquished, along with all its designations. When one gets another body, he gets other designations. Suppose in the present lifetime one is an American. The next body he gets may be Chinese. Therefore, since we are always changing our bodily designations, we should stop identifying them as our self. When one is determined to free himself of all these nonsensical designations, then he can attain *bhakti.*

In the above verse from the *Nārada-pañcarātra,* the word *nirmalam* means "completely pure." What is that purity? One should be convinced, "I am spirit (*ahaṁ brahmāsmi*). I am not this material body, which is simply my covering. I am an eternal servant of Kṛṣṇa; that is my real identity." One who is freed from false designations and fixed in his real constitutional position always renders service to Kṛṣṇa with his senses (*hṛṣīkena hṛṣīkeśa-sevanaṁ bhaktir ucyate*). The word *hṛṣīka* means "the senses." Now our senses are designated, but when our senses are free from designations, and when with that freedom and in that purity we serve Kṛṣṇa – that is devotional service.

Śrīla Rūpa Gosvāmī explains pure devotional service in this verse from *Bhakti-rasāmṛta-sindhu* [1.1.11]:

anyābhilāṣitā-śūnyaṁ
jñāna-karmādy-anāvṛtam
ānukūlyena kṛṣṇānu-
śīlanaṁ bhaktir uttamā

"When first-class devotional service develops, one must be devoid of all material desires, of knowledge tainted by monistic philosophy, and of fruitive action. A pure devotee must constantly serve Kṛṣṇa favorably, as Kṛṣṇa desires." We have to serve Kṛṣṇa favorably, not unfavorably. Also, we should be free from material desires (*anyābhilāṣitā-śūnyam*). Usually one wants to serve God for some material purpose. Of course, that is also good. If someone goes to God for some material gain, he's far greater than the person who never goes to God. That is admitted in *Bhagavad-gītā* [7.16]:

catur-vidhā bhajante māṁ
janāḥ sukṛtino 'rjuna
ārto jijñāsur arthārthī
jñānī ca bharatarṣabha

"O best among the Bhāratas [Arjuna], four kinds of pious men begin to render devotional service unto Me – the distressed, the desirer of wealth, the inquisitive, and he who is searching for knowledge of the Absolute." But it is best that we not go to God with some desire for material benefit. We should be free of this impurity (*anyābhilāṣitā-śunyam*).

The next words Rūpa Gosvāmī uses to describe pure *bhakti* are *jñāna-karmādy-anāvṛtam*. The word *jñāna* refers to the effort to understand Kṛṣṇa by mental speculation. Of course, we *should* try to understand Kṛṣṇa, but we should always remember that He is unlimited and that we can never fully understand Him. It is not possible for us to do this. Therefore, we have to accept whatever is presented to us in the revealed scriptures. The *Bhagavad-gītā,* for example, is presented by Kṛṣṇa for our understanding. We should try to understand Him simply by hearing from books like *Bhagavad-gītā* and *Śrīmad-Bhāgavatam.* The word *karma* means "work with some fruitive result." If we want to practice pure *bhakti,* we should work in Kṛṣṇa consciousness selflessly – not just to get some profit out of it.

Next Śrīla Rūpa Gosvāmī says that pure *bhakti* must be *ānukūlyena,* or favorable. We must culture Kṛṣṇa consciousness favorably. We should find out what will please Kṛṣṇa, and we should do that. How can we know what will please Kṛṣṇa? By hearing *Bhagavad-gītā* and taking the right interpretation from the right person. Then we'll know what Kṛṣṇa wants, and we can act accordingly. At that time we will be elevated to first-class devotional service.

So, *bhakti-yoga* is a great science, and there is immense literature to help us understand it. We should utilize our time to understand this science and thus prepare ourselves to receive the supreme benefit at the time of our death – to attain to the spiritual planets, where the Supreme Personality of Godhead resides.

There are millions of planets and stars within this universe, yet this entire universe is only a small particle within the total creation. There are many universes like ours, and, as mentioned before, the spiritual sky is three times as large as the total material creation. In other words, three fourths of the total manifestation is in the spiritual sky.

We get information from *Bhagavad-gītā* that on every spiritual planet in the spiritual sky there is an expansion of Kṛṣṇa. They are all *puruṣa,* or persons; they are not impersonal. In *Bhagavad-gītā* Kṛṣṇa says, *puruṣaḥ sa paraḥ pārtha bhaktyā labhyas tv ananyayā:* One can approach the Supreme Person only by devotional service – not by challenge, not by philosophical speculation, and not by exercising in this *yoga* or that *yoga.* No. It is clearly stated that one can approach Kṛṣṇa only by surrender and devotional service. It is not stated that one can reach Him by philosophical speculation or mental concoction or some physical exercise. One can reach Kṛṣṇa only by practicing devotion, without deviating to fruitive activities, philosophical speculation, or physical exercise. Only by unalloyed devotional service, without any admixture, can we reach the spiritual world.

Now, *Bhagavad-gītā* further says, *yasyāntaḥ-sthāni bhūtāni yena sarvam idaṁ tatam.* Kṛṣṇa is such a great person that although situated in His own abode, He is still all-pervading, and everything is within Him. How can this be? The sun is located in one place, but the sun rays are distributed all over the universe. Similarly, although God is situated in His own abode in the spiritual sky, His energy is distributed everywhere. Also, He's not different from His energy, just as the sun and the sunshine are not different, in the sense that they are composed of the same illuminating substance. So, Kṛṣṇa distributes Himself everywhere by His energies, and when we become advanced in devotional service we can see Him everywhere, just as one can light a lamp anywhere by plugging it into the electric circuit.

In his *Brahma-saṁhitā,* Lord Brahmā describes the qualifications we require to see God: *premāñjana-cchurita-bhakti-vilocanena santaḥ sadaiva hṛdayeṣu vilokayanti.* Those who have developed love of God can constantly see God before them, twenty-four hours a day. The word *sadaiva* means "constantly, twenty-four hours a day." If one is actually God-realized, he doesn't say, "Oh, I saw God yesterday night, but now He's not visible." No, He's *always* visible, because He's everywhere.

Therefore, the conclusion is that we can see Kṛṣṇa everywhere, but we have to develop the eyes to see Him. We can do that by the process of Kṛṣṇa consciousness. When we see Kṛṣṇa, and when we approach Him in His spiritual abode, our life will be successful, our aims will be fulfilled, and we'll be happy and prosperous eternally.

3

The Pleasure Principle

Pleasing the Perfect Master

During a lecture given in September 1968 in Seattle, Washington, Śrīla Prabhupāda says, "Can anybody in this meeting say that he's not the servant of anybody or anything? No, because our constitutional position is to serve." Then he proposes an idea new to most of his listeners: "If you agree to serve Kṛṣṇa, gradually you will realize that Kṛṣṇa is also serving you." Śrīla Prabhupāda goes on to explain how by pleasing Kṛṣṇa the soul can enjoy unlimited happiness.

In this material world, everyone is trying to search out happiness and get relief from misery. There are three kinds of miseries caused by our material condition: *ādhyātmika, ādhibhautika,* and *ādhidaivika. Ādhyātmika* miseries are those caused by the body and mind themselves. For example, when there is some disarrangement of the different functions of metabolism within the body, we get a fever or some pain. Another kind of *ādhyātmika* misery is caused by the mind. Suppose I lose someone who is dear to me. Then my mind will be disturbed. This is also suffering. So diseases of the body or mental disturbances are *ādhyātmika* miseries.

Then there are *ādhibhautika* miseries, sufferings caused by other living entities. For example, human beings are sending millions of poor animals to the slaughterhouse daily. The animals cannot express themselves, but they are undergoing great suffering. And we also suffer miseries caused by other living entities.

Finally, there are *ādhidaivika* miseries, those caused by higher authorities such as the demigods. There may be famine, earthquake, flood, pestilence – so many things. These are *ādhidaivika* sufferings.

So we are always suffering one or more of these miseries. This material nature is constituted in such a way that we have to suffer; it is God's law. And we are trying to relieve the suffering by patchwork remedies. Everyone is trying to get relief from suffering; that is a fact. The whole struggle for existence is aimed at getting out of suffering.

There are various kinds of remedies that we use to try to relieve our suffering. One remedy is offered by the modern scientists, one by the philosophers, another by the atheists, another by the theists, another by the fruitive workers. There are so many ideas. But according to the philosophy of Kṛṣṇa consciousness, you can get free of all your sufferings if you simply change your consciousness to Kṛṣṇa consciousness. That's all.

All our sufferings are due to ignorance. We have forgotten that we are eternal servants of Kṛṣṇa. There is a nice Bengali verse that explains this point:

kṛṣṇa-bahirmukha hañā bhoga-vāñchā kare
nikaṭa-stha māyā tāre jāpaṭiyā dhare

As soon as our original Kṛṣṇa consciousness becomes polluted with the consciousness of material enjoyment – the idea that I want to lord it over the resources of matter – our troubles begin. Immediately we fall into *māyā,* illusion. Everyone in the material world is thinking, "I can enjoy this world to my best capacity." From the tiny ant up to the highest living creature, Brahmā, everyone is trying to become a lord. In your country many politicians are canvassing to become the president. Why? They want to become some kind of lord. This is illusion.

In the Kṛṣṇa consciousness movement our mentality is just the opposite. We are trying to become the servant of the servant of the servant of the servant of Kṛṣṇa (*gopī-bhartuḥ pada-kamalayor dāsa-dāsānudāsaḥ*). Instead of wanting to become a lord, we want to become the servant of Kṛṣṇa.

Now, people may say this is a slave mentality: "Why should I become a slave? I shall become the master." But they do not know that this consciousness – "I shall become the master" – is the cause of all their suffering. This has to be understood. In the name of becoming master of this material world, we have become the servants of our senses.

We cannot avoid serving. Every one of us sitting in this meeting is a servant. These boys and girls who have taken to Kṛṣṇa consciousness have agreed to become servants of Kṛṣṇa. So their problem is solved. But others are thinking, "Why should I become a servant of God? I shall become the master." Actually, no one can become the master. And if someone tries to become the master, he simply becomes the servant of his senses. That's all. He becomes the servant of his lust, the servant of his avarice, the servant of his anger – the servant of *so* many things.

In a higher stage, one becomes the servant of humanity, the servant of society, the servant of his country. But the actual purpose is to become the master. That is the disease. The candidates for the presidency are presenting their different manifestos: "I shall serve the country very nicely. Please give me your vote." But their real idea is somehow or other to become the master of the country. This is illusion.

So, we should understand this important point of philosophy: Constitutionally we are servants. Nobody can say, "I am free; I am the master." If someone thinks like that, he's in illusion. Can anybody in this meeting say that he's not the servant of anybody or anything? No, because our constitutional position is to serve.

We may serve Kṛṣṇa, or we may serve our senses. But the difficulty is that by serving our senses we simply increase our misery. For the time being you may satisfy yourself by taking some intoxicant. And under the spell of the intoxicant you may think that you are nobody's servant, that you are free. But this idea is artificial. As soon as the hallucination is gone, again you see that you are a servant.

So we are being forced to serve, but we don't wish to serve. What is the adjustment? Kṛṣṇa consciousness. If you become the servant of Kṛṣṇa, your aspiration to become the master is immediately achieved. For example, here we see a picture of Kṛṣṇa and Arjuna. [*Śrīla Prabhupāda points to a painting of Kṛṣṇa and Arjuna on the Battlefield of Kurukṣetra.*] Kṛṣṇa is the Supreme Lord; Arjuna is a human being. But Arjuna loves Kṛṣṇa as a friend, and in response to Arjuna's friendly love Kṛṣṇa has become his chariot driver, his servant. Similarly, if we become reinstated in our transcendental loving relationship with Kṛṣṇa, our aspiration for mastership will be fulfilled. If you agree to serve Kṛṣṇa, gradually you will see that Kṛṣṇa is also serving you. This is a question of realization.

So, if we want to get free of the service of this material world, the service of our senses, then we must direct our service toward Kṛṣṇa. This is Kṛṣṇa consciousness.

Śrīla Rūpa Gosvāmī quotes a nice verse in his *Bhakti-rasāmṛta-sindhu* concerning the service of the senses: *kāmādīnāṁ kati na katidhā pālitā durnideśā*. Here a devotee is saying to Kṛṣṇa that he has served his senses for a very long time (*kāmādīnāṁ kati na katidhā*). *Kāma* means "lust." He says, "By the dictation of my lust I have done what I should not have done." When someone is a slave, he's forced to do things he does not wish to do. He's forced. So, here the devotee is admitting that under the dictation of his lust he has done sinful things.

Then someone may say to the devotee: "All right, you have served your senses. But now you are done serving them. Now everything is all right." But the difficulty is this: *teṣāṁ jātā mayi na karuṇā na trapā nopaśāntiḥ*. The devotee says, "I have served my senses so much, but I find they are not satisfied. That is my difficulty. My senses are not satisfied, nor am I satisfied, nor are my senses kind enough to give me relief, to give me pension from their service. That is my position. I had hoped that by serving my senses for many years they would have been satisfied. But no, they're not. They are still dictating to me."

Here I may disclose something one of my students told me: In old age his mother is going to marry. And somebody else complained that his grandmother has also married. Just see: Fifty years old, seventy-five years old, and the senses are still so strong that they're dictating, "Yes, you must marry." Try to understand how strong the senses are. It is not simply young men who are servants of their senses. One may be seventy-five years old, eighty years old, or even at the point of death – still one is the servant of the senses. The senses are never satisfied.

So this is the material situation. We are servants of our senses, but by serving our senses we are not satisfied, nor are our senses satisfied, nor are they merciful to us. There is chaos!

The best thing, therefore, is to become a servant of Kṛṣṇa. In *Bhagavad-gītā* [18.66] Kṛṣṇa says,

sarva-dharmān parityajya
mām ekaṁ śaraṇaṁ vraja

ahaṁ tvāṁ sarva-pāpebhyo
mokṣayiṣyāmi mā śucaḥ

You have served your senses in so many lives, life after life, in 8,400,000 species. The birds are serving their senses, the beasts are serving their senses, the human beings, the demigods – everyone within this material world is after sense gratification. "So," Kṛṣṇa says, "just surrender unto Me. Just agree to serve Me, and I will take charge of you. You will be free from the dictation of your senses."

Because of the dictation of the senses, we are committing sinful activities life after life. Therefore we are in different grades of bodies. Don't think that every one of you is of the same standard. No. According to one's activities, one gets a certain type of body. And these different types of bodies afford one different grades of sense gratification. There is sense gratification in the hog's life also, but it is of a very low grade. The hog is so sensual that it does not hesitate to have sex with its mother, its sister, or its daughter. Even in human society there are people who don't care whether they have sex with their mother or sister. The senses are so strong.

So, we should try to understand that serving the dictations of our senses is the cause of all our misery. The threefold miseries that we are suffering – the miseries we are trying to get free of – are due to this dictation of the senses. But if we become attracted to serving Kṛṣṇa, we will no longer be forced to follow the dictation of our senses. One name for Kṛṣṇa is Madana-mohana, "He who conquers Cupid, or lust." If you transfer your love from your senses to Kṛṣṇa, you will be free from all misery. Immediately.

So this endeavor to be the master – "I am the monarch of all I survey" – should be given up. Every one of us is constitutionally a servant. Now we are serving our senses, but we should direct this service to Kṛṣṇa. And when you serve Kṛṣṇa, gradually Kṛṣṇa reveals Himself to you as you become sincere. Then the reciprocation of service between Kṛṣṇa and you will be so nice. You can love Him as a friend or as a master or as a lover – there are so many ways to love Kṛṣṇa.

So, you should try to love Kṛṣṇa, and you will see how much you are satisfied. There is no other way to become fully satisfied.

Earning great amounts of money will never give you satisfaction. I once knew a gentleman in Calcutta who was earning six thousand dollars a month. He committed suicide. Why? That money could not give him satisfaction. He was trying to have something else.

So my humble request to you all is that you try to understand this sublime benediction of life, Kṛṣṇa consciousness. Simply by chanting Hare Kṛṣṇa you will gradually develop a transcendental loving attitude for Kṛṣṇa, and as soon as you begin to love Kṛṣṇa, all your troubles will be eradicated and you will feel complete satisfaction.

Thank you very much. Are there any questions?

Question: When we engage the material energy in the service of Kṛṣṇa, what happens to it? Does it become spiritualized?

Śrīla Prabhupāda: When a copper wire is in touch with electricity, it is no longer copper; it is electricity. Similarly, when you apply your energy to the service of Kṛṣṇa, it is no longer material energy; it is spiritual energy. So as soon as you engage yourself in the service of Kṛṣṇa, you become free from the dictates of the material energy. Kṛṣṇa states that in the *Bhagavad-gītā* [14.26]:

māṁ ca yo 'vyabhicāreṇa
bhakti-yogena sevate
sa guṇān samatītyaitān
brahma-bhūyāya kalpate

"Anyone who seriously engages in My service immediately becomes transcendental to the material qualities and comes to the platform of Brahman, or spirit."

So, when you apply your energy in the service of Kṛṣṇa, do not think that it remains material. Everything used in Kṛṣṇa's service is spiritual. For example, each day we distribute fruit *prasādam* [fruit that has been offered to Kṛṣṇa]. Now, one may ask, "Why is this fruit different from ordinary fruit? It has been purchased at the market like any other fruit. We also eat fruit at home. What is the difference?" No. Because we offer the fruit to Kṛṣṇa, it immediately becomes spiritual. The result? Just go on eating *kṛṣṇa-prasādam,* and you will see how you are making progress in Kṛṣṇa consciousness.

Here is another example. If you drink a large quantity of milk, there may be some disorder in your bowels. If you go to a physician (at least, if you go to an Āyur-vedic physician), he'll offer you a medical preparation made with yogurt. And that yogurt with a little medicine in it will cure you. Now, yogurt is nothing but milk transformed. So, your disease was caused by milk, and it is also cured by milk. How is that? Because you are taking the medicine under the direction of a qualified physician. Similarly, if you engage the material energy in the service of Kṛṣṇa under the direction of a bona fide spiritual master, that same material energy which has been the cause of your bondage will bring you to the transcendental stage beyond all misery.

Question: How can you make everything so simple to understand?

Śrīla Prabhupāda: Because the whole philosophy is so simple. God is great. You are not great. Don't claim that you are God. Don't claim that there is no God. God is infinite, and you are infinitesimal. Then what is your position? You have to serve God, Kṛṣṇa. This is simple truth. The rebellious attitude against God is *māyā,* illusion. Anyone who is declaring that he is God, that you are God, that there is no God, that God is dead – he is under the spell of *māyā.*

When a man is haunted by a ghost, he speaks all kinds of nonsense. Similarly, when a person is haunted by *māyā,* he says, "God is dead. I am God. Why are you searching for God? There are so many Gods loitering in the street." People who speak like this are all ghostly haunted, deranged.

So you have to cure them by vibrating the transcendental sound of the Hare Kṛṣṇa *mantra.* This is the cure. Simply let them hear, and gradually they will be cured. When a man is sleeping very soundly, you can cry out beside his ear and he'll awaken. So the Hare Kṛṣṇa *mantra* can awaken the sleeping human society. The *Vedas* say, *uttiṣṭhata jāgrata prāpya varān nibodhata:* "O human being, please get up! Don't sleep any more. You have the opportunity of a human body. Utilize it. Get yourself out of the clutches of *māyā.*" This is the declaration of the *Vedas.* So continue to chant Hare Kṛṣṇa. Awaken your countrymen from illusion, and help them get relief from their miseries.

Liberation to a Higher Pleasure

"Everyone is inviting, 'Come on, enjoy sex.' But no matter how hard you try to enjoy sex, you cannot be satisfied. That is certain. Unless you come to the spiritual platform of enjoyment, you will never be satisfied." In this explanation of a Bengali song written several centuries ago by a great Kṛṣṇa conscious spiritual master, Śrīla Prabhupāda proposes that there is a pleasure higher than sex and tells us how to begin experiencing it.

Narottama dāsa Ṭhākura, who has written this song, is a famous *ācārya* [spiritual master], and his compositions are accepted as Vedic truth. In this song he represents himself as a common man, as one of us. He laments, appealing to Hari, Lord Kṛṣṇa, *hari hari biphale janama goṅāinu:* "My dear Lord, I have uselessly spoiled my life, because I have not worshiped You."

People do not know that they are spoiling their life. They are thinking, "I've got a very nice apartment, a very nice car, a very nice wife, a very nice income, a very nice social position." All these material attractions make us forget the purpose of our life – to worship Kṛṣṇa.

In one verse [5.5.8], the *Śrīmad-Bhāgavatam* summarizes the material attractions:

puṁsah striyā mithunī-bhāvam etaṁ
tayor mitho hṛdaya-granthim āhuḥ
ato gṛha-kṣetra-sutāpta-vittair
janasya moho 'yam ahaṁ mameti

The basic principle of material attraction is sex: *puṁsaḥ striyā mithunī-bhāvam etam.* A man hankers after a woman, and a woman hankers after a man. And when they actually engage in sex, they become very much attracted to each other: *tayor mitho hṛdaya-granthim āhuḥ*. *Hṛdaya* means "heart," and *granthim* means "hard knot." So when a man and a woman engage in sex, the hard knot in the heart is tied. "I cannot leave you," he says. "You are my life and soul." And she says, "I cannot leave you. You are my life and soul."

For a few days. Then divorce.

But the beginning is sex. The basic principle of material attraction is sex. We have organized sex life in many social conventions. Marriage is a social convention that gives sex a nice finishing touch, that's all. Sometimes it is said that marriage is legalized prostitution. But for keeping up social relations one has to accept some regulative principles, some restrictions on sense gratification. Therefore civilized human beings recognize that there is a difference between sex in marriage and sex outside of marriage, which is just like sex between animals.

In any case, when two people unite some way or other, their next demand is a nice apartment (*gṛha*) and some land (*kṣetra*). Then children (*suta*). When you have an apartment and a wife, the next requirement is to have children, because without children no home life is pleasant. *Pūtra-hīnaṁ gṛhaṁ śūnyam:* "Home life without children is just like a desert." Children are the real pleasure of home life. Finally there is the circle of relatives, or society (*āpta*). And all these paraphernalia have to be maintained with money (*vittaiḥ*). So money is required.

In this way one becomes entangled in the material world and covered by illusion. Why illusion? Why are such important things – wife, children, money – illusion? Because although at the present moment you may think everything is all right – you have a nice arrangement of home life, apartment, wife, children, society, and position – as soon as your body is finished everything is finished. You're forced to leave everything and move on to your next platform. And you do not know what your next platform will be. Your next body may be that of a human being or a cat or a dog or a demigod or anything. You do not know. But whatever it is, as soon as you leave your present body you will forget everything. There will be no remembrance of who you were, who your wife was, what your home was like, how big your bank balance was, and so on. Everything will be finished.

Everything will be finished in a flash, just like a bubble bursting in the ocean. The thrashing of the waves in the ocean generates millions and billions of bubbles, but the next moment they are all finished. Finished.

In this way material life is going on. The living entity travels through many species of life, many planets, until he comes to the human form of life. Human life is an opportunity to understand how we are transmigrating from one place to another, from one life to another, and simply wasting our time, not understanding what our constitutional position is and why we are suffering so much distress.

These things are to be understood in this human form of life. But instead of inquiring about our real position, we are simply engaged with *mithunī-bhāvam* and *gṛha-kṣetra-sutāpta-vittaiḥ* – sex, wife, home, property, children, society, money, and position. We are captivated with these things, and we are spoiling our life.

So Narottama dāsa Ṭhākura, representing us, is lamenting, "My dear Lord, I have spoiled my life." Why? *Manuṣya-janama pāiyā rādhā-kṛṣṇa nā bhajiyā:* "This human form of life is meant for understanding Rādhā-Kṛṣṇa [the Lord and His energy] and worshiping Rādhā-Kṛṣṇa. But instead of making contact with Rādhā-Kṛṣṇa, I am simply spoiling my life in sense gratification."

Then his lament goes on. *Golokera prema-dhana hari-nāma-saṅkīrtana rati nā janmilo kene tāy:* "Alas, why have I no attraction for chanting Hare Kṛṣṇa?" The chanting of the Hare Kṛṣṇa *mantra* is a transcendental vibration; it is not a material thing. It is imported from the transcendental abode of Kṛṣṇa. From there the transcendental sound of Hare Kṛṣṇa has come. This sound is like the sunshine coming from the sun. Although you cannot go to the sun – it is far, far beyond your reach – you can understand that the sunshine is coming from the sun globe. There is no doubt about it. Similarly, the vibration of the Hare Kṛṣṇa *mantra* is coming from Kṛṣṇa's planet, Goloka (*golokera prema-dhana*). And this chanting produces love of Kṛṣṇa. (*Prema-dhana* means "the treasure of love for Kṛṣṇa.")

Narottama dāsa Ṭhākura laments, *hari-nāma-saṅkīrtana rati nā janmilo kene tāy:* "Alas, why do I have no attachment for the chanting of Hare Kṛṣṇa?" Why should one be attached to this chanting? That is explained in the next line. *Saṁsāra-biṣānale dibā-niśi hiyā jvale jurāite:* "Chanting Hare Kṛṣṇa is the only remedy to relieve the heart from the burning poison of sense gratification." *Hiyā* means "heart." Our heart is always burning. Why? Because it is in touch with the sense-gratificatory process. No sense-gratificatory process can give me satisfaction, even though I try this way and that way, this way and that way. People are trying sense gratification in so many ways, and now they have come to the last point: the naked dance and . . . what is that short skirt?

Devotee: Miniskirt.

Śrīla Prabhupāda: Miniskirt, yes. [*Laughs.*] So, because in the material world the basic principle is sex, everyone is inviting, "Yes, come on, enjoy sex. Come on, enjoy sex." But no matter how you try to enjoy sex, you cannot be satisfied. That is certain, because sense gratification is not your real platform of enjoyment. You are a spirit soul, and unless you come to the spiritual platform you will never be satisfied by any sense gratification. You'll simply go on hankering after pleasure, but you will find no satisfaction.

Therefore, Narottama dāsa Ṭhākura says we are suffering in *saṁsāra-biṣānale. Saṁsāra* indicates our material demands for eating, sleeping, mating, and defending. These are just like fiery poison. Then he says, "My heart is burning from this poison, but I have not searched out the means of relief: the chanting of Hare Kṛṣṇa. I have no attachment for this chanting, and therefore I have spoiled my life."

Then he says, *vrajendra-nandana jei śacī-suta hoilo sei.* The chanting of Hare Kṛṣṇa was introduced by Lord Kṛṣṇa Himself, Vrajendra-nandana, in the form of Lord Caitanya, Śacī-suta. Kṛṣṇa took the part of the son of Mahārāja Nanda, the king of Vṛndāvana. Therefore Kṛṣṇa is called Vrajendra-nandana. And Lord Caitanya took the role of the son of mother Śacī; so He is known as Śacī-suta. The Supreme Lord takes pleasure when He is addressed with His devotee's name, with His energy's name. (His devotees are also His energy.) Although He has no father – He is the father of everyone – He accepts some devotee as His father when He appears on earth. When a pure devotee wants Kṛṣṇa as his son, Kṛṣṇa accepts the devotee as His parent.

So Narottama dāsa Ṭhākura says that Vrajendra-nandana (Kṛṣṇa) has now appeared as Śacī-suta (Lord Caitanya), and Balarāma (Kṛṣṇa's brother) has become Nitāi. And what is Their business? *Dīna-hīna-jata chilo hari-nāme uddhārilo:* saving all kinds of wretched, sinful conditioned souls by teaching them the chanting of Hare Kṛṣṇa. In this age, Kali-yuga, you cannot find a pious man or a saintly person. Everyone is addicted to sinful activities. But simply by distributing the chanting of Hare Kṛṣṇa, Lord Caitanya saved everyone, however fallen he might have been. "Come on!" He said. "Chant Hare Kṛṣṇa and be delivered."

What is the evidence that Lord Caitanya saved even the most fallen? *Tāra sākṣī jagāi mādhāi.* Jagāi and Mādhāi were two brothers who engaged in all kinds of sinful affairs. They were born into a very high *brāhmaṇa* family, but by bad association they became sinful. Similarly, in the present age, although the people of the West are descending from Āryan families, very nice families, by association they have become fallen. Their environment is full of illicit sex, intoxication, meat-eating, and gambling. So Jagāi and Mādhāi are specimens of the modern population, and Lord Caitanya delivered them simply by inducing them to chant the Hare Kṛṣṇa *mantra.*

So chanting Hare Kṛṣṇa will actually deliver all fallen souls, without doubt. This is not bogus propaganda. Whatever his past life, anyone who takes to this chanting process will become saintly. He will become a pure, Kṛṣṇa conscious person.

Chanting Hare Kṛṣṇa will purify our heart, our burning heart. Then we will understand, "I am an eternal servant of the Supreme Lord, Kṛṣṇa." Ordinarily we can come to this understanding only after many, many births, as Kṛṣṇa confirms in the *Bhagavad-gītā* [7.19]. *Bahūnāṁ janmanām ante jñānavān māṁ prapadyate:* "After many, many births, when a person becomes a man of wisdom, he surrenders unto Me." Why? *Vāsudevaḥ sarvam iti:* Because he knows that Vāsudeva, Kṛṣṇa, is everything. But that kind of great soul is very rare (*sa mahātmā su-durlabhaḥ*).

But Lord Caitanya has made it easy to become such a great soul. How? Simply by chanting Hare Kṛṣṇa. Therefore at the end of his song Narottama dāsa Ṭhākura says, *hā hā prabhu nanda-suta vṛṣabhānu-sutā-juta koruṇā karoho ei-bāro:* "My dear Lord Kṛṣṇa, You are now present before me with Your internal potency, Your pleasure potency, Rādhārāṇī. Please be merciful to me. Don't neglect me because I am so sinful. My past life is so black, but don't neglect me. Please accept me. Don't kick me away. I surrender unto You."

So, all of us should follow in the footsteps of Narottama dāsa Ṭhākura. The purificatory process is chanting Hare Kṛṣṇa. And as soon as our heart is purified, we will become completely convinced that Kṛṣṇa is the Supreme Lord and that we are His eternal servants. We have forgotten this. We are serving, but instead of serving the Lord we are serving our senses. We have never become the master. We are not the masters of our senses; we are the servants of our senses. That is our position.

So why not become the servant of the Supreme Lord instead of remaining the servant of your senses? Actually, you can become the master of your senses only when you become the servant of Kṛṣṇa. Otherwise, it is not possible. Either *godāsa* or *gosvāmī:* that is your choice. A person who is the servant of his senses is called *godāsa,* and a person who is the master of his senses is called *gosvāmī.* He controls his senses. When his tongue wants to eat something that is not offered to Kṛṣṇa, he thinks, "O tongue, you cannot taste this thing. It is not *kṛṣṇa-prasādam* [food offered to Kṛṣṇa]." In this way one becomes a *gosvāmī,* a master of his senses.

When a person does not allow his senses to do anything for sense gratification but acts only for the service of Kṛṣṇa, that is called devotional service. *Hṛṣīkeṇa hṛṣīkeśa-sevanaṁ bhaktir ucyate:* Devotional service means to engage your senses in satisfying the master of the senses. The supreme master of the senses is Kṛṣṇa. Now we are trying to use our senses for our personal service. This is called *māyā,* illusion. But when we engage the same senses in the service of Kṛṣṇa, that is perfection. We don't stop the activities of the senses, but we purify the senses by engaging them in the service of the Lord. This is Kṛṣṇa consciousness.

Thank you very much. Any questions?

Devotee: Śrīla Prabhupāda, how is it that Lord Jesus is called the son of God? If Kṛṣṇa is usually the son, how is Jesus—

Śrīla Prabhupāda: Not "usually." Kṛṣṇa is the supreme father, but He becomes His devotee's son out of His love. Being a son is not Kṛṣṇa's constitutional position; being the father is His constitutional position (*ahaṁ bīja-pradaḥ pitā*). But sometimes He voluntarily becomes a son to taste His devotee's fatherly or motherly love for Him.

When a pure devotee prays, "My dear Lord, I want You for my son,"

Kṛṣṇa accepts his prayer. Vasudeva and Devakī became Kṛṣṇa's parents in this way. In a previous life they underwent severe austerities. They were married, but they had no sex. They were determined that unless they could get the Lord as their son they would not have a child. So they performed severe austerities for many thousands of years. Then the Lord appeared to them and asked, "What do you want?"

"Sir, we want a son like You."

"How can you get a son like Me? I'll become your son!"

So Kṛṣṇa, the Lord, is the father of everyone, but He voluntarily becomes the son of His devotee. Otherwise, His position is always the supreme father.

Devotee: Śrīla Prabhupāda, I read in the *Śrīmad-Bhāgavatam* that when one becomes a liberated soul he attains perfect freedom and that sometimes his freedom is on the same level as Kṛṣṇa's or even more than Kṛṣṇa's. Can you explain this?

Śrīla Prabhupāda: Yes. Take Vasudeva, for example. He's more than Kṛṣṇa. Or mother Yaśodā. You have seen the picture of Yaśodā binding Kṛṣṇa?

Devotee: Kṛṣṇa looks like a little baby?

Śrīla Prabhupāda: Yes. The Supreme Personality of Godhead is feared by everyone, but He becomes fearful of mother Yaśodā: "My dear mother, kindly do not bind Me. I shall obey your orders."

So mother Yaśodā has become more than God, more than Kṛṣṇa. The *māyāvādī* [impersonalistic] philosophers want to become one with the Lord, but our philosophy is to become *more* than Kṛṣṇa. Why *one* with Kṛṣṇa? *More* than Kṛṣṇa. And, actually, Kṛṣṇa does make His devotee more than Himself. Another example is Arjuna. Kṛṣṇa took the part of his chariot driver. Kṛṣṇa was actually the hero of the Battle of Kurukṣetra, but He gave that position to His devotee: "Arjuna, you become the hero. I shall be your charioteer."

Kṛṣṇa is just like a father who wants to see his son become more than himself. If the father has an M.A., he wants to see his son get a Ph.D. Then the father is satisfied. He'll not tolerate an outsider's becoming more than him, but he's glad if his son becomes more than him. Similarly, Kṛṣṇa, the Supreme Lord, wants to see His devotee become more than Himself. That is His pleasure.

Kṛṣṇa, Enchanter of the Soul

"A man is attracted by a woman, a woman is attracted by a man, and when they are united in sex, their attachment for this material world increases more and more. . . . But our business is not to be attracted by the glimmer of this material world; our business is to be attracted by Kṛṣṇa. And when we become attracted by the beauty of Kṛṣṇa, we will lose our attraction for the false beauty of this material world."

In this material world everyone is attracted by sex. This is a fact. As the *Śrīmad-Bhāgavatam* says, *yan maithunādi-gṛhamedhi-sukhaṁ hi tuccham:* "The happiness – the so-called happiness – of household life begins from *maithuna,* or sexual intercourse."

Generally, a man marries to satisfy sex desire. Then he begets children. Then, when the children are grown up, the daughter marries a boy and the son marries a girl for the same purpose: sex. Then, grandchildren.

In this way, material happiness expands as *śryaiśvarya-prajepsavaḥ*. *Śrī* means "beauty," *aiśvarya* means "wealth," and *prajā* means "children." People think they are successful if they have a beautiful wife, a good bank balance, and good sons, daughters, daughters-in-law, and so on. If one's family consists of beautiful women and riches and many children, one is supposed to be a most successful man.

What is this success? The *śāstra* [scripture] says this success is simply an expansion of sexual intercourse. That's all. We may polish it in different ways, but this same sex happiness is also there in the hogs. The hogs eat the whole day, here and there – "Where is stool? Where is stool?" – and then have sex without any discrimination. The hog does not discriminate whether he has sex with his mother, sister, or daughter.

So, the *śāstra* says we are encaged in this material world only for sex. In other words, we are victims of Cupid. Cupid, or Madana, is the god of sex. Unless one is induced by Madana, one cannot be engladdened in sex life. And one of Kṛṣṇa's names is Madana-mohana, "He who vanquishes Cupid." In other words, one who is attracted to Kṛṣṇa will forget the pleasure derived from sex. This is the test of advancement in Kṛṣṇa consciousness.

Another meaning of *madana* is "to intoxicate or madden." Everyone is maddened by the force of sex desire. The *Śrīmad-Bhāgavatam* says, *puṁsaḥ striyā mithunī-bhāvam etaṁ tayor mitho hṛdaya-granthim āhuḥ:* "The whole material world is going on because of the attraction between male and female." A man is attracted by a woman, a woman is attracted by a man, and when they are united in sex their attachment for this material world increases more and more. After marriage, the man and woman seek a nice home and a job or some land for farming, because they have to earn money to get food and other things. Then come *suta* (children), *āpta* (friends and relatives), and *vittaiḥ* (wealth). In this way the attraction for the material world becomes tighter and tighter. And it all begins with our attraction for *madana,* the pleasure of sex.

But our business is not to be attracted by the glimmer of this material world; our business is to be attracted by Kṛṣṇa. And when we become attracted by the beauty of Kṛṣṇa, we will lose our attraction for the false beauty of this material world. As Śrī Yāmunācārya says,

yad-avadhi mama cetaḥ kṛṣṇa-pādāravinde
nava-nava-rasa-dhāmany udyataṁ rantum āsīt
tad-avadhi bata nārī-saṅgame smaryamāṇe
bhavati mukha-vikāraḥ suṣṭhu niṣṭhīvanaṁ ca

"Since I have been attracted by the beauty of Kṛṣṇa and have begun to serve His lotus feet, I am getting newer and newer pleasure, and as soon as I think of sexual intercourse my mouth immediately turns aside and I spit."

So, Kṛṣṇa is Madana-mohana, the conqueror of Madana, or Cupid. Madana is attracting everyone, but when one is attracted by Kṛṣṇa, Madana is defeated. And as soon as Madana is defeated, we conquer this material world. Otherwise, it is very difficult. As Kṛṣṇa says in the *Bhagavad-gītā* [7.14],

daivī hy eṣā guṇa-mayī
mama māyā duratyayā
mām eva ye prapadyante
māyām etāṁ taranti te

This material world is very difficult to overcome, but if one surrenders unto Kṛṣṇa and catches His lotus feet very strongly – "Kṛṣṇa, save me!" – Kṛṣṇa promises, "Yes, I'll save you. Don't worry, I shall save you." *Kaunteya pratijānīhi na me bhaktaḥ praṇaśyati:* "My dear Arjuna, you can declare to the world that I will protect My devotee who has no other desire but to serve Me."

Unfortunately, people do not know that our only business is to take shelter of the lotus feet of Kṛṣṇa. We have no other business. Any other business we may do simply entangles us in this material world. The aim of human life is to get out of the clutches of the material world. But, as the *Bhāgavatam* says, *na te viduḥ svārtha-gatiṁ hi viṣṇum:* "People do not know that their ultimate goal in life is to realize Viṣṇu, or Kṛṣṇa."

So, it is very difficult to turn people to Kṛṣṇa consciousness in this age. Still, Caitanya Mahāprabhu has ordered us to distribute this knowledge all over the world. So let us try. Even if the people do not take our instruction, that is no disqualification for us. Our only qualification is simply to try our best. *Māyā* [illusion] is very strong. Therefore to take the living entities out of the clutches of *māyā* is not a very easy thing. My Guru Mahārāja had so many temples all over India, and sometimes he would say, "If by selling all these temples I could turn one man to Kṛṣṇa consciousness, my mission would be successful." He used to say that.

Our purpose is not to construct big, big buildings, although that is sometimes required for spreading Kṛṣṇa consciousness and for giving shelter to people. But our main business is to turn the faces of the bewildered conditioned souls toward Kṛṣṇa. That is our main purpose. Therefore Bhaktivinoda Ṭhākura and other Vaiṣṇavas have warned us to be careful about constructing too many big temples, because our attention may be diverted toward material things. In other words, we may become forgetful of Kṛṣṇa.

Of course, ultimately nothing is material. Thinking something is material is simply an illusion. Actually, there is nothing but spirit. How can there be anything material? The Supreme Lord is the Supreme Spirit, and since everything is coming from Him, what we call the material energy is also coming from Him and is thus ultimately spiritual.

But the difficulty is that in this material world, Kṛṣṇa's inferior energy, there is the possibility of forgetting Kṛṣṇa. People are engaged in so many activities – we can see this very clearly in the Western countries – and they are inventing so many modern facilities, but the result is that they are forgetting Kṛṣṇa. *That* is material – this forgetfulness of Kṛṣṇa.

Actually, there is nothing except Kṛṣṇa and His energies. As Nārada Muni says, *idaṁ hi viśvaṁ bhagavān ivetaraḥ:* "This world is Kṛṣṇa, Bhagavān." But to those in ignorance it appears different from Bhagavān. For a *mahā-bhāgavata,* a pure devotee, there is no conception of material and spiritual, because he sees Kṛṣṇa everywhere. As soon as he sees anything we call material, he sees it as a transformation of Kṛṣṇa's energy (*pariṇāma-vāda*). Lord Caitanya gave the following example:

sthāvara-jaṅgama dekhe, nā dekhe tāra mūrti
sarvatra haya nija iṣṭa-deva-sphūrti

A pure devotee may see a tree, but he forgets the tree and sees the energy of Kṛṣṇa. And as soon as he sees the energy of Kṛṣṇa, he sees Kṛṣṇa. Therefore, instead of seeing the tree he sees Kṛṣṇa.

Another example is the sun and the sunshine. As soon as you see the sunshine, you can immediately think of the sun. Is that not so? In the morning, as soon as you see the sunshine shining in your window, you can immediately remember the sun. You are confident the sun is there, because you know that without the sun there cannot be any sunshine. Similarly, whenever we see something, we should immediately think of Kṛṣṇa with reference to that particular thing, because that thing is a manifestation of Kṛṣṇa's energy. And because the energy is not different from the energetic, those who have understood Kṛṣṇa along with His energies do not see anything except Kṛṣṇa. Therefore for them there is no material world. To a perfect devotee, everything is spiritual (*sarvaṁ khalv idaṁ brahma*).

His Divine Grace A. C. Bhaktivedanta Swami Prabhupāda

Founder-*Ācārya* of the International Society for Krishna Consciousness

As the embodied soul continuously passes, in this body, from boyhood to youth to old age, the soul similarly passes into another body at death. (p. 24)

Lord Caitanya and His associates propagate the congregational chanting of the Lord's holy name, the easiest means of self-realization for the modern age. (p. 142)

Kṛṣṇa and Arjuna on the Battlefield of Kurukṣetra. Śrīla Prabhupāda explains: "Kṛṣṇa is the Supreme Lord; Arjuna is a human being. Arjuna loves Kṛṣṇa as a friend, and in response to Arjuna's friendly love Kṛṣṇa has become his chariot driver, his servant. Similarly, if we become

reinstated in our transcendental loving relationship with Kṛṣṇa, our aspiration for mastership will be fulfilled. If you agree to serve Kṛṣṇa, gradually you will see that Kṛṣṇa is also serving you. This is a question of realization." (p. 105)

The Vedic conception of evolution: Eternal, unchanging spirit souls transmigrate through successively higher bodily forms and evolve successively higher levels of consciousness. (p. 283)

The original feature of God as the all-attractive Supreme Personality, Kṛṣṇa, is fully manifest in Goloka Vṛndāvana, the Lord's spiritual abode. (p. 155)

By the inexorable law of *karma,* one who eats meat – and thus conspires in the barbaric practice of cow slaughter – must be killed in turn in a future life. (pp. 221–29)

So, we have to train our eyes to see Kṛṣṇa everywhere. And this training is devotional service to Kṛṣṇa, which is a process of purification:

sarvopādhi-vinirmuktaṁ
tat-paratvena nirmalam
hṛṣīkeṇa hṛṣīkeśa-
sevanaṁ bhaktir ucyate

As soon as we are in Kṛṣṇa consciousness, we give up our false designations, and our seeing, touching, smelling, and so on become *nirmala,* or purified, by being engaged in the service of Kṛṣṇa. Then we can immediately see Kṛṣṇa everywhere. As long as our eyes are not purified we cannot see Kṛṣṇa, but as soon as they are purified by the process of devotional service, we will see nothing *but* Kṛṣṇa.

So, Cupid is one of the agents of the illusory, material energy, but if we are perfectly in Kṛṣṇa consciousness, Cupid cannot pierce our heart with his arrows. It is not possible. A good example is Haridāsa Ṭhākura. When Haridāsa Ṭhākura was a young man, a nicely dressed young prostitute came to him in the middle of the night and revealed her desire to unite with him. Haridāsa Ṭhākura said, "Yes, please sit down. I shall fulfill your desire, but just let me finish my chanting of Hare Kṛṣṇa." Just see! It's the dead of night, and in front of Haridāsa Ṭhākura is a beautiful young girl proposing to have sex with him. But still he's steady, chanting Hare Kṛṣṇa, Hare Kṛṣṇa, Kṛṣṇa Kṛṣṇa, Hare Hare/ Hare Rāma, Hare Rāma, Rāma Rāma, Hare Hare. But he never finished his chanting, so her plan was unsuccessful.

So, Cupid cannot pierce our heart when we are fully absorbed in Kṛṣṇa consciousness. There may be thousands of beautiful women before a devotee, but they cannot disturb him. He sees them as energies of Kṛṣṇa. He thinks, "They are Kṛṣṇa's; they are meant for His enjoyment."

A devotee's duty is to try to engage all beautiful women in the service of Kṛṣṇa, not to try to enjoy them. A devotee is not pierced by the arrows of Cupid, because he sees everything in relationship with Kṛṣṇa. That is real renunciation. He does not accept anything for his own sense gratification but engages everything and everyone in the service of Kṛṣṇa. This is the process of Kṛṣṇa consciousness.

Thank you very much.

4

The Spiritual Master

Show-Bottle Spiritualists Exposed

Los Angeles, December 30, 1968: A CBS television news reporter asks for Śrīla Prabhupāda's comments on the many newly-arisen "gurus" *of the late '60s who were promising – among other things – power, influence, stress control, and salvation. This no-holds-barred interview exposes many current "religious" philosophies and practices. Śrīla Prabhupāda declares, "The man who says he's God – he's rascal number one."*

Journalist: I think an awful lot of our readers, and an awful lot of people in the United States, are terribly confused with the many people who claim to be *gurus* and gods and who pop up in this country, one after the other after the other, and they say that—

Śrīla Prabhupāda: I can declare that they are all nonsense.

Journalist: I wonder if you could elaborate on that a little bit.

Śrīla Prabhupāda: I can say, furthermore, they're all rascals.

Journalist: For example, the famous one who sells meditation *mantras*?

Śrīla Prabhupāda: He is rascal number one. I say it publicly.

Journalist: Could you explain, give me a little background on that, and why, because our readers—

Śrīla Prabhupāda: From his behavior I can understand he is rascal number one. I do not want to know about him, but what he has done makes it obvious. But the wonderful thing is that people in the Western countries are supposed to be so advanced – how are they befooled by these rascals?

Journalist: Well, I think that people are looking for something, and he comes along—

Śrīla Prabhupāda: Yes, but they want something very cheap – that is their fault. Now, for our disciples, we don't give anything cheap. Our first condition is character – moral character. You see? Unless one is strictly following moral principles, we don't initiate him, we don't allow him in this institution. And this so-called *guru* has been telling people, "Just do whatever you like. You simply pay me thirty-five dollars, and I'll give you a *mantra*." You see? So people want to be cheated, and so many cheaters come. People do not wish to undergo any discipline. They have got money, so they think, "We shall pay, and immediately we'll get whatever we want."

Journalist: Instant heaven.

Śrīla Prabhupāda: Yes. That is their foolishness.

Journalist: Let me ask you – I have my opinion, but let me ask you – why do you feel that the younger people today are turning more and more toward the Eastern-oriented religions?

Śrīla Prabhupāda: Because your materialistic way of life no longer satisfies them. In America, especially, you have got enough for enjoyment. You have got enough food, enough women, enough wine, enough houses – enough of everything. But still you have confusion and dissatisfaction – more in your country than in India, which is said to be poverty-stricken. But you'll find in India that although they are poverty-stricken, they are continuing their old spiritual culture. So the people are not as disturbed. This shows that material advancement alone cannot give one satisfaction. If they really want satisfaction, people must take to spiritual life. That will make them happy. All these people – they are in darkness. There is no hope. They do not know where they are going; they have no aim. But when you are spiritually situated, you know what you are doing and where you are going. Everything is clear.

Journalist: In other words, you feel that the Western-oriented church – whether it be a synagogue or a church or whatever – has failed to present spiritual life. Would you say that their message is not relevant? Or is it that they have failed to present their message properly?

Śrīla Prabhupāda: Take the Bible. It was spoken long, long ago to primitive people who were living in the desert. These people were not very advanced. So at that time, in the Old Testament, it was sufficient to say, "There is a God, and God created the world." That is a fact. But now people are scientifically advanced, and they want to know in detail how the creation has taken place. You see? Unfortunately, that detailed, scientific explanation is not there in the Bible. And the church can't give any more than that. Therefore people are not satisfied. Simply officially going to the church and offering prayers does not appeal to them.

Besides that, the so-called religious leaders are not following even the most basic religious principles. For instance, in the Old Testament there are the Ten Commandments, and one commandment is "Thou shalt not kill." But killing is very prominent in the Christian world. The religious leaders are sanctioning slaughterhouses, and they have manufactured a theory that animals have no soul. "Give the dog a bad name and hang it."

So when we ask, "Why are you committing this sinful act of killing?" the priests refuse to discuss the matter. Everyone is silent. That means they are deliberately disobeying the Ten Commandments. So where are the religious principles? It is plainly stated, "Thou shalt not kill." Why are they killing? How do you answer?

Journalist: Are you asking me?

Śrīla Prabhupāda: Yes.

Journalist: Well, "Thou shalt not kill" is obviously an ethic . . . and it's timeless, and it's valid. But man is not really interested—

Śrīla Prabhupāda: Yes, that's right. They are not really interested in religion. It is simply show-bottle. If you do not follow the regulative principles, then where is your religion?

Journalist: I'm not arguing with you. I couldn't agree with you more. I'm in total agreement. It doesn't make any sense. "Thou shalt not kill." "Thou shalt worship no other gods before Me." "Thou shalt not covet thy neighbor's goods." "Thou shalt honor thy father and thy mother." . . . Those are beautiful—

Śrīla Prabhupāda: "Thou shalt not covet thy neighbor's wife" – but who is following this?

Journalist: Very few.

Śrīla Prabhupāda: So how can they say they're religious? And without religion, human society is animal society.

Journalist: All right, but let me ask you this. How does your interpretation differ from the basic Judeo-Christian ethic of the Ten Commandments?

Śrīla Prabhupāda: There is no difference. But as I have told you, none of them are strictly *following* the Ten Commandments. So I simply say, "Please follow God's commandments." That is my message.
Journalist: In other words, you're asking them to obey those principles.
Śrīla Prabhupāda: Yes. I don't say that Christians should become Hindu. I simply say, "Please obey your commandments." I'll make you a better Christian. That is my mission. I don't say, "God is not in your tradition – God is only here in ours." I simply say, "Obey God." I don't say, "You have to accept that God's name is Kṛṣṇa and no other." No. I say, "Please obey God. Please try to love God."
Journalist: Let me put it this way. If your mission and the mission of the Western Judeo-Christian ethic are the same, again let me ask, Why is it that the younger people, or people in general, are disenchanted, are trying to go toward the Eastern-oriented religions? Why are they going toward the Eastern if both are the same?
Śrīla Prabhupāda: Because Judaism and Christianity are not teaching them *practically*. I am teaching them *practically*.
Journalist: In other words, you're teaching them what you feel is a practical, everyday method for attaining this fulfillment of man's spirit.
Śrīla Prabhupāda: Love of Godhead is being taught both in the Bible and in the *Bhagavad-gītā*. But today's religionists are not actually teaching how to love God. I am teaching people how to love God – that is the difference. Therefore, young people are attracted.
Journalist: All right. So the end is the same, but it's the method of getting there that's different?
Śrīla Prabhupāda: No – the end is the same and the method is also the same. But these so-called religious leaders are not teaching people to follow the method. I am teaching them practically how to follow it.
Journalist: Let me ask you something that we've run into a great deal just recently. The biggest problem holding men and women back from love of God and following the Ten Commandments is the problem – how should I put it? – well, the sexual problem. Now, I'm stating something that's obvious. We've all gone through this.
Śrīla Prabhupāda: Yes, everyone.
Journalist: And there is nothing in Western culture or religion that teaches or helps a young person to cope with this difficult problem. I

went through it. We all have. Now do you, in your message, give the young people something to hang on to? And if so, what?

Śrīla Prabhupāda: I ask my disciples to get married. I don't allow this nonsense of boys living with girlfriends. No. "You must get yourself married and live like a gentleman."

Journalist: Well, let me get a little more basic. How about when one is fourteen, fifteen, sixteen years old?

Śrīla Prabhupāda: One thing is that we teach our boys how to become *brahmacārī* – how to live the life of celibacy, how to control their senses. In Vedic culture, marriage generally doesn't take place until the boy is about twenty-four or twenty-five and the girl is about sixteen or seventeen. And because they are experiencing the spiritual pleasure of Kṛṣṇa consciousness, they are not simply interested in sex life. So we don't say, "Don't mix with women," "Stop sex life." But we regulate everything under the higher principle of Kṛṣṇa consciousness. In this way everything goes nicely.

Journalist: So your disciples don't just bite their tongue or their lip and say, "I won't touch her (or him)." There is a substitute?

Śrīla Prabhupāda: Yes, a higher taste. That is Kṛṣṇa consciousness. And it is working: I'm already teaching Western men and women how to control their sexual impulse. My disciples that you see here are all Americans. They are not imported from India.

Journalist: One thing I want to know is what you think about people like this famous *mantra*-selling *guru,* who turned me off and so many other people. My daughter was very involved in that kind of thing for awhile. She's terribly disillusioned.

Śrīla Prabhupāda: The psychology is that the Western people, especially youngsters, are hankering after spiritual life. Now, if somebody comes to me and says, "Svāmījī, initiate me," I immediately say, "You have to follow these four principles – no meat-eating, no gambling, no intoxication, and no illicit sex." Many go away. But this *mantra* seller – he does not put any restrictions. That's just like a physician who says, "You can do whatever you like; you simply take my medicine and you'll be cured." That physician will be very popular.

Journalist: Yes. He'll kill a lot of people, but he'll be very well liked.

Śrīla Prabhupāda: Yes. [*Laughs.*] And a real physician says, "You cannot do this. You cannot do that. You cannot eat this." This is a botheration for people. They want something very cheap. Therefore the cheaters come and cheat them. They take the opportunity – because people want to be cheated.

"Oh, let us take advantage!" You see? So the rascals advise people, "You are God – everyone is God. You just have to realize yourself – you have simply forgotten. You take this *mantra,* and you'll become God. You'll become powerful. There is no need to control the senses. You can drink. You can have unrestricted sex life and whatever you like."

People like this. "Oh, simply by fifteen minutes' meditation I shall become God, and I have to pay only thirty-five dollars." Many millions of people will be ready to do it. For Americans, thirty-five dollars is not very much. But multiplied by a million, it becomes thirty-five million dollars. [*Laughs.*]

We cannot bluff like that. We say that if you actually want spiritual life, you have to follow the restrictions. The commandment is, "You shall not kill." So I shall not say, "Yes, you can kill – the animal has no feeling, the animal has no soul." We cannot bluff in this way, you see.

Journalist: This kind of thing has disenchanted an awful lot of young people.

Śrīla Prabhupāda: So please try to help us. This movement is very nice. It will help your country. It will help the whole human society. It is a genuine movement. We are not bluffing or cheating. It is authorized.

Journalist: Authorized by whom?

Śrīla Prabhupāda: Authorized by Kṛṣṇa, God. In India this Kṛṣṇa consciousness philosophy has millions and millions of followers – eighty percent of the population. If you ask any Indian he will be able to tell you so many things about Kṛṣṇa consciousness.

Journalist: Do you really think, from a very practical standpoint, that your movement has a chance to make it here in America?

Śrīla Prabhupāda: From what I've seen it has a great chance. We don't say, "Give up your religion and come to us." We say, "At least follow your own principles. And then if you want to, study with us." Sometimes it happens that although students have received their M.A. degree, they go to foreign universities to study more. Why does it happen? They want more enlightenment. Similarly, any religious scripture you may follow will give you enlightenment. But if you find more in this Kṛṣṇa consciousness movement, then why should you not accept it? If you are serious about God, why should you say, "Oh, I am Christian," "I am Jewish," "I cannot attend your meeting"? Why should you say, "Oh, I cannot allow you to speak in my church"? If I am speaking about God, what objection can you have?

Journalist: Well, I couldn't agree with you more.

Śrīla Prabhupāda: I am prepared to talk with any God conscious man. Let us chalk out a program so that people may be benefited. But they want to go on in their stereotyped way. If we see that by following a particular type of religious principle one is developing love of God, that is first-class religion. But if one is merely developing his love for mammon, then what kind of religion is that?

Journalist: Right you are.

Śrīla Prabhupāda: That is our test – you have to develop love for God. We don't say that you must follow Christianity or Mohammedanism or Judaism or Hinduism. We simply look to see whether you are developing your love of Godhead. But they say, "Who is God? I am God." You see? Everyone is taught nowadays that everyone is God.

Journalist: Have you seen pictures of a smiling man with a mustache and a pushed-in nose? Before he died, he said he was God.

Śrīla Prabhupāda: He was God? He was another rascal. Just see – this is going on. He was making propaganda that he was God. That means that people do not know what God is. Suppose I come to you and say that I am the President of the United States. Will you accept me?

Journalist: [*Laughs.*] No, I don't think I would.

Śrīla Prabhupāda: These rascals! The people are accepting them as God because they do not know what God *is* – that is the problem.

Journalist: It's just absolutely absurd that somebody comes along and tells you he's God.

Śrīla Prabhupāda: But whoever accepts him as God is just as much a rascal. The man who says he's God – he's rascal number one. He's a cheater. And the man who is cheated – he's also a rascal. He does not know what God is. He thinks that God is so cheap that you can find Him in the marketplace.

Journalist: Of course, the Western concept is that man is created in the image of God. Consequently, God must look somewhat like man.
Śrīla Prabhupāda: You have got so many scientists. So just find out what the actual image of God is, what His form is really like. Where is that department? You have got so many departments – research department, technology department. But where is that department that researches what God is? Is there any such department of knowledge?
Journalist: There's no God department working tonight – I'll tell you that right now.
Śrīla Prabhupāda: That is the difficulty. But the Kṛṣṇa consciousness movement is the department of how to know God. If you study with us, then you'll not accept any rascal as God. You'll accept only God as God. We are teaching about another nature, beyond this material nature. This material nature is coming into existence and again dissolving, but God and His spiritual nature are eternal. We living entities are also eternal – without any end or any beginning. This Kṛṣṇa consciousness movement is teaching how we can transfer ourselves to that eternal, spiritual nature where God is residing.
Journalist: That's man's quest.
Śrīla Prabhupāda: Yes, that is the quest. Everyone is trying to be happy, because that is the living entity's prerogative. He is meant by nature to be happy, but he does not know where he can be happy. He is trying to be happy in a place where there are four miserable conditions – namely birth, old age, disease, and death. The scientists are trying to be happy and make other people happy. But what scientist has stopped old age, disease, death, and rebirth? Has any scientist succeeded?
Journalist: I don't think so.
Śrīla Prabhupāda: So what is this? Why do they not consider, "We have made so much improvement, but what improvement have we made in these four areas?" They have not made *any.* And still they are very much proud of their advancement in education and technology. But the four primary miseries remain as they are. You see?

The scientists may have made advancements in medicine, but is there any remedy that can allow us to claim, "Now there is no more disease"? Is there any such remedy? No. So then what is the scientists' advancement? Rather, disease is increasing in so many new forms.

They have invented nuclear weapons. What good is that? Simply for killing. Have they invented something so that no more men will die? That would be to their credit. But people are dying at every moment, and the scientists have simply invented something to accelerate their death. That's all. Is that to their credit? So there is still no solution to death.

And they are trying to stop overpopulation. But where is their solution? Every minute the population is increasing by one hundred persons. These are the statistics.

So there is no solution for birth. There is no solution for death. There is no solution for disease. And there is no solution for old age. Even a great scientist like Professor Einstein had to undergo old age and death. Why could he not stop old age? Everyone is trying to remain youthful, but what is the process? The scientists do not care to solve this problem – because it is beyond their means.

They are giving some kind of bluff, that's all. But Kṛṣṇa consciousness is the solution, and the whole thing is described in *Bhagavad-gītā*. Let them try to understand it. At least let them make an experiment.

The Bona Fide Spiritual Master

"The spiritual master will never say, 'I am God.' . . . The spiritual master will say, "I am a servant of God." Addressing the student body of Stockholm University in September 1973, Śrīla Prabhupāda delineates the eight principal features that, according to Vedic teachings, characterize a genuine spiritual master and thus enable us to distinguish the saint from the charlatan.

In order to enter into spiritual life, two things are required. As enunciated by Śrī Caitanya Mahāprabhu, one needs the mercy of the Supreme Lord and the mercy of the spiritual master:

brahmāṇḍa bhramite kona bhāgyavān jīva
guru-kṛṣṇa-prasāde pāya bhakti-latā-bīja

The living entities are wandering throughout the universe changing bodies, transmigrating from one body to another, from one place to another, and from one planet to another. *Brahmāṇḍa bhramite:* they are rotating within this material universe. This science is unknown to the modern educators – how the spirit soul is transmigrating from one body to another, and how he is being transferred from one planet to another. But we have explained this in our book *Easy Journey to Other Planets.*

In fact, the *guru* can help you transmigrate from this planet directly to the spiritual sky, Vaikuṇṭhaloka, where there are innumerable spiritual planets. The topmost planet in the spiritual sky is Kṛṣṇa's planet, called Goloka Vṛndāvana. The Kṛṣṇa consciousness movement is trying to give information of how one can be transferred directly to the Goloka Vṛndāvana planet, Kṛṣṇaloka. That is our mission.

What is the difference between this material world and the spiritual world? The difference is that in the material world you have to change your body, although you are eternal. *Ajo nityaḥ śāśvato 'yaṁ purāṇo na hanyate hanyamāne śarīre.* You are not destroyed after the annihilation of your material body, but you transmigrate to another body, which may be one of 8,400,000 forms. *Jalajā nava-lakṣāṇi.* There are 900,000 forms in the water, 2,000,000 forms of trees and plants, 1,100,000 forms of insects, 1,000,000 forms of birds, and 3,000,000 forms of beasts. Then you come to this human form of life. Now it is your choice whether to be transferred again, by the cycle of transmigration, from one body to another in the lower species of life, or whether to be transferred to the spiritual sky – to the highest spiritual planet, known as Goloka Vṛndāvana. That is your choice. You have been given the chance of this human form of body to make your choice. In the lower species you are completely under the control of material nature, but when the material nature gives you a chance to get this human form of body, you can choose whatever you like.

That is confirmed in the *Bhagavad-gītā* [9.25]:

yānti deva-vratā devān
pitṝn yānti-pitṛ-vratāḥ
bhūtāni yānti bhūtejyā
yānti mad-yājino 'pi mām

Those who are trying to be elevated to the higher planets – *deva-loka,* or the planets of the demigods, where the standard of living and the life span are very great – may worship the demigods. Or if you want you may be transferred to the Pitṛloka, to the planets of the ghosts, or to the planet where Kṛṣṇa lives (*yānti mad-yājino 'pi mām*). This all depends on your activities. But *saṁsāra* – rotating, wandering within this material world from one body to another or from one planet to another – is not advised. Material existence is called *saṁsāra. Bhūtvā bhūtvā pralīyate:* You take your birth in some form of body, you live for some time, then you have to give up this body. Then you have to accept another body, again live for some time, then give up that body, and then again accept another body. This is called *saṁsāra.*

The material world is compared to *dāvānala,* a forest fire. As we have experienced, no one goes to the forest to set a fire, but still it takes place. Similarly, no one within this material world wants to be unhappy. Everyone is trying to be very happy, but one is forced to accept unhappiness. In this material world, from time immemorial to the present moment, there have been occasional wars, world wars, even though people have devised various means to stop wars. When I was a young man there was the League of Nations. In 1920, after the First World War, different nations formed the League of Nations, just to arrange for peaceful living among themselves. No one wanted war, but again there was a forest fire – the Second World War. Now they have devised the United Nations, but war is still going on – the Vietnam War, the Pakistan War, and many others. So you may try your best to live very peacefully, but nature will not allow you. There must be war. And this warlike feeling is always going on, not only between nation and nation, but also between man and man, neighbor and neighbor – even between husband and wife and father and son. This warlike feeling is going on. This is called *dāvānala*, a forest fire. No one goes to the forest to set fire, but automatically, by the friction of dried bamboo, sparks arise, and the forest catches fire. Similarly, although we do not want unhappiness, by our dealings we create enemies, and there is fighting and war. This is called *saṁsāra-dāvānala.*

This forest fire of material existence goes on perpetually, and the authorized person who can deliver you from this fire is called *guru,* the spiritual master.

How does he deliver you? What is his means? Consider the same example. When there is a fire in the forest, you cannot send a fire brigade or go there yourself with bucketfuls of water to extinguish it. That is not possible. Then how will it be extinguished? You need water to extinguish fire, but where will the water come from – from your bucket or your fire brigade? No, it must come from the sky. Only when there are torrents of rain from the sky will the blazing forest fire be extinguished. These rains from the sky do not depend on your scientific propaganda or manipulation. They depend on the mercy of the Supreme Lord. So the spiritual master is compared to a cloud. Just as there are torrents of rain from a cloud, so the spiritual master brings mercy from the Supreme Personality of Godhead. A cloud takes water from the sea. It doesn't have its own water but takes water from the sea. Similarly, the spiritual master brings mercy from the Supreme Personality of Godhead. Just see the comparison. He has no mercy of his own, but he carries the mercy of the Supreme Personality of Godhead. That is the qualification of the spiritual master.

The spiritual master will never say, "I am God – I can give you mercy." No. That is not a spiritual master; that is a bogus pretender. The spiritual master will say, "I am a servant of God; I have brought His mercy. Please take it and be satisfied." This is the spiritual master's business. He is just like a mailman. When a mailman delivers you some large amount of money, it is not his own money. The money is sent by someone else, but he honestly delivers it – "Sir, here is your money. Take it." So you become very much satisfied with him, although it is not his money he is giving you. When you are in need and you get money from your father or someone else – brought by the mailman – you feel very much satisfaction.

Similarly, we are all suffering in this blazing fire of material existence. But the spiritual master brings the message from the Supreme Lord and delivers it to you, and if you kindly accept it, then you'll be satisfied. This is the business of the spiritual master.

saṁsāra-dāvānala-līḍha-loka-
trāṇāya kāruṇya-ghanāghanatvam
prāptasya kalyāṇa-guṇārṇavasya
vande guroḥ śrī-caraṇāravindam

Thus the spiritual master is offered obeisances: "Sir, you have brought mercy from the Supreme Lord; therefore, we are much obliged to you. You have come to deliver us, so we offer our respectful obeisances." That is the meaning of this verse: The first qualification of the spiritual master, or *guru*, is that he brings you the message to stop the blazing fire in your heart. This is the test.

Everyone has a blazing fire within his heart – a blazing fire of anxiety. That is the nature of material existence. Always, everyone has anxiety; no one is free from it. Even a small bird has anxiety. If you give the small bird some grains to eat, he'll eat them, but he won't eat very peacefully. He'll look this way and that way – "Is somebody coming to kill me?" This is material existence. Everyone, even a president like Mr. Nixon, is full of anxieties, what to speak of others. Even Gandhi, in our country – he was full of anxiety. All politicians are full of anxiety. They may hold a very exalted post, but still the material disease – anxiety – is there.

So if you want to be anxiety-less, then you must take shelter of the *guru*, the spiritual master. And the test of the *guru* is that by following his instructions you'll be free from anxiety. This is the test. Don't try to find a cheap *guru* or a fashionable *guru*. Just as you sometimes keep a dog as a fashion, if you want to keep a *guru* as a fashion – "I have a *guru*" – that will not help. You must accept a *guru* who can extinguish the blazing fire of anxiety within your heart. That is the first test of the *guru*.

The second test is, *mahāprabhoḥ kīrtana-nṛtya-gīta-vāditra-mādyan-manaso rasena*. The second symptom of the *guru* is that he is always engaged in chanting, glorifying Lord Caitanya Mahāprabhu – that is his business. *Mahāprabhoḥ kīrtana-nṛtya-gīta*. The spiritual master is chanting the holy name of the Lord and dancing, because that is the remedy for all calamities within this material world.

At the present moment, no one can meditate. The so-called meditation now popular in the West is humbug. It is very difficult to meditate in this disturbing age of Kali [the age of quarrel and hypocrisy]. Therefore *śāstra* [scripture] says, *kṛte yad dhyāyato viṣṇum*. In the Satya-yuga [the age of truth], when people used to live for one hundred thousands years, Vālmīki Muni attained perfection by meditating for sixty thousand years. But now we have no guarantee that we are going to live for sixty years or even sixty hours. So meditation is not possible in this age. In the next age [the Tretā-yuga], people performed rituals, as they are described in the Vedic *śāstra*. *Tretāyāṁ yajato makhaiḥ*. *Makhaiḥ* means performing big, big sacrifices. That requires huge amounts of money. In the present age people are very poor, so they cannot perform these sacrifices. *Dvāpare paricaryāyām* – in the Dvāpara-yuga [the age just prior to the present age] it was possible to worship the Deity opulently in the temple, but nowadays, in the Kali-yuga, that is also an impossible task. Therefore, the general recommendation is *kalau tad dhari-kīrtanāt:* in this age of Kali one can attain all perfection simply by chanting the holy name of the Lord. The Kṛṣṇa consciousness movement is meant to spread such chanting. Śrī Caitanya Mahāprabhu inaugurated this movement of chanting and dancing. It has been going on for the last five hundred years. In India it is very popular, but in the Western countries we have just introduced it five or six years ago. Now people are taking to it, and they are feeling happy. This is the only process for this age.

Therefore, the *guru* is always engaged in chanting. *Mahāprabhoḥ kīrtana-nṛtya-gīta* – chanting and dancing. Unless he performs it himself, how can he teach his disciples? So his first symptom is that he will give you such instructions that immediately you will feel relief from all anxiety, and his second symptom is that he is always personally engaged in chanting the holy name of the Lord and dancing. *Mahāprabhoḥ kīrtana-nṛtya-gīta-vāditra-mādyan-manaso rasena* – the spiritual master enjoys transcendental bliss within his mind by chanting and dancing. Unless you become blissful, you cannot dance. You cannot dance artificially. When devotees dance, it is not artificial. They feel some transcendental bliss, and therefore they dance. It is not that they are dancing dogs. No. Their dancing is performed from the spiritual platform. *Romāñca-kampāśru-taraṅga-bhājaḥ.* There are sometimes transformations of the body with spiritual symptoms – sometimes crying, sometimes the hairs standing on end. There are so many symptoms. These are natural. These symptoms are not to be imitated, but when one is spiritually advanced, they are visible.

The third symptom of the *guru* is:

śrī-vigrahārādhana-nitya-nānā-
śṛṅgāra-tan-mandira-mārjanādau
yuktasya bhaktāṁś ca niyuñjato 'pi
vande guroḥ śrī-caraṇāravindam

The spiritual master's duty is to engage the disciples in worshiping the Deity, *śrī-vigraha.* In all of our one hundred centers, we engage in Deity worship. Here in Stockholm this worship has not yet been fully established, but we worship the pictures of Lord Caitanya and the *guru.* In other centers, such as the ones in England and America, there is Deity worship. *Śrī-vigrahārādhana-nitya-nānā-śṛṅgāra-tan-mandira-mārjanādau:*

Deity worship means to dress the Deity very nicely, to cleanse the temple very nicely, to offer nice foodstuffs to the Deity, and to accept the remnants of the Deity's foodstuffs for our eating. This is the method of Deity worship. Deity worship is done by the *guru* himself, and he also engages his disciples in that worship. This is the third symptom.

The fourth symptom is:

catur-vidha-śrī-bhagavat-prasāda-
svādv-anna-tṛptān hari-bhakta-saṅghān
kṛtvaiva tṛptiṁ bhajataḥ sadaiva
vande guroḥ śrī-caraṇāravindam

The spiritual master encourages distribution of *prasādam* (remnants of Kṛṣṇa's food) to the public. Ours is not a dry philosophy – simply talk and go away. No. We distribute *prasādam,* very sumptuous *prasādam.* In every temple, we offer *prasādam* to anyone who comes. In each and every temple we already have from fifty to two hundred devotees, and outsiders also come and take *prasādam.* So *prasādam* distribution is another symptom of the genuine spiritual master.

If you eat *bhagavat-prasādam,* then gradually you become spiritualized; it has this potency. Therefore it is said that realization of God begins with the tongue. *Sevonmukhe hi jihvādau:* If you engage your tongue in the service of the Lord, then you realize God. So what is that engagement of the tongue? You chant the holy name of the Lord, and you take this *prasādam,* remnants of food offered to the Lord. Then you become self-realized, God-realized – by these two methods. You don't have to be very highly educated or be a philosopher, a scientist, or a rich man to realize God. If you just sincerely engage your tongue in the service of the Lord, you will realize Him. It is so simple. It is not very difficult. Therefore the *guru,* the spiritual master, introduces this *prasādam* program. *Svādv-anna-tṛptān hari-bhakta-saṅghān. Hari-bhakta-saṅghān* means "in the association of devotees." You cannot do it outside. *Kṛtvaiva tṛptiṁ bhajataḥ sadaiva:* When the *guru* is fully satisfied that *prasādam* distribution is going on, he is very much pleased, and he engages himself in the devotional service of the Lord by chanting and dancing. This is the fourth symptom.

The fifth symptom is:

śrī-rādhikā-mādhavayor apāra-
mādhurya-līlā-guṇa-rūpa-nāmnām
prati-kṣaṇāsvādana-lolupasya
vande guroḥ śrī-caraṇāravindam

The spiritual master is always thinking of the pastimes of Kṛṣṇa with His consort – Śrīmatī Rādhārāṇī – and the *gopīs.* Sometimes he is thinking about Kṛṣṇa's pastimes with the cowherd boys. This means that he is always thinking of Kṛṣṇa engaged in some kind of pastime. *Pratikṣaṇāsvādana-lolupasya. Prati-kṣaṇa* means he is thinking that way twenty-four hours a day. That is Kṛṣṇa consciousness. One must be engaged twenty-four hours a day in thinking of Kṛṣṇa. You have to make yourself a program like this. We, at least, have made such a program – all the boys and girls in the Kṛṣṇa consciousness movement are engaged twenty-four hours daily – not just officially, not that once a week they meditate or go to some temple. No, they engage twenty-four hours a day.

The next symptom is:

nikuñja-yūno rati-keli-siddhyai
yā yālibhir yuktir apekṣaṇīyā
tatrāti-dākṣyād ati-vallabhasya
vande guroḥ śrī-caraṇāravindam

The spiritual master's ultimate goal is that he wants to be transferred to the planet of Kṛṣṇa, where he can associate with the *gopīs* to help them serve Kṛṣṇa. Some spiritual masters are thinking of becoming assistants to the *gopīs,* some are thinking of becoming assistants to the cowherd boys, some are thinking of becoming assistants to Nanda and mother Yaśodā, and some are thinking of becoming God's servants. Some are thinking of becoming flower trees, fruit trees, calves, or cows in Vṛndāvana. There are five kinds of mellows: *śānta* [veneration], *dāsya* [servitorship], *sakhya* [friendship], *vātsalya* [parenthood], and *mādhurya* [conjugal love]. Everything is there in the spiritual world. *Cintāmaṇi-prakara-sadmasu.* In the spiritual sky, even the land is spiritual. The trees are spiritual, the fruit is spiritual, the flowers are spiritual, the water is spiritual, the servants are spiritual, the friends are spiritual, the mothers are spiritual, the fathers are spiritual, the Lord is spiritual, and His associates are spiritual. It is all absolute, although there are varieties.

In the material world these spiritual varieties are merely reflected, just like trees on a riverbank. A tree is reflected in the water, but reflected how? Upside down. Similarly, this material world is a reflection of the spiritual world, but a perverted reflection. In the spiritual world there is love between Rādhā and Kṛṣṇa. Kṛṣṇa is always young – *nava-yauvana*. And Rādhārāṇī is always young, because She is Kṛṣṇa's pleasure potency. *Śrī-rādhikā-mādhavayor apāra. Jaya rādhā-mādhava.* We worship not Kṛṣṇa alone but Kṛṣṇa with His eternal consort, Śrīmātī Rādhārāṇī. There is eternal love between Rādhārāṇī and Kṛṣṇa. Therefore the *Vedānta-sūtra* says, *janmādy asya yataḥ:* The Absolute Truth is that from which everything emanates. In this world we find love between mother and son, love between wife and husband, love between master and servant, between friend and friend, between the master and the dog or the cat or the cow. But these are only reflections of the spiritual world. Kṛṣṇa is also the good lover of the animals, the calves and cows. Just as here we love dogs and cats, there Kṛṣṇa loves cows and calves. You have seen this in pictures of Kṛṣṇa. So the propensity to love even an animal is there in the spiritual world. Otherwise, how can it be reflected? This world is simply a reflection. If in the reality there is nothing like that, how can it be reflected here? So everything is there in the spiritual world. But to understand that original propensity to love, you have to practice Kṛṣṇa consciousness.

Here in this world we are experiencing frustration. Here we love – a man loves a woman, or a woman loves a man – but there is frustration. After some time they are divorced, because their love is a perverted reflection. There is no real love in this world. It is simply lust. Real love is in the spiritual world, between Rādhā and Kṛṣṇa. Real love is there between Kṛṣṇa and the *gopīs.* Real love is there in the friendship between Kṛṣṇa and His cowherd boys. Real love is there between Kṛṣṇa and the cows and calves. Real love is there between Kṛṣṇa and the trees, flowers, and water. In the spiritual world, everything is love. But within this material world, we are satisfied merely by the reflection of the things in the spiritual world. So, now that we have this opportunity of human life, let us understand Kṛṣṇa. That is Kṛṣṇa consciousness – let us understand Kṛṣṇa. And as the *Bhagavad-gītā* [4.9] says, *janma karma ca me divyam evaṁ yo vetti tattvataḥ* – you should understand Kṛṣṇa in truth, not superficially. Learn the science of Kṛṣṇa. This is the instruction – you should simply try to love Kṛṣṇa. The process is that you worship the Deity, you take *prasādam,* you chant Kṛṣṇa's holy names, and you follow the instruction of the spiritual master. In this way you'll learn how to understand Kṛṣṇa, and then your life will be successful. This is our Kṛṣṇa consciousness movement. Thank you very much.

5

Yoga and Meditation

Meditation Through Transcendental Sound

Lecturing at Boston's Northeastern University in the summer of 1969, Śrīla Prabhupāda introduces a meditation system renowned for its extraordinary power and the fact that it can be easily practiced almost anywhere and at any time. "If you take up this simple process," he says, "chanting Hare Kṛṣṇa, Hare Kṛṣṇa, Kṛṣṇa Kṛṣṇa, Hare Hare/ Hare Rāma, Hare Rāma, Rāma Rāma Hare Hare, you are immediately elevated to the transcendental platform." He adds, "No other meditation is possible while you are walking on the street."

My dear boys and girls, I thank you very much for attending this meeting. We are spreading this Kṛṣṇa consciousness movement because there is a great need of this consciousness throughout the world. And the process is very easy – that is the advantage.

First of all, we must try to understand what the transcendental platform is. As far as our present condition is concerned, we are on various platforms. So we have to first of all stand on the transcendental platform; then there can be a question of transcendental meditation.

In the third chapter of *Bhagavad-gītā*, you'll find an explanation of the various statuses of conditioned life. The first is the bodily conception of life (*indriyāṇi parāṇy āhuḥ*). Everyone in this material world is under this bodily concept of life. Someone is thinking, "I am Indian." You are thinking, "I am American." Somebody's thinking, "I am Russian." Somebody's thinking he is something else. So everyone is thinking, "I am the body."

This bodily standard of conditioned life is called the sensual platform, because as long as we have a bodily conception of life we think happiness means sense gratification. That's all. This bodily concept of life is very prominent at the present moment – not only at the present moment, but since the creation of this material world. That is the disease: "I am the body."

Śrīmad-Bhāgavatam says, *yasyātma-buddhiḥ kuṇape tri-dhātuke:* Thinking we are the body means we have a concept of ourself as a bag of skin and bones. The body is a bag of skin, bones, blood, urine, stool, and so many other nice things. So when we think, "I am the body," we are actually thinking, "I am a bag of bones and skin and stool and urine. That is my beauty; that is my everything." So this bodily concept of life is not very intelligent, and improvement of the body is not a right calculation of self-realization.

Those who are too engrossed with the bodily concept of life are recommended to practice the *dhyāna-yoga* system, the *yoga* of meditation. That is mentioned in the *Śrīmad Bhagavad-gītā*. In the sixth chapter, verses 13 and 14, Kṛṣṇa explains, "One should hold one's body, neck, and head erect in a straight line and stare steadily at the tip of the nose. Thus, with an unagitated, subdued mind, devoid of fear, completely free from sex life, one should meditate upon Me within the heart and make Me the ultimate goal of life."

Earlier Lord Kṛṣṇa gives preliminary instructions on how one should practice this transcendental meditation. One has to restrict sense gratification, especially sex. One has to select a very solitary place, a sacred place, and sit down alone. This meditation process is not practiced in a place like this, a big city, where many people are gathered. One must go to a solitary place and practice alone. And then you have to carefully select your sitting place, you have to sit in a certain way . . . There are so many things. Of course, those things cannot be explained within a few minutes. If you are very much interested, you'll find a full description in *Bhagavad-gītā*, in the chapter called *"Dhyāna-yoga."*

So from the bodily concept of life one has to transcend, to the spiritual platform. That is the goal of any genuine process of self-realization. I began by saying that at first we are all thinking we are the body. *Indriyāṇi parāṇy āhuḥ*. Then, one who has transcended the bodily concept of life comes to the platform of mind. *Indriyebhyaḥ paraṁ manaḥ.* The word *manaḥ* means "mind." Practically the whole population of the world is under the bodily concept of life, but above them are some people who are under the mental concept of life. They are thinking they are the mind. And a few people are on the intellectual platform: *manasas tu parā buddhiḥ. Buddhiḥ* means "intelligence." And when you transcend the intellectual platform also, then you come to the spiritual platform. That is the first realization required.

Before you practice transcendental meditation, you have to reach the transcendental platform. That transcendental platform is called *brahma-bhūtaḥ.* Perhaps you have heard this word – Brahman. The transcendentalist thinks, "*Ahaṁ brahmāsmi:* I am not the body; I am not the mind; I am not the intelligence; I am spirit soul." This is the transcendental platform.

We are talking of transcendental meditation. So, by transcending the bodily concept of life, transcending the mental concept of life, and transcending the intellectual concept of life, you come to the real, spiritual platform, which is called the *brahma-bhūtaḥ* stage. You cannot simply say some words – "Now I have realized Brahman." There are symptoms. Everything has symptoms, and how you can know if someone has realized transcendence, Brahman, is explained in *Bhagavad-gītā* [18.54]: *brahma-bhūtaḥ prasannātmā.* When one is on the transcendental platform, the *brahma-bhūtaḥ* stage, his symptom is that he's always joyful. There is no moroseness.

And what does *joyful* mean? That is also explained: *na śocati na kāṅkṣati.* Someone on the transcendental platform does not hanker after anything, nor does he lament. On the material platform we have two symptoms: hankering and lamenting. The things we do not possess we hanker after, and the things we have lost we lament for. These are the symptoms of the bodily concept of life.

The whole material world is hankering after sex. That is the basic principle of hankering. *Puṁsaḥ striyā mithunī-bhāvam etam. Mithunī-bhāvam* means sex. Whether you look at the human society or the animal society or the bird society or the insect society, everywhere you will find that sex is very prominent. That is the materialistic way of life. A boy is hankering after a girl, a girl is hankering after a boy; a man is hankering after a woman, a woman is hankering after a man. This is going on.

And as soon as the man and woman unite, the hard knot in the heart is tied. *Tayor mitho hṛdaya-granthim āhuḥ.* They think, "I am matter, this body. This body belongs to me. This woman or man belongs to me. This country belongs to me. This world belongs to me." That is the hard knot. Instead of transcending the bodily concept of life, they become still more implicated. The situation becomes very difficult. Therefore Kṛṣṇa recommends in *Bhagavad-gītā* that if you are at all interested in practicing *yoga* and meditation, in trying to rise to the transcendental platform, you must cease from sex.

But in the present age that is not possible. So in our method, Kṛṣṇa consciousness, we don't say, "Stop sex." We say, "Don't have illicit sex." Of course, what to speak of transcendental life, giving up illicit sex is a requirement of *civilized* life. In every civilized society there is a system of marriage, and if there is sex outside of marriage, that is called illicit sex. That is never allowed for people in any civilized society, what to speak of those trying for transcendental life. Transcendental life must be purified of all mental and bodily concepts of self.

But in this age of Kali, where everyone is disturbed, always full of anxieties, and where life is very short, people are generally not interested in any transcendental subject matter. They are interested only in the bodily concept of life. When one is always disturbed by so many anxieties, how can he ascend to the platform of transcendental realization? It is very difficult in this age. It was difficult even five thousand years ago, when Arjuna took instruction on meditation from Kṛṣṇa in *Bhagavad-gītā*. Arjuna was a royal prince; he was very much advanced in so many ways. Yet on the Battlefield of Kurukṣetra he said, "My dear Kṛṣṇa, it is not possible for me to practice this transcendental meditation, this *dhyāna-yoga* process. I am a family man; I have come here to fight for my political interest. How can I practice this system, in which I have to go to a solitary place, I have to sit down, I have to cease from sex? It is not possible." Arjuna was so much more qualified than we are, yet he refused to practice this meditation process.

So, reaching the transcendental platform by the *haṭha-yoga* or *dhyāna-yoga* system is not at all possible in this age. And if somebody is trying to practice such so-called meditation, he is not actually practicing transcendental meditation. You cannot perform this transcendental meditation in the city. It is not possible. That is very clearly stated in *Bhagavad-gītā*. But you are living in the city, you are living with your family, you are living with your friends. It is not possible for you to go to the forest and find a secluded place. But Kṛṣṇa says you must do this to practice transcendental meditation.

So here, in this age, if you want to rise to the transcendental platform, then you must follow the recommendations of the Vedic literature: *kalau tad dhari-kīrtanāt*. In this age, simply by chanting the holy name of God one can reach all perfection. We are not introducing this chanting system by our mental concoction, to make things very easy. No, Lord Caitanya Mahāprabhu introduced this process of transcendental meditation five hundred years ago. Also, the Vedic literature recommends it, and it is practical. You have seen that my disciples, these boys and girls, immediately experience a transcendental feeling as soon as they begin chanting Hare Kṛṣṇa. If you practice, you will also see how you are rising to the transcendental platform. So chanting Hare Kṛṣṇa, Hare Kṛṣṇa, Kṛṣṇa Kṛṣṇa, Hare Hare/ Hare Rāma, Hare Rāma, Rāma Rāma, Hare Hare is the easiest process of transcendental meditation.

This transcendental sound vibration will immediately carry you to the transcendental platform, especially if you try to hear so that your mind is absorbed in the sound. This Hare Kṛṣṇa sound vibration is nondifferent from Kṛṣṇa, because Kṛṣṇa is absolute. Since God is absolute, there is no difference between God's name and God Himself. In the material world there is a difference between water and the word *water*, between a flower and the word *flower*. But in the spiritual world, in the absolute world, there is no such difference. Therefore, as soon as you vibrate Hare Kṛṣṇa, Hare Kṛṣṇa, you immediately associate with the Supreme Lord and His energy.

The word *Hare* indicates the energy of the Supreme Lord. Everything is being done by the energy of the Supreme Lord. *Parasya brahmaṇaḥ śaktiḥ*. Just as the planets are a creation of the energy of the sun, so the whole material and spiritual manifestation is a creation of the energy of the Supreme Lord. So when we chant Hare Kṛṣṇa we are praying to the energy of the Supreme Lord and to the Supreme Lord Himself: "Please pick me up. Please pick me up. I am in the bodily concept of life. I am in this material existence. I am suffering. Please pick me up to the spiritual platform, so that I will be happy."

You haven't got to change your situation. If you are a student, remain a student. If you are a businessman, remain a businessman. Woman, man, black, white – anyone can chant Hare Kṛṣṇa. It is a simple process, and there is no charge. We are not saying, "Give me so many dollars, and I shall give you this Hare Kṛṣṇa *mantra*." No, we are distributing it publicly. You simply have to catch it up and try it. You'll very quickly come to the transcendental platform. When you hear the chanting, that is transcendental meditation.

This process is recommended in all the scriptures of the Vedic literature, it was taught by Lord Caitanya and followed by His disciplic succession for the last five hundred years, and people are achieving good results from it today, not only in India but here also. If you try to understand what this Kṛṣṇa consciousness movement is, you'll understand how transcendental meditation is possible. We are not sentimentalists; we have many books: *Bhagavad-gītā As It Is, Śrīmad-Bhāgavatam, Teachings of Lord Caitanya, Īśopaniṣad*. And we have our magazine, *Back to Godhead*. It is not that we are sentimentalists. We are backed up by high philosophical thought. But if you take up this simple process – chanting Hare Kṛṣṇa, Hare Kṛṣṇa, Kṛṣṇa Kṛṣṇa, Hare Hare/ Hare Rāma, Hare Rāma, Rāma Rāma, Hare Hare – you are immediately elevated to the transcendental platform, even without reading so much philosophical literature. This Hare Kṛṣṇa *mantra* is Lord Caitanya Mahāprabhu's gift to the conditioned souls of the present age, in accordance with the Vedic sanction.

So our request is that you give it a try. Simply chant, at home or anywhere. There is no restriction: "You have to chant this Hare Kṛṣṇa *mantra* in such-and-such a place, in such-and-such a condition." No. *Niyamitaḥ smaraṇe na kālaḥ*. There is no restriction of time, circumstances, or atmosphere. Anywhere, at any time, you can meditate by chanting Hare Kṛṣṇa. No other meditation is possible while you are walking on the street, but *this* meditation is possible. You are working with your hands? You can chant Hare Kṛṣṇa. It is so nice.

Kṛṣṇa is the perfect name for God. The Sanskrit word *kṛṣṇa* means "all-attractive." And *rāma* means "the supreme pleasure." So if God is not all-attractive and full of supreme pleasure, then what is the meaning of God? God must be the source of supreme pleasure; otherwise how could you be satisfied with Him? Your heart is hankering after so many pleasures. If God cannot satisfy you with all pleasures, then how can He be God? And He must also be all-attractive. If God is not attractive to every person, how can He be God? But Kṛṣṇa actually *is* all-attractive.

So the Hare Kṛṣṇa *mantra* is not sectarian. Because we are chanting these three names – *Hare, Kṛṣṇa,* and *Rāma* – someone may think, "These are Hindu names. Why should we chant these Hindu names?" There are some sectarian people who may think like that. But Lord Caitanya says, "It doesn't matter. If you have some other bona fide name of God, you can chant that. But chant God's name." That is the instruction of this Kṛṣṇa consciousness movement. So do not think that this movement is trying to convert you from Christian to Hindu. Remain a Christian, a Jew, a Muslim. It doesn't matter. But if you really want to perfect your life, then try to develop your dormant love for God. That is the perfection of life.

Sa vai puṁsāṁ paro dharmo yato bhaktir adhokṣaje. You may profess any religion, but to test whether your religion is perfect or whether you are perfect, you have to see whether you have developed your love for God. Now we are distributing our love among so many things. But when all this love is concentrated simply on God, that is the perfection of love. Our love is there, but because we have forgotten our relationship with God, we are directing our love toward dogs. That is our disease. We have to transfer our love from so many dogs to God. That is the perfection of life.

So we are not teaching any particular type of religion. We are simply teaching that you should learn to love God. And this is possible by chanting the Hare Kṛṣṇa *mantra.*

The Way of Yoga

We generally regard yoga *merely as a form of physical exercise. But in the following lecture, delivered in February 1969 in Los Angeles, Śrīla Prabhupāda reveals the inner meaning and nature of yoga as taught and practiced in India for centuries. He explains how expert* yogīs *can – by practicing austerities – travel to any planet in the universe. But, he concludes, at the time of death the most successful* yogīs *transfer themselves to "the spiritual world and enter into the Kṛṣṇaloka, or the Kṛṣṇa planet, and enjoy with Kṛṣṇa."*

sarva-dvārāṇi saṁyamya
mano hṛdi nirudhya ca
mūrdhny ādhāyātmanaḥ prāṇam
āsthito yoga-dhāraṇām

"The yogic situation is that of detachment from all sensual engagements. Closing all the doors of the senses and fixing the mind on the heart and the life air at the top of the head, one establishes himself in *yoga*." [*Bhagavad-gītā* 8.12]

There are different kinds of transcendentalists, or *yogīs:* the *jñāna-yogī,* the *dhyāna-yogī,* and the *bhakti-yogī.* All of them are eligible to be transferred to the spiritual world, because the *yoga* system is meant for reestablishing our link with the Supreme Lord.

Actually, we are eternally connected with the Supreme Lord, but somehow or other we are now entangled in material contamination. So the process is that we have to go back again. That linking process is called *yoga.*

The actual meaning of the word *yoga* is "plus." Now, at the present moment, we are minus God, minus the Supreme. But when we make ourselves plus, or connected with God, then our human form of life is perfect.

By the time death comes, we must reach that stage of perfection. As long as we are alive, we have to practice how to approach that point of perfection. And at the time of death, when we give up this material body, that perfection must be realized. *Prayāṇa-kāle manasācalena. Prayāṇa-kāle* means "at the time of death." For instance, a student may prepare two years, three years, or four years in his college education, and the final test is his examination. If he passes the examination, then he gets his degree. Similarly, if we prepare for the examination of death and we pass the examination, then we are transferred to the spiritual world. All that we have learned in this life is examined at the time of death.

So here in the *Bhagavad-gītā*, Lord Kṛṣṇa is describing what we should do at the point of death, when we are giving up this present body.

For the *dhyāna-yogīs* the prescription is: *sarva-dvārāṇi saṁyamya mano hṛdi nirudhya ca.* In the technical language of the *yoga* system, this process is called *pratyāhāra. Pratyāhāra* means "just the opposite." For example, suppose my eyes are engaged in seeing worldly beauty. So I would have to refrain from enjoying that external beauty and instead engage in meditation to see the beauty within. That is called *pratyāhāra*. Similarly, I would have to hear *oṁkāra* – the sound representation of the Lord – from within. And in the same way, all the senses must be withdrawn from their external activities and engaged in meditation on God. That is the perfection of *dhyāna-yoga:* to concentrate the mind on Viṣṇu, or God. The mind is very agitating. So it has to be fixed on the heart: *mano hṛdi nirudhya*. Then we have to transfer the life air to the top of the head: *mūrdhny ādhāyātmanaḥ prāṇam āsthito yoga-dhāraṇām*. That is the perfection of *yoga*.

A perfect *dhyāna-yogī* can choose his own destination after death. There are innumerable material planets, and beyond the material planets is the spiritual world. *Yogīs* have information about all the different planets. Where did they get this information? From the Vedic scriptures. For instance, before I came to your country, I got the description of your country from books. Similarly, we can get the descriptions of higher planets and the spiritual world from the *Śrīmad-Bhāgavatam*.

The *yogī* knows everything, and he can transfer himself to any planet he likes. He does not require the help of any spaceship. The scientists have been trying to reach other planets for so many years with their spaceships, and they will go on trying for one hundred or one thousand years. But they'll never be successful. Rest assured. This is not the process to reach another planet. Maybe, by scientific progress, one man or two men can succeed, but that is not the general process. The general process is that if you want to transfer yourself to any better planet, then you have to practice this *dhyāna-yoga* system – or the *jñāna* system. But not the *bhakti* system.

The *bhakti* system is not meant for attaining any material planet. Those who render devotional service to Kṛṣṇa, the Supreme Lord, are not interested in any planet of this material world. Why? Because they know that regardless of what planet you elevate yourself to, the four principles of material existence will still be there. What are those principles? Birth, death, disease, and old age. You will find these on any planet you go to. On some higher planets your duration of life may be very, very much longer than on this earth, but still, death is there. Material life means birth, death, disease, and old age. And spiritual life means relief from these botherations. No more birth, no more death, no more ignorance, and no more misery. So those who are intelligent do not try to elevate themselves to any planet of this material world.

Now the scientists are trying to reach the moon planet, but it is very difficult for them to gain entrance, because they do not have a suitable body. But if we enter into the higher planets by this *yoga* system, then we will get a body suitable for those planets. For every planet there is a suitable body. Otherwise, you cannot enter. For example, although we cannot live in the water with this body, we can live in the water with oxygen tanks – for fifteen or sixteen hours. But the fish, the aquatic animals, have a suitable body – they are living their whole life underwater. And of course, if you take the fish out of the water and put them on the land, they'll die instantly. So you see, even on this planet you have to have a suitable kind of body to live in a particular place. Similarly, if you want to enter into another planet, you have to prepare yourself by getting a particular type of body.

In the higher planets, our year is equal to one day and night, and you live for ten thousand of such years. That is the description in the Vedic literature. So you get a very long duration of life undoubtedly. But then there is death. After ten thousand years, or twenty thousand years, or millions of years – it doesn't matter. It is all counted, and death is there. But you, the spirit soul, are not subject to death – that is the beginning of *Bhagavad-gītā. Na hanyate hanyamāne śarīre:* you are an eternal spirit soul.

Why should you subject yourself to this birth and death? To ask this question is a sign of real intelligence. Those persons who are in Kṛṣṇa consciousness are very intelligent. They aren't interested in promotion to any planet where there is death, regardless of how long you live. They want a spiritual body, just like God's. God's body is *sac-cid-ānanda-vigraha: īśvaraḥ paramaḥ kṛṣṇaḥ sac-cid-ānanda-vigrahaḥ. Sat* means "eternal," *cit* means "full of knowledge," and *ānanda* means "full of pleasure." If we leave this body and transfer ourselves to the spiritual world – to live with Kṛṣṇa Himself – then we get a body similar to His: *sac-cid-ānanda* – eternal, full of knowledge, and full of bliss. Those who are trying to be Kṛṣṇa conscious have a different aim of life than those who are trying to promote themselves to any of the better planets in this material world.

You are a very minute, spiritual particle within this body, and you are being sustained in the *prāṇa-vāyu,* or life airs. The *dhyāna-yoga* system – the *ṣaṭ-cakra* system – aims to get the soul from its position in the heart to the topmost part of the head. And the perfection is when you can place yourself at the top of the head and, by rupturing this topmost part of the head, transfer yourself into the higher planets, as you like. A *dhyāna-yogī* can transfer into any planet – wherever he likes.

So if you like – just like you are inquisitive about the moon planet – become a *yogī* and go there. A *yogī* thinks, "Oh, let me see what the moon planet is like. Then I shall transfer myself to higher planets." It is the same with ordinary travelers. They come to New York, then go to California, then go to Canada. Similarly, you can transfer yourself to so many planets by this *yoga* system. But anywhere you go, the same systems – visa system and customs system – are there. So a Kṛṣṇa conscious person is not interested in these temporary planets. Life there may be of a long duration, but he is not interested.

For the *yogī* there is a process of giving up this body:

oṁ ity ekākṣaraṁ brahma
vyāharan mām anusmaran
yaḥ prayāti tyajan dehaṁ
sa yāti paramāṁ gatim

At the time of death – *"Oṁ . . ."* He can pronounce *oṁ,* the *oṁkāra. Oṁkāra* is the concise form of transcendental sound vibration. *Oṁ ity ekākṣaraṁ brahma vyāharan:* If he can vibrate this sound, *oṁkāra,* and at the same time remember Kṛṣṇa, or Viṣṇu (*mām anusmaran*), he can enter into the spiritual kingdom.

The whole *yoga* system is meant for concentrating the mind on Viṣṇu. But the impersonalists imagine that this *oṁkāra* is the form of Viṣṇu, or the Lord. Those who are personalists do not imagine. They see the actual form of the Supreme Lord. Anyway, whether you concentrate your mind by imagining or you see factually, you have to fix your mind on the Viṣṇu form. Here *mām* means "unto the Supreme Lord, Viṣṇu." *Yaḥ prayāti tyajan deham:* Anyone who quits his body remembering Viṣṇu – *sa yāti paramāṁ gatim* – he enters into the spiritual kingdom.

Those who are actual *yogīs* do not desire to enter any other planet in the material world, because they know that life there is temporary. That is intelligence. Those who are satisfied with temporary happiness, temporary life, and temporary facilities are not intelligent, according to the *Bhagavad-gītā: antavat tu phalaṁ teṣāṁ tad bhavaty alpa-medhasām.* I am permanent. I am eternal. Who wants nonpermanent existence? Nobody wants it.

Suppose you are living in an apartment and the landlord asks you to vacate. You are sorry. But you'll not be sorry if you go to a better apartment. So this is our nature: Wherever we live, because we are permanent, we want a permanent residence. That is our inclination. We don't wish to die. Why? Because we are permanent. We don't want to be diseased. These are all artificial, external things – disease, death, birth, miseries. They are external things.

Just like sometimes you are attacked with fever. You are not meant for suffering from fever, but sometimes it comes upon you. So you have to take precautions to get out of it. Similarly, these four kinds of external afflictions – birth, death, disease, and old age – are due to this material body. If we can get out of this material body, we can get out of these afflictions.

So for the *yogī* who is an impersonalist, the recommended process is vibrating this transcendental sound, *oṁ*, while leaving this body. Anyone who is able to quit this material body while uttering the transcendental sound *oṁ*, with full consciousness of the Supreme Lord, is sure to be transferred to the spiritual world.

But those who are not personalists cannot enter into the spiritual planets. They remain outside. Just like the sunshine and the sun planet. The sunshine is not different from the sun disk. But still, the sunshine is not the sun disk. Similarly, those impersonalists who are transferred to the spiritual world remain in the effulgence of the Supreme Lord, which is called the *brahma-jyotir.* Those who are not personalists are placed into the *brahma-jyotir* as one of the minute particles.

We are minute particles, spiritual sparks, and the *brahma-jyotir* is full of such spiritual sparks. So you become one of the spiritual sparks. That is, you merge into the spiritual existence. You keep your individuality, but because you don't want any personal form, you are held there in the impersonal *brahma-jyotir.* Just as the sunshine is small molecules, shining molecules – those who are scientists know – similarly, we are tiny particles, smaller than an atom. Our magnitude is one ten-thousandth of the tip of a hair. So that small particle remains in the *brahma-jyotir.*

The difficulty is that, as a living entity, I want enjoyment. Because I am not only simply existing. I have got bliss. I am composed of three spiritual qualities: *sac-cid-ānanda.* I am eternal, and I am full of knowledge, and I am full of bliss. Those who enter into the impersonal effulgence of the Supreme Lord can remain eternally with full knowledge that they are now merged with Brahman, or the *brahma-jyotir.* But they cannot have eternal bliss, because that part is wanting.

If you are confined in a room alone, you may read a book or think some thought, but still you cannot remain alone all the time, for all the years of your life. That is not possible. You'll find some association, some recreation. That is our nature. Similarly, if we merge into the impersonal effulgence of the Supreme Lord, then there is a chance of falling down again to this material world. That is stated in the *Śrīmad-Bhāgavatam* [10.2.32]:

ye 'nye 'ravindākṣa vimukta-māninas
tvayy asta-bhāvād aviśuddha-buddhayaḥ
āruhya kṛcchreṇa paraṁ padaṁ tataḥ
patanty adho 'nādṛta-yuṣmad-aṅghrayaḥ

It's just like the astronauts who go higher and still higher – twenty-five thousand or thirty thousand or a hundred thousand miles up. But they have to come to rest on some planet. So coming to rest is required. In the impersonal form the resting place is uncertain. Therefore the *Bhāgavatam* says, *āruhya kṛcchreṇa paraṁ padaṁ tataḥ.* Even after so much endeavor, if the impersonalist gets into the spiritual world and remains in that impersonal form, the risk is *patanty adhaḥ,* that he will come down into material existence again. Why? *Anādṛta-yuṣmad-aṅghrayaḥ:* because he has neglected to serve the Supreme Lord with love and devotion.

So, as long as we are here we have to practice loving Kṛṣṇa, the Supreme Lord. Then we can enter the spiritual planets. This is the training. If you are not trained in that way, then by impersonal endeavor you can enter into the spiritual kingdom, but there is the risk of falling down again – because that loneliness will create some disturbance, and you'll try to have association. And because you have no association with the Supreme Lord, you'll have to come back and associate with this material world.

So better that we know the nature of our constitutional position. Our constitutional position is that we want eternity, we want complete knowledge, and we want pleasure also. If we are kept alone, we cannot have pleasure. We'll feel uncomfortable, and for want of pleasure we'll accept any kind of material pleasure. That is the risk. But in Kṛṣṇa consciousness, we'll have full pleasure. The highest pleasure of this material world is sex life, and that is also perverted – so diseased. So even in the spiritual world there is sex pleasure in Kṛṣṇa. But we should not think that this is something like sex life in the material world. No. But, *janmādy asya yataḥ:* unless that sex life is there, it cannot be reflected here. It is simply a perverted reflection. The actual life is there, in Kṛṣṇa. Kṛṣṇa is full of pleasure.

So the best thing is to train ourselves in Kṛṣṇa consciousness. Then at the time of death it will be possible to transfer ourselves to the spiritual world and enter into Kṛṣṇaloka, Kṛṣṇa's own planet, and enjoy with Him.

cintāmaṇi-prakara-sadmasu kalpa-vṛkṣa-
lakṣāvṛteṣu surabhīr abhipālayantam
lakṣmī-sahasra-śata-sambhrama-sevyamānaṁ
govindam ādi-puruṣam tam ahaṁ bhajāmi

These are the descriptions of Kṛṣṇaloka. *Cintāmaṇi-prakara-sadmasu:* the houses are made of touchstone. Perhaps you know touchstone. If a small particle of it is touched to an iron beam, the iron will at once become gold. Of course, none of you have seen this touchstone, but there is such a thing. So all the buildings there are touchstone. *Cintāmaṇi-prakara-sadmasu. Kalpa-vṛkṣa:* The trees are desire trees. Whatever you like, you can get. Here, from mango trees you get only mangoes, and from apple trees you get apples. But there, from any tree, anything you like you can have. These are some of the descriptions of Kṛṣṇaloka.

So the best thing is not to try elevating ourselves to another material planet, because on any material planet you enter, you find the same principles of miserable life. We are accustomed to them. We have been acclimated to birth and death. We don't care. The modern scientists are very proud of their advancement, but they have no solution to any of these unpleasant things. They cannot make anything that will check death or disease or old age. That is not possible. You can manufacture something that will *accelerate* death, but you cannot manufacture anything that will *stop* death. That is not in your power.

So, those who are very intelligent are concerned about finding a permanent solution to these four problems – *janma-mṛtyu-jarā-vyādhi:* birth, death, old age, and disease. They are concerned about attaining their spiritual life, full of bliss and full of knowledge. And that is possible when you enter into the spiritual planets. As Kṛṣṇa states in *Bhagavad-gītā* [8.14]:

ananya-cetāḥ satataṁ
yo māṁ smarati nityaśaḥ

tasyāhaṁ sulabhaḥ pārtha
nitya-yuktasya yoginaḥ

Nitya-yuktaḥ means "continuously in trance." This is the highest *yogī:* one who is continuously thinking of Kṛṣṇa, who is always engaged in Kṛṣṇa consciousness. Such a perfect *yogī* does not divert his attention to this sort of process or that sort of *yoga* system or the *jñāna* or *dhyāna* systems. Simply one system: Kṛṣṇa consciousness. *Ananya-cetāḥ:* without any deviation. He's not disturbed by anything. He simply thinks of Kṛṣṇa. *Ananya-cetāḥ satatam. Satatam* means "everywhere and at all times."

For example, my residence is at Vṛndāvana. That is the place of Kṛṣṇa, where Kṛṣṇa advented Himself. So now I am in America, in your country. But that does not mean I'm out of Vṛndāvana, because if I think of Kṛṣṇa always, it is as good as being in Vṛndāvana. I am in New York, in this apartment, but my consciousness is there in Vṛndāvana. Kṛṣṇa consciousness means you already live with Kṛṣṇa in His spiritual planet. You simply have to wait to give up this body.

So this is the process of Kṛṣṇa consciousness: *ananya-cetāḥ satataṁ yo māṁ smarati nityaśaḥ. Smarati* means "remembering"; *nityaśaḥ,* "continuously." Kṛṣṇa declares that He becomes easily available to someone who is always remembering Him. The highest, most valuable thing becomes very inexpensive for one who takes up this process of Kṛṣṇa consciousness. *Tasyāhaṁ sulabhaḥ pārtha nitya-yuktasya yoginaḥ:* "Because he's continuously engaged in such a process of *yoga, bhakti-yoga* – oh, I am very cheap. I am easily available."

Why should you try for any hard process? Simply chant Hare Kṛṣṇa, Hare Kṛṣṇa, Kṛṣṇa Kṛṣṇa, Hare Hare/ Hare Rāma, Hare Rāma, Rāma Rāma, Hare Hare. And you can chant twenty-four hours a day. There are no rules or regulations. Either in the street or in the subway, at your home or in your office – there is no tax, no expense. Why don't you do it?

Thank you very much.

Making Friends with the Mind

Is the mind the ultimate reservoir of human resources? Or is there a greater source of knowledge beyond our minds? In the following lecture, recorded in February 1969 in Los Angeles, Śrīla Prabhupāda explains why the mind must be brought under the control of spiritual energy. His theme is based on the following famous verse from India's most widely read and respected scripture, the Bhagavad-gītā:

bandhur ātmātmanas tasya
yenātmaivātmanā jitaḥ
anātmanas tu śatrutve
vartetātmaiva śatru-vat

"For one who has conquered the mind, the mind is the best of friends, but for one who has failed to do so, the mind will remain the greatest enemy." [*Bhagavad-gītā* 6.6]

The whole purpose of the *yoga* system is to make the mind our friend. The mind in material contact is our enemy, just like the mind of a person in a drunken condition. In *Caitanya-caritāmṛta* [*Madhya* 20.117] it is said, *kṛṣṇa bhuli' se jīva anādi-bahirmukha ataeva māyā tāre deya saṁsāra-duḥkha:* "Forgetting Kṛṣṇa, the living entity has been attracted by the Lord's external feature from time immemorial. Therefore, the illusory energy [*māyā*] gives him all kinds of misery in his material existence." I am a spiritual soul, part and parcel of the Supreme Lord, but as soon as my mind is contaminated I rebel, because I have a little independence. "Why shall I serve Kṛṣṇa, or God? *I* am God." When this idea is dictated from the mind, my whole situation turns. I come under a false impression, an illusion, and my whole life is spoiled. So, we are trying to conquer so many things – empires and so on – but if we fail to conquer our minds, then even if we conquer an empire we are failures. Our very mind will be our greatest enemy.

The purpose of practicing eightfold *yoga* is to control the mind in order to make it a friend in discharging the human mission. Unless the mind is controlled, the practice of *yoga* is simply a waste of time; it is simply for show. One who cannot control his mind lives always with the greatest enemy, and thus his life and its mission are spoiled. The constitutional position of the living entity is to carry out the order of the superior. As long as one's mind remains an unconquered enemy, one has to serve the dictations of lust, anger, avarice, illusion, and so on. But when the mind is conquered, one voluntarily agrees to abide by the dictation of the Personality of Godhead, who is situated within the heart of everyone as the Supersoul (Paramātmā). Real *yoga* practice entails meeting the Paramātmā within the heart and then following His dictation. For one who takes to Kṛṣṇa consciousness directly, perfect surrender to the dictation of the Lord follows automatically.

jitātmanaḥ praśāntasya
paramātmā samāhitaḥ
śītoṣṇa-sukha-duḥkheṣu
tathā mānāpamānayoḥ

"For one who has conquered the mind, the Supersoul is already reached, for he has attained tranquillity. To such a man happiness and distress, heat and cold, honor and dishonor are all the same." [*Bhagavad-gītā* 6.7]

Actually, every living entity is intended to abide by the dictation of the Supreme Personality of Godhead, who is seated in everyone's heart as Paramātmā. When the mind is misled by the external energy, one becomes entangled in material activities. Therefore, as soon as one's mind is controlled through one of the *yoga* systems, one is to be considered as having already reached the destination. One has to abide by superior dictation. When one's mind is fixed on the superior nature, one has no alternative but to follow the dictation of the Supreme from within. The mind must admit some superior dictation and follow it. The effect of controlling the mind is that one automatically follows the dictation of the Paramātmā, or Supersoul. Because this transcendental position is at once achieved by one who is in Kṛṣṇa consciousness, the devotee of the Lord is unaffected by the dualities of material existence – distress and happiness, cold and heat, and so on. This state is practical *samādhi*, or absorption in the Supreme.

jñāna-vijñāna-tṛptātmā
kūṭa-stho vijitendriyaḥ
yukta ity ucyate yogī
sama-loṣṭrāśma-kāñcanaḥ

"A person is said to be established in self-realization and is called a *yogī*, or mystic, when he is fully satisfied by virtue of acquired knowledge and realization. Such a person is situated in transcendence and is self-controlled. He sees everything – whether it be pebbles, stones, or gold – as the same." [*Bhagavad-gītā* 6.8]

Book knowledge without realization of the Supreme Truth is useless. In the *Padma Purāṇa* this is stated as follows:

ataḥ śrī-kṛṣṇa-nāmādi
na bhaved grāhyam indriyaiḥ
sevonmukhe hi jihvādau
svayam eva sphuraty adaḥ

"No one can understand the transcendental nature of the name, form, qualities, and pastimes of Śrī Kṛṣṇa through his materially contaminated senses. Only when one becomes spiritually saturated by transcendental service to the Lord are the transcendental name, form, quality, and pastimes of the Lord revealed to him."

This is very important. Now, we accept Kṛṣṇa as the Supreme Lord. And why do we accept that Kṛṣṇa is the Supreme Lord? Because it is stated in the Vedic literature. The *Brahma-saṁhitā*, for example, says, *īśvaraḥ paramaḥ kṛṣṇaḥ sac-cid-ānanda-vigrahaḥ:* "The supreme controller is Kṛṣṇa, who has an eternal, blissful, spiritual body." Those who are in the modes of passion and ignorance simply imagine the form of God. And when they are confused, they say, "Oh, there is no personal God. The Absolute is impersonal or void." This is frustration.

Actually, God has a form. Why not? The *Vedānta-sūtra* says, *janmādy asya yataḥ:* "The Supreme Absolute Truth is that from whom or from which everything emanates." Now, *we* have forms. And not only we but all the different kinds of living entities have forms. Wherefrom have they come? Wherefrom have these forms originated? These are very commonsense questions. If God is not a person, then how have His sons become persons? If my father is not a person, how have I become a person? If my father has no form, wherefrom did I get my form? Nonetheless, when people are frustrated, when they see that their bodily forms are troublesome, they develop an opposite conception of form, and they imagine that God must be formless. But the *Brahma-saṁhitā* says no. God has a form, but His form is eternal, full of knowledge and bliss (*īśvaraḥ paramaḥ kṛṣṇaḥ sac-cid-ānanda-vigrahaḥ*). *Sat* means "eternity," *cit* means "knowledge," and *ānanda* means "pleasure." So God has a form, but His form is full of pleasure, full of knowledge, and eternal.

Now, let's compare our body to God's. Our body is neither eternal nor full of pleasure nor full of knowledge. So our form is clearly different from God's. But as soon as we think of form, we think the form must be like ours. Therefore we think that since God must be the opposite of us, He must have no form. This is speculation, however, not knowledge. As it is said in the *Padma Purāṇa, ataḥ śrī-kṛṣṇa-nāmādi na bhaved grāhyam indriyaiḥ:* "One cannot understand the form, name, quality, or paraphernalia of God with one's material senses." Our senses are imperfect, so how can we see the Supreme Person? It is not possible.

Then how is it possible to see Him? *Sevonmukhe hi jihvādau:* If we train our senses, if we purify our senses, those purified senses will help us see God. It is just as if we had cataracts on our eyes. Because our eyes are suffering from cataracts, we cannot see. But this does not mean that there is nothing to be seen – only that *we* cannot see. Similarly, now we cannot conceive of the form of God, but if our cataracts are removed, we can see Him. The *Brahma-saṁhitā* says, *premāñjana-cchurita-bhakti-vilocanena santaḥ sadaiva hṛdayeṣu vilokayanti:* "The devotees whose eyes are anointed with the love-of-God ointment see God, Kṛṣṇa, within their hearts twenty-four hours a day." So, we require to purify our senses. Then we'll be able to understand what the form of God is, what the name of God is, what the qualities of God are, what the abode of God is, and what the paraphernalia of God are, and we'll be able to see God in everything.

The Vedic literature is full of references to God's form. For example, it is said that God has no hands or legs but that He can accept anything you offer: *apāṇi-pādo javano grahītā*. Also, it is said that God has no eyes or ears but that He can see everything and hear everything. So, these are apparent contradictions, because whenever we think of someone seeing, we think he must have eyes like ours. This is our material conception. Factually, however, God does have eyes, but His eyes are different from ours. He can see even in the darkness, but we cannot. God can hear, also. God is in His kingdom, which is millions and millions of miles away, but if we are whispering something – conspiracy – He can hear it, because He is sitting within us.

So, we cannot avoid God's seeing or God's hearing or God's touching. In the *Bhagavad-gītā* [9.26] Lord Kṛṣṇa says,

patraṁ puṣpaṁ phalaṁ toyaṁ
yo me bhaktyā prayacchati
tad ahaṁ bhakty-upahṛtam
aśnāmi prayatātmanaḥ

"If somebody offers Me flowers, fruits, vegetables, or milk with devotional love, I accept and eat it." Now, how is He eating? We cannot see Him eat, but He is eating. We experience this daily: When we offer Kṛṣṇa food according to the ritualistic process, we see that the taste of the food changes immediately. This is practical. So God eats, but because He is full in Himself, He does not eat like us. If someone offers me a plate of food, I may finish it, but God is not hungry, so when He eats He leaves the things as they are. *Pūrṇasya pūrṇam ādāya pūrṇam evāvaśiṣyate:* God is so full that He can eat all the food that we offer and still it remains as it is. He can eat with His eyes. This is stated in the *Brahma-saṁhitā: aṅgāni yasya sakalendriya-vṛttimanti.* "Every limb of the body of God has all the potencies of the other limbs." For example, we can see with our eyes, but we cannot *eat* with our eyes. But if God simply sees the food we have offered, that is His eating.

Of course, these things cannot be understood by us at the present moment. Therefore, the *Padma Purāṇa* says that only when one becomes spiritually saturated by transcendental service to the Lord are the transcendental name, form, qualities, and pastimes of the Lord revealed to him. We cannot understand God by our own endeavor, but God can reveal Himself to us. Trying to see God by our own efforts is just like trying to see the sun when it is dark outside. If we say, "Oh, I have a very strong flashlight, and I shall search out the sun," we will not be able to see it. But in the morning, when the sun rises out of its own will, we can see it. Similarly, we cannot see God by our own endeavor, because our senses are all imperfect. We have to purify our senses and wait for the time when God will be pleased to reveal Himself before us. This is the process of Kṛṣṇa consciousness. We cannot challenge, "Oh, my dear God, my dear Kṛṣṇa, You must come before me. I shall see You." No, God is not our order-supplier, our servant. When He is pleased with us, we'll see Him.

So, our *yoga* process tries to please God so that He will reveal Himself to us. That is the real *yoga* process. Without this process, people are accepting so many nonsensical "Gods." Because people cannot see God, anybody who says "I am God" is accepted. No one knows who God is. Somebody may say, "I am searching after truth," but he must know what truth is. Otherwise, how will he search out truth? Suppose I want to purchase gold. I must know what gold is, or at least have some experience of it. Otherwise, people will cheat me. So, people are being cheated – accepting so many rascals as God – because they do not know what God is. Anyone can come and say, "I am God," and some rascal will accept him as God. The man who says "I am God" is a rascal, and the man who accepts him as God is also a rascal. God cannot be known like this. One has to qualify himself to see God, to understand God. That is Kṛṣṇa consciousness. *Sevonmukhe hi jihvādau svayam eva sphuraty adaḥ:* If we engage ourselves in the service of the Lord, then we'll become qualified to see God. Otherwise, it is not possible.

Now, this *Bhagavad-gītā* is the science of Kṛṣṇa consciousness. No one can become Kṛṣṇa conscious simply by mundane scholarship. Simply because one has some titles – M.A., B.A., Ph.D. – that does not mean he'll understand the *Bhagavad-gītā*. This is a transcendental science, and one requires different senses to understand it. So one has to purify his senses by rendering service to the Lord. Otherwise, even if one is a great scholar – a doctor or a Ph.D. – he will make mistakes in trying to find out what Kṛṣṇa is. He will not understand – it is not possible. This is why Kṛṣṇa appears in the material world as He is. Although He is unborn (*ajo 'pi sann avyayātmā*), He comes to make us know who God is. But since He is not personally present now, to know Him one must be fortunate enough to associate with a person who is in pure Kṛṣṇa consciousness. A Kṛṣṇa conscious person has realized knowledge, by the grace of Kṛṣṇa, because He is satisfied with pure devotional service. So we have to acquire the grace of Kṛṣṇa. Then we can understand Kṛṣṇa, then we can see Kṛṣṇa, then we can talk with Kṛṣṇa – then we can do everything.

Kṛṣṇa is a *person*. He is the supreme *person*. That is the Vedic injunction: *nityo nityānāṁ cetanaś cetanānām* – "We are all eternal persons, and God is the supreme eternal person." Now we are meeting birth and death because we are encaged within this body. But actually, being eternal spirit souls, we have no birth and death at all. According to our work, according to our desire, we are transmigrating from one kind of body to another, another, and another. Yet actually, we have no birth and death. As explained in the *Bhagavad-gītā* [2.20], *na jāyate mriyate vā:* "The living entity never takes birth, nor does he ever die." Similarly, God is also eternal. *Nityo nityānāṁ cetanaś cetanānām:* "God is the supreme living entity among all living entities, and He is the supreme eternal person among eternal persons." So, by practicing Kṛṣṇa consciousness, by purifying our senses, we can reestablish our eternal relationship with the supreme eternal person, the complete eternal person. Then we will see God.

Through realized knowledge one becomes perfect. Through transcendental knowledge one can remain steady in his convictions, but with mere academic knowledge one can be easily deluded and confused by apparent contradictions. It is the realized soul who is actually self-controlled, because he is surrendered to Kṛṣṇa. And he is transcendental, because he has nothing to do with mundane scholarship. For him, mundane scholarship and mental speculation (which may be as good as gold to others) are of no greater value than pebbles or stones.

Even if one is illiterate, even if he does not know the ABC's, he can realize God – provided he engages himself in submissive transcendental loving service to God. On the other hand, although one is a very learned scholar, he may not be able to realize God. God is not subject to any material condition, because He is the supreme spirit. Similarly, the process of realizing God is also not subject to any material condition. It is not true that because one is a poor man he cannot realize God, or that because one is a very rich man he shall realize God. No. God is beyond our material conditions (*apratihatā*). In the *Śrīmad-Bhāgavatam* [1.2.6] it is said, *sa vai puṁsāṁ paro dharmo yato bhaktir adhokṣaje:* "That religion is first class which helps one advance his devotional service and love of God."

The *Bhāgavatam* does not mention that the Hindu religion is first class or the Christian religion is first class or the Mohammedan religion is first class or some other religion is first class. The *Bhāgavatam* says that that religion is first class which helps one advance his devotional service and love of God. That's all. This is the definition of a first-class religion. We do not analyze that one religion is first class or that another religion is last class. Of course, there are three qualities in the material world (goodness, passion, and ignorance), and religious conceptions are created according to these qualities. But the *purpose* of religion is to understand God and to learn how to love God. *Any* religious system, if it teaches one how to love God, is first class. Otherwise, it is useless. One may prosecute his religious principles very rigidly and very nicely, but if his love of God is nil, if his love of matter is simply enhanced, then his religion is no religion.

In the same verse, the *Bhāgavatam* says that real religion must be *ahaitukī* and *apratihatā:* without selfish motivation and without any impediment. If we can practice such a system of religious principles, then we'll find that we are happy in all respects. Otherwise there is no possibility of happiness. *Sa vai puṁsāṁ paro dharmo yato bhaktir adhokṣaje.* One of God's names is Adhokṣaja. *Adhokṣaja* means "one who conquers all materialistic attempts to be seen." *Akṣaja* means "direct perception by experimental knowledge," and *adhaḥ* means "unreachable." We cannot understand God by experimental knowledge. No. We have to learn of Him in a different way – by submissive aural reception of transcendental sound and by the rendering of transcendental loving service. Then we can understand God.

So, a religious principle is perfect if it teaches us how to develop our love for the Godhead. But our love must be without selfish motive. If I say, "I love God because He supplies me very nice things for my sense gratification," that is not love. Real love is without any selfish motive (*ahaitukī*). We must simply think, "God is great; God is my father. It is my duty to love Him." That's all. *No exchange* – "Oh, God gives me my daily bread; therefore I love God." No. God gives daily bread even to the animals – the cats and dogs. God is the father of everyone, and He supplies food to everyone. So, appreciating God because He gives me bread – that is not love. Love without motive. I must think, "Even if God does not supply me daily bread, I'll love Him." This is real love. As Caitanya Mahāprabhu says, *āśliṣya vā pāda-ratāṁ pinaṣṭu mām adarśanān marma-hatāṁ karotu vā:* "O Lord, You may embrace me, or You may trample me down with Your feet. Or You may never come before me, so that I become brokenhearted without seeing You. Still, I love You." This is pure love of God. When we come to this stage of loving God, then we'll find ourselves full of pleasure. Just as God is full of pleasure, we'll also be full of pleasure. This is perfection.

The Ultimate Yoga

In this 1969 discourse, Śrīla Prabhupāda focuses on the perfected stage of yoga *practice. According to ancient Vedic teachings, the* yoga *system – beginning with* haṭha-yoga, prāṇāyāma *(physical exercises and breath control), and* karma-yoga *– culminates in* bhakti-yoga, *the* yoga *of devotion to the Personality of Godhead. "If one is fortunate enough to come to the point of* bhakti-yoga, *it is to be understood that one has surpassed all other* yogas," *says Śrīla Prabhupāda. "And the test of one's mastery of* bhakti-yoga *is based on how much one is developing one's love for God."*

yoginām api sarveṣāṁ
mad-gatenāntar-ātmanā
śraddhāvān bhajate yo māṁ
sa me yuktatamo mataḥ

"And of all *yogīs,* the one with great faith who always abides in Me, thinks of Me within himself, and renders transcendental loving service to Me – he is the most intimately united with Me in *yoga* and is the highest of all. That is My opinion." [*Bhagavad-gītā* 6.47]

Here it is clearly stated that out of all the different kinds of *yogīs* – the *aṣṭāṅga-yogī,* the *haṭha-yogī,* the *jñāna-yogī,* the *karma-yogī,* and the *bhakti-yogī* – the *bhakti-yogī* is on the highest platform of *yoga.* Kṛṣṇa directly says, "Of all *yogīs,* the one with great faith who always abides in Me . . . is the most intimately united with Me in *yoga* and is the highest of all." Since Kṛṣṇa is speaking, the words *in Me* mean "in Kṛṣṇa." In other words, if one wants to become a perfect *yogī* on the highest platform, one should keep oneself in Kṛṣṇa consciousness.

In this regard, the word *bhajate* in this verse is significant. *Bhajate* has its root in the verb *bhaj,* which is used to indicate devotional service. The English word *worship* cannot be used in the same sense as *bhaja. To worship* means "to adore" or "to show respect and honor to a worthy one." But service with love and faith is especially meant for the Supreme Personality of Godhead. One can avoid worshiping a respectable man or a demigod and be called merely discourteous, but one cannot avoid serving the Supreme Lord without being thoroughly condemned.

So, worship is very different from devotional service. Worship involves some selfish motive. We may worship some very big businessman because we know that if we please him, he may give us some business and we'll derive some profit. The worship of the demigods is like that. People often worship one of the demigods for some particular purpose, but this is condemned in *Bhagavad-gītā* [7.20]: *kāmais tais tair hṛta-jñānāḥ prapadyante 'nya-devatāḥ* – "Those who have lost their sense and are bewildered by lust worship demigods with a selfish motive."

Thus when we speak of worship, there is a selfish motive, but when we speak of devotional service, there is no motive except the desire to please the beloved. Devotional service is based on love. For example, when a mother renders service to her child, there is no personal motive: she serves only out of love. Everyone else may neglect the child, but the mother cannot, because she loves him. Similarly, when there is a question of service to God, there should be no question of a personal motive. That is perfect Kṛṣṇa consciousness, and that is recommended in *Śrīmad-Bhāgavatam* [1.2.6] in the description of the first-class system of religious principles: *sa vai puṁsāṁ paro dharmo yato bhaktir adhokṣaje* – "The first-class system of religious principles is that which enables one to develop one's God consciousness, or love of God." If one can develop one's love for God, one may follow any religious principle – it doesn't matter. But the test is how much one is developing one's love for God.

But if one has some personal motive and thinks, "By practicing this system of religion, my material necessities will be fulfilled," that is not first-class religion. That is third-class religion. First-class religion is that by which one can develop one's love of God, and that love must be without any personal motive and without any impediment (*ahaituky apratihatā*). That is first-class religion, as recommended here by Kṛṣṇa in this final verse of the sixth chapter of *Bhagavad-gītā.*

Kṛṣṇa consciousness is the perfection of *yoga,* but even if one looks at it from a religious viewpoint it is first class – because it is performed with no personal motive. My disciples are not serving Kṛṣṇa so that He will supply them with this or that. There may be this or that, but that doesn't matter. Of course, there is no scarcity; devotees get everything they need. We shouldn't think that by becoming Kṛṣṇa conscious one becomes poor. No. If Kṛṣṇa is there, everything is there, because Kṛṣṇa *is* everything. But we shouldn't make any business with Kṛṣṇa: "Kṛṣṇa, give me this, give me that." Kṛṣṇa knows what we require better than we do, just as a father knows the necessities of his child. Why should we ask? Since God is all-powerful, He knows our wants and He knows our necessities. This is confirmed in the *Vedas: eko bahūnāṁ yo vidadhāti kāmān* – "God is supplying all the necessities of the innumerable living entities."

We should simply try to love God, without demanding anything. Our needs will be supplied. Even the cats and dogs are getting their necessities. They don't go to church and ask God for anything, but they are getting their necessities. So why should a devotee not get his necessities? If the cats and dogs can get their necessities of life without demanding anything from God, why should we demand from God, "Give me this, give me that"? No. We should simply try to love Him and serve Him. That will fulfill everything, and that is the highest platform of *yoga.*

Service to God is natural; since I am part and parcel of God, my natural duty is to serve Him. The example of the finger and the body is appropriate. The finger is part and parcel of the body. And what is the duty of the finger? To serve the whole body, that's all. If you are feeling some itch, immediately your finger is working. If you want to see, your eyes immediately work. If you want to go somewhere, your legs immediately take you there. So, the bodily parts and limbs are helping the whole body.

Similarly, we are all part and parcel of God, and we are all meant simply for rendering service to Him. When the limbs of the body serve the whole body, the energy automatically comes to the limbs. Similarly, when we serve Kṛṣṇa, we get all our necessities automatically. *Yathā taror mūla-niṣecanena.* If one pours water on the root of a tree, the energy is immediately supplied to the leaves, the twigs, the branches, and so on.

Similarly, simply by serving Kṛṣṇa, or God, we serve all other parts of creation. There is no question of serving each living entity separately.

Another point is that by serving God, we will automatically have sympathy for all living beings – not only for human beings, but even for animals. Therefore God consciousness, Kṛṣṇa consciousness, is the perfection of religion. Without Kṛṣṇa consciousness our sympathy for other living entities is very limited, but with Kṛṣṇa consciousness our sympathy for other living entities is full.

Every living entity is part and parcel of the Supreme Lord, and thus every living entity is intended to serve the Supreme Lord by his own constitution. Failing to do this, he falls down. *Śrīmad-Bhāgavatam* [11.5.3] confirms this as follows:

ya eṣāṁ puruṣaṁ sākṣād
ātma-prabhavam īśvaram
na bhajanty avajānanti
sthānād bhraṣṭāḥ patanty adhaḥ

"Anyone who does not render service and neglects his duty unto the primeval Lord, who is the source of all living entities, will certainly fall down from his constitutional position."

How do we fall down from our constitutional position? Once again, the example of the finger and the body is appropriate. If one's finger becomes diseased and cannot render service to the whole body, it simply gives one pain. Similarly, any person who is not rendering service to the Supreme Lord is simply disturbing Him, giving Him pain and trouble. Therefore, such a person has to suffer, just like a man who is not abiding by the laws of the state. Such a criminal simply gives pain to the government, and he's liable to be punished. He may think, "I'm a very good man," but because he's violating the laws of the state, he's simply torturing the government. This is easy to understand.

So, any living entity who is not serving Kṛṣṇa is causing Him a kind of pain. And that is sinful – to make Kṛṣṇa feel pain. Just as the government collects all the painful citizens and keeps them in the prison house – "You criminals must live here so you can't disturb people in the open state" – so God puts all the criminals who have violated His laws, who have simply given Him pain, into this material world. *Sthānād bhraṣṭāḥ patanty adhaḥ:* They fall down from their constitutional position in the spiritual world. Again we may cite the example of the finger. If your finger is extremely painful, the doctor may advise, "Mr. So-and-so, your finger has to be amputated. Otherwise, it will pollute your whole body." *Sthānād bhraṣṭāḥ patanty adhaḥ:* The finger then falls down from its constitutional position as part of the body.

Having rebelled against the principles of God consciousness, we have all fallen down to this material world. If we want to revive our original position, we must again establish ourselves in the service attitude. That is the perfect cure. Otherwise, we shall suffer pain, and God will be suffering pain on account of us. We are just like bad sons of God. If a son is not good, he suffers, and the father suffers along with the son. Similarly, when we are suffering, God is also suffering. Therefore, the best thing is to revive our original Kṛṣṇa consciousness and engage in the service of the Lord.

The word *avajānanti* used in the verse cited from *Śrīmad-Bhāgavatam* is also used by Kṛṣṇa in *Bhagavad-gītā* [9.11]:

avajānanti māṁ mūḍhā
mānuṣīṁ tanum āśritam
paraṁ bhāvam ajānanto
mama bhūta-maheśvaram

"Fools deride Me when I descend in the human form. They do not know My transcendental nature and My supreme dominion over all that be." Only the fools and rascals deride the Supreme Personality of Godhead, Lord Kṛṣṇa. The word *mūḍha* means "fool" or "rascal." Only a rascal does not care for Kṛṣṇa. Not knowing that he will suffer for this attitude, he dares neglect Him. Without knowing the supreme position of the Lord, the rascals worship some cheap "God." God has become so cheap that many people say, "I am God, you are God." But what is the meaning of the word *God*? If everyone is God, then what is the meaning of God?

So, the word *avajānanti* is very appropriate. *Avajānanti* means "neglectful," and it perfectly describes the person who says, "What is God? I am God. Why should I serve God?" This is *avajānanti* – neglecting

God's real position. A criminal may have the same attitude toward the government: "Oh, what is the government? I can do whatever I like. I don't care for the government." This is *avajānanti*. But even if we say, "I don't care for the government," the police department is there. It will give us pain; it will punish us. Similarly, even if we don't care for God, the material nature will punish us with birth, old age, disease, and death. To get out of this suffering, we must practice *yoga*.

The culmination of all kinds of *yoga* practice lies in *bhakti-yoga*. All other *yogas* are but means to come to the point of *bhakti-yoga*. *Yoga* actually *means bhakti-yoga;* all other *yogas* are progressions toward this destination. From the beginning of *karma-yoga* to the end of *bhakti-yoga* is a long way to self-realization. *Karma-yoga,* executed without fruitive desires, is the beginning of this path. (Fruitive activities, or *karma,* include sinful activities also. *Karma-yoga,* however, does not include sinful activities but only good, pious activities, or prescribed activities. This is *karma-yoga*.) Then, when *karma-yoga* increases in knowledge and renunciation, the stage is called *jñāna-yoga*. When *jñāna-yoga* increases in meditation on the Supersoul by various physical processes, and when the mind is on Him, one has reached the stage called *aṣṭāṅga-yoga*. And when one surpasses *aṣṭāṅga-yoga* and comes to the point of serving the Supreme Personality of Godhead, Kṛṣṇa, one has reached *bhakti-yoga,* the culmination.

Factually, *bhakti-yoga* is the ultimate goal, but to analyze *bhakti-yoga* minutely one has to understand these other, minor *yogas*. The *yogī* who is progressive is therefore on the true path of eternal auspiciousness, whereas one who sticks to a particular point and does not make further progress is called by that particular name: *karma-yogī, jñāna-yogī,* or *aṣṭāṅga-yogī*. But if one is fortunate enough to come to the point of *bhakti-yoga,* it is to be understood that one has surpassed all the other *yogas*. Therefore, to become Kṛṣṇa conscious is the highest stage of *yoga,* just as, when we speak of the Himālayas, we refer to the world's highest mountains, of which the highest peak, Mount Everest, is considered the culmination.

If someone practicing *jñāna-yoga* thinks that he is finished, that is wrong. He has to make further progress. For example, suppose you want to go to the highest floor of a building – say, the hundredth floor – by walking up a staircase. You will pass the thirtieth floor, the fiftieth floor, the eightieth floor, and so on. But suppose when you come to the fiftieth or eightieth floor you think, "I have reached my goal." Then you are unsuccessful. To reach your destination you have to go to the hundredth floor. Similarly, all the processes of *yoga* are connected, like a staircase, but we shouldn't be satisfied to stop on the fiftieth floor or the eightieth floor. We should go to the highest platform, the hundredth floor – pure Kṛṣṇa consciousness.

Now, if somebody who wants to reach the hundredth floor is given a chance to use the elevator, within a minute he will be able to come to the top. Of course, he may still say, "Why should I take advantage of this elevator? I shall go step by step." He can do this, but there is a chance he will not reach the top floor. Similarly, if one takes help from the "elevator" of *bhakti-yoga,* within a short time he can reach the "hundredth floor" – the perfection of *yoga,* Kṛṣṇa consciousness.

Kṛṣṇa consciousness is the direct process. You may go step by step, following all the other *yoga* systems, or you may take directly to Kṛṣṇa consciousness. Lord Caitanya has recommended that in this age, since people are very short-lived, disturbed, and full of anxiety, they should take up the direct process. And by His grace, by His causeless mercy, He has given us the chanting of the Hare Kṛṣṇa *mantra,* which lifts us immediately to the platform of *bhakti-yoga.* It is immediate; we don't have to wait. That is the special gift of Lord Caitanya. Therefore Śrīla Rūpa Gosvāmī prayed, *namo mahā-vadānyāya kṛṣṇa-prema-pradāya te:* "O Lord Caitanya, You are the most munificent incarnation because You are directly giving love of Kṛṣṇa." Ordinarily, to attain love of Kṛṣṇa one has to pass through so many steps and stages of *yoga,* but Lord Caitanya gave it directly. Therefore He is the most munificent incarnation. This is the position of Lord Caitanya.

The only way to know God in truth is through *bhakti-yoga.* In *Bhagavad-gītā* [18.55] Kṛṣṇa confirms this. *Bhaktyā mām abhijānāti yāvān yaś cāsmi tattvataḥ:* "Only by devotional service can one understand the Supreme Personality of Godhead as He is." The *Vedas* confirm that only through *bhakti,* or devotional service, can one attain the highest perfectional stage. If one practices other *yoga* systems, there must be a mixture of *bhakti* if one is to make any progress. But because people don't have sufficient time to execute all the practices of any other *yoga* system, the direct process of *bhakti-yoga,* unadulterated devotion, is recommended for this age. Therefore, it is by great fortune that one comes to Kṛṣṇa consciousness, the path of *bhakti-yoga,* and becomes well situated according to the Vedic directions.

The ideal *yogī* concentrates his attention on Kṛṣṇa, who is as beautifully colored as a cloud, whose lotuslike face is as effulgent as the sun, whose dress is brilliant with jewels, and whose body is flower-garlanded. Illuminating all sides is His gorgeous luster, which is called the *brahmajyotir.* He incarnates in different forms, such as Rāma, Varāha, and Kṛṣṇa, the Supreme Personality of Godhead. He descends as a human being – as the son of mother Yaśodā – and He is known as Kṛṣṇa, Govinda, and Vāsudeva. He is the perfect child, husband, friend, and master, and He is full with all opulences and transcendental qualities. One who remains fully conscious of these features of the Lord is the highest *yogī.* This stage of perfection in *yoga* can be attained only by *bhakti-yoga,* as confirmed in all Vedic literature.

6

Material Problems, Spiritual Solutions

Focus for Global Unity

December 1969: Speaking in Boston before the International Student Society, Śrīla Prabhupāda provides a practical, simple, yet profound solution for world peace and harmony. Noting the increasing number of flags at the United Nations building in New York, he states that internationalism is failing because "your international feeling and my international feeling are overlapping and conflicting. We have to find the proper center for our loving feelings. . . . That center is Kṛṣṇa."

Thank you very much for participating with us in this Kṛṣṇa consciousness movement. I understand that this society is known as the International Student Society. There are many other international societies, such as the United Nations. So the idea of an international society is very nice, but we must try to understand what the central idea of an international society should be.

If you throw a stone into the middle of a pool of water, a circle will expand to the limit of the bank. Similarly, radio waves expand in a circle, and when you capture the waves with your radio you can hear the message. In the same way, our loving feeling can also expand.

At the beginning of our life, we simply want to eat. Whatever a small child grabs, he wants to eat. He has only personal interest. Then, when the child grows a little, he tries to participate with his brothers and sisters: "All right. You also take a little." This is an increase in the feeling of fellowship. Then, as he grows up, he begins to feel some love for his parents, then for his community, then for his country, and at last for all nations. But unless the center is right, that expansion of feeling – even if it is national or international – is not perfect.

For example, the meaning of the word *national* is "one who has taken birth in a particular country." You feel for other Americans because they are born in this country. You may even sacrifice your life for your countrymen. But there is a defect: If the definition of *national* is "one who is born in a particular country," then why are the animals born in America not considered Americans? The problem is that we are not expanding our feelings beyond the human society. Because we don't think animals are our countrymen, we send them to the slaughterhouse.

So the center of our national feeling or our international feeling is not fixed on the proper object. If the center is right, then you can draw any number of circles around that center and they'll never overlap. They'll simply keep growing, growing, growing. They'll not intersect with one another if the center is all right. Unfortunately, although everyone is feeling nationally or internationally, the center is missing. Therefore your international feeling and my international feeling, your national feeling and my national feeling, are overlapping and conflicting. So we have to find the proper center for our loving feelings. Then you can expand your circle of feelings and it will not overlap or conflict with others'.

That center is Kṛṣṇa.

Our society, the International Society for Krishna Consciousness, is teaching the people of all countries that the center of their affection should be Kṛṣṇa. In other words, we are teaching people to be *mahātmās*. You may have heard this word *mahātmā* before. It is a Sanskrit word that is applied to a person whose mind is expanded, whose circle of feelings is very much expanded. This is a *mahātmā*. *Mahā* means "big" or "great," and *ātmā* means "soul." So he who has expanded his soul very wide is called a *mahātmā*.

The *Bhagavad-gītā* [7.19] gives a description of the person who has expanded his feelings very wide:

bahūnāṁ janmanām ante
jñānavān māṁ prapadyate
vāsudevaḥ sarvam iti
sa mahātmā su-durlabhaḥ

The first idea in this verse is that one can become a *mahātmā* only after many, many births (*bahūnāṁ janmanām ante*). The soul is transmigrating through many bodies, one after another. There are 8,400,000 different species of life, and we evolve through them until at last we come to the human form of life. Only then can we become a *mahātmā*. This is why Kṛṣṇa says *bahūnāṁ janmanām ante:* "After many, many births one may become a *mahātmā*."

In the *Śrīmad-Bhāgavatam* there is a similar verse. *Labdhvā su-durlabham idaṁ bahu-sambhavānte:* "After many, many births you have achieved a human body, which is very difficult to get." This human form of life is not cheap. The bodies of cats and dogs and other animals are cheap, but this human form is not. After being born in at least 8,000,000 different species, we get this human form. So the *Bhāgavatam* and the *Bhagavad-gītā* say the same thing. All Vedic literatures corroborate one another, and the person who can understand them doesn't find any contradiction.

So the human form of life is obtained after many, many births in other-than-human forms of life. But even in this human form of life, many, many births are required for one who is cultivating knowledge of the central point of existence. If one is actually cultivating spiritual knowledge – not in one life but in many, many lives – one eventually comes to the highest platform of knowledge and is called *jñānavān,* "the possessor of true knowledge." Then, Kṛṣṇa says, *māṁ prapadyate:* "He surrenders unto Me, Kṛṣṇa, or God." (When I say "Kṛṣṇa" I mean the Supreme Lord, the all-attractive Supreme Personality of Godhead.)

Now, why does a man in knowledge surrender to Kṛṣṇa? *Vāsudevaḥ sarvam iti:* Because he knows that Vāsudeva, Kṛṣṇa, is everything – that He is the central point of all loving feelings. Then, *sa mahātmā su-durlabhaḥ*. Here the word *mahātmā* is used. After cultivating knowledge for many, many births, a person who expands his consciousness up to the point of loving God – he is a *mahātmā,* a great soul. God is great, and His devotee is also great. But, Kṛṣṇa says, *sa mahātmā su-durlabhaḥ:* That sort of great soul is very rarely to be seen. This is the description of a *mahātmā* we get from the *Bhagavad-gītā*.

Now we have expanded our feelings of love to various objects. We may love our country, we may love our community, we may love our family, we may love our cats and dogs. In any case, we have love, and we expand it according to our knowledge. And when our knowledge is perfect, we come to the point of loving Kṛṣṇa. That is perfection. Love of Kṛṣṇa is the aim of all activities, the aim of life.

The *Śrīmad-Bhāgavatam* [1.2.8] confirms that the goal of life is Kṛṣṇa:

dharmaḥ svanuṣṭhitaḥ puṁsāṁ
viṣvaksena-kathāsu yaḥ
notpādayed yadi ratiṁ
śrama eva hi kevalam

The first words in this verse are *dharmaḥ svanuṣṭhitaḥ puṁsām.* This means that everyone is doing his duty according to his position. A householder has some duty, a *sannyāsī* [renunciant] has some duty, a *brahmacārī* [celibate student] has some duty. There are different types of duties according to different occupations or professions. But, the *Bhāgavatam* says, if by performing your duties very nicely you still do not come to the understanding of Kṛṣṇa, then whatever you have done is simply useless labor (*śrama eva hi kevalam*). So if you want to come to the point of perfection, you should try to understand and love Kṛṣṇa. Then your national or international feelings of love will actually expand to their limit.

Now, suppose a man says, "Yes, I have expanded my feelings of love very widely." That is all right, but he must show the symptoms of how his feelings of love are expanded. As Kṛṣṇa says in the *Bhagavad-gītā* [5.18]:

vidyā-vinaya-sampanne
brāhmaṇe gavi hastini
śuni caiva śva-pāke ca
paṇḍitāḥ sama-darśinaḥ

If one is actually a *paṇḍita,* someone who is elevated to the stage of perfect wisdom, then he must see everyone on an equal platform (*sama-darśinaḥ*). Because the vision of a *paṇḍita* is no longer absorbed simply with the body, he sees a learned *brāhmaṇa* as a spirit soul, he sees a dog as a spirit soul, he sees an elephant as a spirit soul, and he also sees a lowborn man as a spirit soul. From the highborn *brāhmaṇa* down to the *caṇḍāla* [outcaste], there are many social classes in human society, but if a man is really learned he sees everyone, every living entity, on the same level. That is the stage of true learning.

We are trying to expand our feeling socially, communally, nationally, internationally, or universally. That is our natural function – to expand our consciousness. But my point is that if we actually want to expand our consciousness to the utmost, we must find out the real center of existence. That center is Kṛṣṇa, or God. How do we know Kṛṣṇa is God? Kṛṣṇa declares Himself to be God in the *Bhagavad-gītā*. Please always remember that the Kṛṣṇa consciousness movement is based on understanding *Bhagavad-gītā* as it is. Whatever I am speaking is in the *Bhagavad-gītā*. Unfortunately, the *Bhagavad-gītā* has been misinterpreted by so many commentators that people have misunderstood it. Actually, the purport of the *Bhagavad-gītā* is to develop Kṛṣṇa consciousness, love of Kṛṣṇa, and we are trying to teach that.

In the *Bhagavad-gītā* Kṛṣṇa has given several descriptions of a *mahātmā*. He says, *mahātmānas tu māṁ pārtha daivīṁ prakṛtim āśritāḥ:* "A *mahātmā,* one who is actually wise and broad-minded, is under the shelter of My spiritual energy." He is no longer under the spell of the material energy.

Whatever we see is made up of various energies of God. In the *Upaniṣads* it is said, *parāsya śaktir vividhaiva śrūyate:* "The Supreme Absolute Truth has many varieties of energies." And these energies are acting so nicely that it appears they are working automatically (*svābhāvikī jñāna-bala-kriyā ca*). For example, we have all seen a blooming flower. We may think that it has automatically blossomed and become so beautiful. But no, the material energy of God is acting.

Similarly, Kṛṣṇa has a spiritual energy. And a *mahātmā,* one who is broad-minded, is under the protection of that spiritual energy; he is not under the spell of the material energy. These things are all explained in the *Bhagavad-gītā.* There are many verses in the *Bhagavad-gītā* that describe how Kṛṣṇa's energies are working, and our mission is to present *Bhagavad-gītā* as it is, without any nonsensical commentary. There is no need of nonsensical commentary. *Bhagavad-gītā* is as clear as the sunlight. Just as you don't require a lamp to see the sun, you don't require the commentary of an ignorant, common man to study the *Bhagavad-gītā*. You should study the *Bhagavad-gītā* as it is. Then you will get all spiritual knowledge. You will become wise and will understand Kṛṣṇa. Then you will surrender to Him and become a *mahātmā*.

Now, what are the activities of a *mahātmā*? A *mahātmā* is under the protection of Kṛṣṇa's spiritual energy, but what is the symptom of that protection? Kṛṣṇa says, *mām . . . bhajanty ananya-manasaḥ:* "A *mahātmā* is always engaged in devotional service to Me." That is the main symptom of a *mahātmā:* he is always serving Kṛṣṇa. Does he engage in this devotional service blindly? No. Kṛṣṇa says, *jñātvā bhūtādim avyayam:* "He knows perfectly that I am the source of everything."

So Kṛṣṇa explains everything in the *Bhagavad-gītā*. And our purpose in the Kṛṣṇa consciousness movement is to spread the knowledge contained in the *Bhagavad-gītā* without adding any nonsensical commentary. Then the human society will profit from this knowledge. Now society is not in a sound condition, but if people understand the *Bhagavad-gītā*, and if they actually broaden their outlook, all social, national, and international problems will be solved automatically. There will be no difficulty. But if we don't find out what the center of existence is, if we manufacture our own ways to expand our loving feelings, there will be only conflict – not only between individual persons but between the different nations of the world. The nations are trying to be united; in your country there is the United Nations. Unfortunately, instead of the nations becoming united, the flags are increasing. Similarly, India was once one country, Hindustan. Now there is also Pakistan. And some time in the future there will be Sikhistan and then some other "stan."

Instead of becoming united we are becoming disunited, because we are missing the center. Therefore, my request, since you are all international students, is that you please try to find out the real center of your international movement. Real international feeling will be possible when you understand that the center is Kṛṣṇa. Then your international movement will be perfect.

In the fourteenth chapter of *Bhagavad-gītā* [14.4], Lord Kṛṣṇa says,

sarva-yoniṣu kaunteya
mūrtayaḥ sambhavanti yāḥ
tāsāṁ brahma mahad yonir
ahaṁ bīja-pradaḥ pitā

Here Kṛṣṇa says, "I am the father of all forms of life. The material nature is the mother, and I am the seed-giving father." Without a father and mother, nobody can be born. The father gives the seed, and the mother supplies the body. In this material world the mother of every one of us – from Lord Brahmā down to the ant – is the material nature. Our body is matter; therefore it is a gift of the material nature, our mother. But I, the spirit soul, am part and parcel of the supreme father, Kṛṣṇa. Kṛṣṇa says, *mamaivāṁśo . . . jīva-bhūtaḥ:* "All these living entities are part and parcel of Me."

So if you want to broaden your feelings of fellowship to the utmost limit, please try to understand the *Bhagavad-gītā*. You'll get enlightenment; you'll become a real *mahātmā*. You will feel affection even for the cats and dogs and reptiles. In the Seventh Canto of the *Śrīmad-Bhāgavatam* you'll find a statement by Nārada Muni that if there is a snake in your house, you should give it something to eat. Just see how your feelings can expand! You'll care even for a snake, what to speak of other animals and human beings.

So we cannot become enlightened unless we come to the point of understanding God, or Kṛṣṇa. Therefore we are preaching Kṛṣṇa consciousness all over the world. The Kṛṣṇa consciousness movement is not new. As I told you, it is based on the principles of the *Bhagavad-gītā*, and the *Bhagavad-gītā* is an ancient scripture. From the historical point of view it is five thousand years old. And from a prehistorical point of view it is millions of years old. Kṛṣṇa says in the fourth chapter, *imaṁ vivasvate yogaṁ proktavān aham avyayam:* "I first spoke this ancient science of *yoga* to the sun-god." That means Kṛṣṇa first spoke the *Bhagavad-gītā* some millions of years ago. But simply from a historical point of view, *Bhagavad-gītā* has existed since the days of the Battle of Kurukṣetra, which was fought five thousand years ago. So it is older than any other scripture in the world.

Try to understand *Bhagavad-gītā* as it is, without any unnecessary commentary. The words of the *Bhagavad-gītā* are sufficient to give you enlightenment, but unfortunately people have taken advantage of the popularity of the *Bhagavad-gītā* and have tried to express their own philosophy under the shelter of the *Bhagavad-gītā*. That is useless. Try to understand the *Bhagavad-gītā* as it is. Then you will get enlightenment;

you will understand that Kṛṣṇa is the center of all activities. And if you become Kṛṣṇa conscious, everything will be perfect and all problems will be solved.

Thank you very much. Are there any questions?

Indian student: I don't know the exact Sanskrit from the *Gītā*, but somewhere Kṛṣṇa says, "All roads lead to Me. No matter what one does, no matter what one thinks, no matter what one is involved with, eventually he will evolve toward Me." So is enlightenment a natural evolution?

Śrīla Prabhupāda: No, Kṛṣṇa never says that whatever you do, whatever you think, you will naturally evolve toward Him. To become enlightened in Kṛṣṇa consciousness is not natural for the conditioned soul. You require instruction from a spiritual master. Otherwise, why did Kṛṣṇa instruct Arjuna? You have to get knowledge from a superior person and follow his instructions.

Arjuna was perplexed. He could not understand whether he should fight or not. Similarly, everyone in the material world is perplexed. So we require guidance from Kṛṣṇa or his bona fide representative. Then we can become enlightened.

Evolution is natural up through the animal species. But when we come to the human form of life, we can use our own discretion. As you like, you make your choice of which path to follow. If you like Kṛṣṇa, you can go to Kṛṣṇa; if you like something else, you can go there. That depends on your discretion.

Everyone has a little bit of independence. At the end of the *Bhagavad-gītā* [18.66] Kṛṣṇa says, *sarva-dharmān parityajya mām ekaṁ śaraṇaṁ vraja:* "Just give up everything and surrender unto Me." If this surrender is natural, why would Kṛṣṇa say, "You should do this"? No. Surrendering to Kṛṣṇa is not natural in our materially conditioned state. We have to learn it. Therefore we must hear from a bona fide spiritual master – Kṛṣṇa or His authorized representative – and follow his instructions. This will bring us to the stage of full enlightenment in Kṛṣṇa consciousness.

The Myth of Scarcity

Contrary to popular belief, current statistics show that the earth produces enough food to easily support its entire population. Yet greed and exploitation force over 25 percent of the world's people to be underfed and undernourished. Śrīla Prabhupāda condemns unnecessary industrialization for contributing to the problem of hunger and for creating unemployment, pollution, and a host of other problems. In the following speech, recorded on May 2, 1973, in Los Angeles, he advocates a simpler, more natural, God-centered lifestyle.

ime jana-padāḥ sv-ṛddhāḥ
supakvauṣadhi-vīrudhaḥ
vanādri-nady-udanvanto
hy edhante tava vīkṣitaiḥ

[Queen Kuntī said:] "All these cities and villages are flourishing in all respects because the herbs and grains are in abundance, the trees are full of fruits, the rivers are flowing, the hills are full of minerals, and the oceans are full of wealth. And this is all due to Your glancing over them." [*Śrīmad-Bhāgavatam* 1.8.40]

Human prosperity flourishes by natural gifts and not by gigantic industrial enterprises. The gigantic industrial enterprises are products of a godless civilization, and they cause the destruction of the noble aims of human life. The more we increase such troublesome industries to squeeze out the vital energy of the human being, the more there will be dissatisfaction of the people in general, although a select few can live lavishly by exploitation.

The natural gifts such as grains and vegetables, fruits, rivers, the hills of jewels and minerals, and the seas full of pearls are supplied by the order of the Supreme, and as He desires, material nature produces them in abundance or restricts them at times. The natural law is that the human being may take advantage of these godly gifts of nature and thus satisfactorily flourish without being captivated by the exploitative motive of lording it over material nature.

The more we attempt to exploit material nature according to our whims, the more we shall become entrapped by the reaction of such exploitative attempts. If we have sufficient grains, fruits, vegetables, and herbs, then what is the necessity of running a slaughterhouse and killing poor animals?

A man need not kill an animal if he has sufficient grains and vegetables to eat. The flow of river waters fertilizes the fields, and there is more than what we need. Minerals are produced in the hills, and the jewels in the ocean. If the human civilization has sufficient grains, minerals, jewels, water, milk, etc., then why should we hanker after terrible industrial enterprises at the cost of the labor of some unfortunate men?

But all these natural gifts are dependent on the mercy of the Lord. What we need, therefore, is to be obedient to the laws of the Lord and achieve the perfection of human life by devotional service. The indications by Kuntī-devī are just to the point. She desires that God's mercy be bestowed upon her and her sons so that natural prosperity will be maintained by His grace.

Kuntī-devī mentions that the grains are abundant, the trees full of fruits, the rivers flowing nicely, the hills full of minerals, and the oceans full of wealth, but she never mentions that industry and slaughterhouses are flourishing, for such things are nonsense that men have developed to create problems.

If we depend on God's creation, there will be no scarcity, but simply *ānanda,* bliss. God's creation provides sufficient grains and grass, and while we eat the grains and fruits, the animals like the cows will eat the grass. The bulls will help us produce grains, and they will take only a little, being satisfied with what we throw away. If we take fruit and throw away the skin, the animal will be satisfied with the skin. In this way, with Kṛṣṇa in the center, there can be full cooperation between the trees, animals, human beings, and all living entities. This is Vedic civilization, a civilization of Kṛṣṇa consciousness.

Kuntī-devī prays to the Lord, "This prosperity is due to Your glance." When we sit in the temple of Kṛṣṇa, Kṛṣṇa glances over us, and everything is nice. When sincere souls try to become Kṛṣṇa's devotees, Kṛṣṇa very kindly comes before them in His full opulence and glances upon them, and they become happy and beautiful.

Similarly, the whole material creation is due to Kṛṣṇa's glance (*sa aikṣata*). In the *Vedas* it is said that He glanced over matter, thus agitating it. A woman in touch with a man becomes agitated and becomes pregnant and then gives birth to children. The whole creation follows a similar process. Simply by Kṛṣṇa's glance, matter becomes agitated and then becomes pregnant and gives birth to the living entities. It is simply by His glance that plants, trees, animals, and all other living beings come forth. How is this possible? None of us can say, "Simply by glancing over my wife, I can make her pregnant." But although this is impossible for us, it is not impossible for Kṛṣṇa. The *Brahma-saṁhitā* [5.32] says, *aṅgāni yasya sakalendriya-vṛttimanti:* Every part of Kṛṣṇa's body has all the capabilities of the other parts. With our eyes we can only see, but Kṛṣṇa can make others pregnant merely by looking at them. There is no need of sex, for simply by glancing Kṛṣṇa can create pregnancy.

In *Bhagavad-gītā* [9.10] Lord Kṛṣṇa says, *mayādhyakṣeṇa prakṛtiḥ sūyate sa-carācaram:* "By My supervision, material nature gives birth to all moving and nonmoving beings." The word *akṣa* means "eyes," so *akṣeṇa* indicates that all living entities take birth because of the Lord's glance. There are two kinds of living entities – the moving beings, like insects, animals, and human beings, and the nonmoving beings, like trees and plants. In Sanskrit these two kinds of living entities are called *sthāvara-jaṅgama,* and they both come forth from material nature.

Of course, what comes from material nature is not the life, but the body. The living entities accept particular types of bodies from material nature, just as a child takes its body from its mother. For ten months the child's body develops from the blood and nutrients of the mother's body, but the child is a living entity, not matter. It is the living entity that has taken shelter in the womb of the mother, who then supplies the ingredients for that living entity's body. This is nature's way. The mother may not know how from her body another body has been created, but when the body of the child is fit, the child takes birth.

It is not that the living entity takes birth. As stated in *Bhagavad-gītā* [2.20], *na jāyate mriyate vā:* The living entity neither takes birth nor dies. That which does not take birth does not die; death is meant for that which has been created, and that which is not created has no death. The *Gītā* says, *na jāyate mriyate vā kadācit.* The word *kadācit* means "at any time." At no time does the living entity actually take birth. Although we may see that a child is born, actually it is not born. *Nityaḥ śāśvato 'yaṁ purāṇaḥ.* The living entity is eternal (*śāśvata*), always existing, and very, very old (*purāṇa*). *Na hanyate hanyamāne śarīre:* Don't think that when the body is destroyed the living entity will be destroyed; no, the living entity will continue to exist.

A scientist friend once asked me, "What is the proof of the soul's eternality?" Kṛṣṇa says, *na hanyate hanyamāne śārīre:* "The soul is not killed when the body is killed." This statement in itself is proof. This type of proof is called *śruti,* the proof established by that which is heard through the disciplic succession from the Supreme. One form of proof is proof by logic (*nyāya-prasthāna*). One can get knowledge by logic, arguments, and philosophical research. But another form of proof is *śruti,* proof established by hearing from authorities. A third form of proof is *smṛti,* proof established by statements derived from the *śruti.* The *Purāṇas* are *smṛti,* the *Upaniṣads* are *śruti,* and the *Vedānta* is *nyāya.* Of these three the *śruti-prasthāna,* or the evidence from the *śruti,* is especially important.

Pratyakṣa, the process of receiving knowledge through direct perception, has no value, because our senses are all imperfect. For example, to us the sun looks like a small disk, but in fact it is many times larger than the earth. So what is the value of our direct perception through our eyes? We have so many senses through which we can experience knowledge – the eyes, the ears, the nose, and so on – but because these senses are imperfect, whatever knowledge we get by exercising these senses is also imperfect. Because scientists try to understand things by exercising their imperfect senses, their conclusions are always imperfect. Svarūpa Dāmodara, a scientist among our disciples, inquired from a fellow scientist who says that life comes from matter, "If I give you the chemicals with which to produce life, will you be able to produce it?" The scientist replied, "That I do not know." This is imperfect knowledge. If you do not know, then your knowledge is imperfect. Why then have you become a teacher? That is cheating. Our contention is that to become perfect one must take lessons from the perfect teacher.

Kṛṣṇa is perfect, so we take knowledge from Him. Kṛṣṇa says, *na hanyate hanyamāne śarīre:* "The soul does not die when the body dies." Therefore this understanding that the soul is eternal and the body is temporary is perfect.

Kuntī-devī says, *ime jana-padāḥ sv-ṛddhāḥ supakvauṣadhi-vīrudhaḥ:* "The grains are abundant, the trees are full of fruits, the rivers are flowing, the hills are full of minerals, and the oceans are full of wealth." What more could one want? The oyster produces pearls, and formerly people decorated their bodies with pearls, valuable stones, silk, gold, and silver. But where are those things now? Now, with the advancement of civilization, there are so many beautiful girls who have no ornaments of gold, pearls, or jewels, but only plastic bangles. So what is the use of industry and slaughterhouses?

By God's arrangement one can have enough food grains, enough milk, enough fruits and vegetables, and nice clear river water. But now I have seen, while traveling in Europe, that all the rivers there have become nasty. In Germany, in France, and also in Russia and America I have seen that the rivers are nasty. By nature's way the water in the ocean is kept clear like crystal, and the same water is transferred to the rivers, but without salt, so that one may take nice water from the river. This is nature's way, and nature's way means Kṛṣṇa's way. So what is the use of constructing huge waterworks to supply water?

Nature has already given us everything. If we want wealth we may collect pearls and become rich; there is no need to become rich by starting some huge factory to produce auto bodies. By such industrial enterprises we have simply created troubles. Otherwise, we need only depend on Kṛṣṇa and Kṛṣṇa's mercy, because by Kṛṣṇa's glance (*tava vīkṣitaiḥ*), everything is set right. So if we simply plead for Kṛṣṇa's glance, there will be no question of scarcity or need. Everything will be complete. The idea of the Kṛṣṇa consciousness movement, therefore, is to depend on nature's gifts and the grace of Kṛṣṇa.

People say that the population is increasing, and therefore they are checking this by artificial means. Why? The birds and beasts are increasing their populations and have no contraceptives, but are they in need of food? Do we ever see birds or animals dying for want of food? Perhaps in the city, although not very often. But if we go to the jungle we shall see that all the elephants, lions, tigers, and other animals are very stout and strong. Who is supplying them with food? Some of them are vegetarians and some of them are nonvegetarians, but none of them are in want of food.

Of course, by nature's way the tiger, being a nonvegetarian, does not get food every day. After all, who will face a tiger to become its food? Who will say to the tiger, "Sir, I am an altruist and have come to you to give you food, so take my body"? No one. Therefore the tiger has difficulty finding food. And as soon as the tiger is out, there is an animal that follows it and makes a sound like *"fayo, fayo,"* so that the other animals will know, "Now the tiger is out." So by nature's way the tiger has difficulty. But still Kṛṣṇa supplies it food. After about a week, the tiger will get the chance to catch an animal, and because it does not get fresh food daily, it will keep the carcass in some bush and eat a little at a time. Since the tiger is very powerful, people want to become like a lion or a tiger. But that is not a very good proposition, because if one actually becomes like a tiger one won't get food daily, but will have to search for food with great labor. If one becomes a vegetarian, however, one will get food every day. The food for a vegetarian is available everywhere.

Now in every city there are slaughterhouses, but does this mean that the slaughterhouses can supply enough so that one can live by eating only meat? No, there will not be an adequate supply. Even meat-eaters have to eat grains, fruits, and vegetables along with their slice of meat. Still, for that daily slice of meat they kill so many poor animals. How sinful this is! If people commit such sinful activities, how can they be happy? This killing should not be done, but because it is being done people are unhappy. However, if one becomes Kṛṣṇa conscious and simply depends on Kṛṣṇa's glance (*tava vīkṣitaiḥ*), Kṛṣṇa will supply everything and there will be no question of scarcity.

Sometimes there appears to be scarcity, and sometimes we find that grains and fruits are produced in such a huge quantity that people cannot finish eating them. So this is a question of Kṛṣṇa's glance. If Kṛṣṇa likes, He can produce a huge quantity of grains, fruits, and vegetables, but if Kṛṣṇa desires to restrict the supply, what good will meat do? You may eat me, or I may eat you, but that will not solve the problem.

For real peace and tranquillity and a sufficient supply of milk, water, and everything else we need, we simply have to depend on Kṛṣṇa. This is what Bhaktivinoda Ṭhākura teaches us when he says, *mārabi rākhabi – yo icchā tohārā:* "My dear Lord, I simply surrender unto You and depend on You. Now if You like You may kill me, or else You may give me protection." And Kṛṣṇa says in reply, "Yes. *Sarva-dharmān parityajya mām ekaṁ śaraṇaṁ vraja:* Simply surrender exclusively unto Me." He does not say, "Yes, depend on Me, and also depend on your slaughterhouses and factories." No. He says, "Depend only on Me. *Ahaṁ tvāṁ sarva-pāpebhyo mokṣayiṣyāmi:* I will rescue you from the results of your sinful activities."

Because we have lived so many years without being Kṛṣṇa conscious, we have lived only a sinful life, but Kṛṣṇa assures us that as soon as one surrenders to Him, He immediately squares all accounts and puts an end to all one's sinful activities so that one may begin a new life. When we initiate disciples we therefore tell them, "Now the account is squared. Now don't commit sinful activities any more."

One should not think that because the holy name of Kṛṣṇa can nullify sinful activities, one may commit a little sinful activity and chant Hare Kṛṣṇa to nullify it. That is the greatest offense (*nāmno balād yasya hi pāpa-buddhiḥ*). The members of some religious orders go to church and confess their sins, but then they again commit the same sinful activities. What, then, is the value of their confession? One may confess, "My Lord, out of my ignorance I committed this sin." But one should not plan, "I shall commit sinful activities and then go to church and confess them, and then the sins will be nullified and I can begin a new chapter of sinful life." Similarly, one should not knowingly take advantage of the chanting of the Hare Kṛṣṇa *mantra* to nullify sinful activities so that one may then begin sinful acts again. We should be very careful. Before taking initiation, one promises to have no illicit sex, no intoxicants, no gambling, and no meat-eating, and this vow one should strictly follow. Then one will be clean. If one keeps oneself clean in this way and always engages in devotional service, his life will be a success, and there will be no scarcity of anything he wants.

Spiritual Advice to Businessmen

On January 30, 1973, in Calcutta, Śrīla Prabhupāda speaks to the Bharata Chamber of Commerce, a group of the region's leading businessmen. "We should not be satisfied with becoming a big businessman. We must know what our next life is. . . . If you cultivate this knowledge and at the same time go on doing your business, your life will be successful."

Mr. President, ladies, and gentlemen, I thank you very much for kindly inviting me. I'll serve you to the best of my ability.

Today's subject is "Culture and Business." We understand *business* to mean "occupational duty." According to our Vedic culture, there are different types of business. As described in *Bhagavad-gītā* [4.13], *cātur-varṇyaṁ mayā sṛṣṭaṁ guṇa-karma-vibhāgaśaḥ*. The four divisions of the social system, based on people's qualities and types of work, are the *brāhmaṇas* [intellectuals and teachers], the *kṣatriyas* [military men and state leaders], the *vaiśyas* [farmers and merchants], and the *śūdras* [laborers]. Before doing business, one must know what kinds of work there are and who can do what kind of work. People have different capabilities, and there are different types of work, but now we have created a society where everyone takes up everyone else's business. That is not very scientific.

Society has natural cultural divisions, just as there are natural divisions in the human body. The whole body is one unit, but it has different departments, also – for example, the head department, the arm department, the belly department, and the leg department. This is scientific. So in society the head department is represented by the *brāhmaṇa*, the arm department by the *kṣatriya*, the belly department by the *vaiśya*, and the leg department by the *śūdra*. Business should be divided scientifically in this way.

The head department is the most important department, because without the head the other departments – the arm, the belly, and the leg – cannot function. If the arm department is lacking, business can still go on. If the leg department is lacking, business can go on. But if the head department is not there – if your head is cut off from your body – then even though you have arms, legs, and a belly, they are all useless.

The head is meant for culture. Without culture, every type of business creates confusion and chaos. And that is what we have at the present moment, because of jumbling of different types of business. So there must be one section of people, the head department, who give advice to the other departments. These advisors are the intelligent and qualified *brāhmaṇas*.

śamo damas tapaḥ śaucaṁ
kṣāntir ārjavam eva ca
jñānaṁ vijñānam āstikyaṁ
brahma-karma svabhāva-jam

"Peacefulness, self-control, austerity, purity, tolerance, honesty, knowledge, wisdom, and religiousness – these are the natural qualities by which the *brāhmaṇas* work." [*Bhagavad-gītā* 18.42]

The *brāhmaṇas*, the head of the social body, are meant to guide society in culture. Culture means knowing the aim of life. Without understanding the aim of life, a man is a ship without a rudder. But at the present moment we are missing the goal of life because there is no head department in society. The whole human society is now lacking real *brāhmaṇas* to give advice to the other departments.

Arjuna is a good example of how a member of the *kṣatriya* department should take advice. He was a military man; his business was to fight. In the Battle of Kurukṣetra he engaged in his business, but at the same time he took the advice of the *brahmaṇya-deva*, Lord Kṛṣṇa. As it is said,

namo brahmaṇya-devāya
go-brāhmaṇa-hitāya ca

jagad-dhitāya kṛṣṇāya
govindāya namo namaḥ

"Let me offer my respectful obeisances unto Lord Kṛṣṇa, who is the worshipable Deity for all brahminical men, who is the well-wisher of cows and *brāhmaṇas,* and who is always benefiting the whole world. I offer my repeated obeisances to the Personality of Godhead, known as Kṛṣṇa and Govinda." [*Viṣṇu Purāṇa* 1.19.65]

In this verse the first things taken into consideration are the cows and the *brāhmaṇas* (*go-brāhmaṇa*). Why are they stressed? Because a society with no brahminical culture and no cow protection is not a human society but a chaotic, animalistic society. And any business you do in a chaotic condition will never be perfect. Business can be done nicely only in a society following a proper cultural system.

Instructions for a perfect cultural system are given in *Śrīmad-Bhāgavatam.* At a meeting in the forest of Naimiṣāraṇya, where many learned scholars and *brāhmaṇas* had assembled and Śrīla Sūta Gosvāmī was giving instructions, he stressed the *varṇāśrama* social system (*ataḥ pumbhir dvija-śreṣṭhā varṇāśrama-vibhāgaśaḥ*). The Vedic culture organizes society into four *varṇas* [occupational divisions] and four *āśramas* [spiritual stages of life]. As mentioned before, the *varṇas* are the *brāhmaṇa, kṣatriya, vaiśya,* and *śūdra.* The *āśramas* are the *brahmacārī-āśrama* [celibate student life], *gṛhastha-āśrama* [family life], *vānaprastha-āśrama* [retired life], and *sannyāsa-āśrama* [renounced life]. Unless we take to this institution of *varṇāśrama-dharma,* the whole society will be chaotic.

And the purpose of *varṇāśrama-dharma* is to satisfy the Supreme Lord. As stated in the *Viṣṇu Purāṇa* [3.8.9],

varṇāśramācāra-vatā
puruṣeṇa paraḥ pumān
viṣṇur ārādhyate panthā
nānyat tat-toṣa-kāraṇam

According to this verse, one has to satisfy the Supreme Lord by properly performing one's prescribed duties according to the system of *varṇa* and *āśrama.* In a state, you have to satisfy your government. If you don't, you are a bad citizen and cause chaos in society. Similarly, in the cosmic state – that is, in this material creation as a whole – if you do not satisfy the Supreme Lord, the proprietor of everything, then there will be a chaotic condition. Our Vedic culture teaches that whatever you do, you must satisfy the Supreme Lord. That is real culture.

Sva-karmaṇā tam abhyarcya siddhiṁ vindati mānavaḥ. You may do any business – the *brāhmaṇa's* business, the *kṣatriya's* business, the *vaiśya's* business, or the *śūdra's* business – but by your business you should satisfy the Supreme Personality of Godhead. You may be a merchant, a professional man, a legal advisor, a medical man – it doesn't matter. But if you want perfection in your business, then you must try to satisfy the Supreme Personality of Godhead. Otherwise you are simply wasting your time.

In *Bhagavad-gītā* [3.9], Lord Kṛṣṇa says, *yajñārthāt karmaṇaḥ*. The word *yajña* refers to Viṣṇu, or Kṛṣṇa, the Supreme Lord. You have to work for Him. Otherwise you become bound by the reactions of your activities (*anyatra loko 'yaṁ karma-bandhanaḥ*). And as long as you are in the bondage of *karma*, you have to transmigrate from one body to another.

Unfortunately, at the present moment people do not know that there is a soul and that the soul transmigrates from one body to another. As stated in *Bhagavad-gītā* [2.13], *tathā dehāntara-prāptiḥ:* "When the body dies, the soul transmigrates to another body." I've talked with big, big scientists and professors who do not know that there is life after death. They do not know. But according to our Vedic information, there *is* life after death. And we can experience transmigration of the soul in this present life. It is a very common thing: A baby soon gets the body of a boy, the boy then gets the body of a young man, and the young man gets the body of an old man. Similarly, the old man, after the annihilation of his body, will get another body. It is quite natural and logical.

Actually, we have two bodies, the gross body and the subtle body. The gross body is made up of our senses and the bodily elements – bones, blood, and so on. When we change our body at death, the present gross body is destroyed, but the subtle body, made of mind, intelligence, and ego, is not. The subtle body carries us to our next gross body.

It is just like what happens when we sleep. At night we forget about the gross body, and the subtle body alone works. As we dream we are taken away from our home, from our bed, to some other place, and we completely forget the gross body. When our sleep is over we forget about the dream and become attached again to the gross body. This is going on in our daily experience.

So we are the observer, sometimes of the gross body and sometimes of the subtle body. Both bodies are changing, but we are the unchanging observer, the soul *within* the bodies. Therefore, our inquiry should be, "What is my position? At night I forget my gross body, and during the daytime I forget my subtle body. Then what is my real body?" These are the questions we should ask.

So you may do your business, as Arjuna did his business. He was a fighter, a *kṣatriya,* but he did not forget his culture, hearing *Gītā* from the master. But if you simply do business and do not cultivate your spiritual life, then your business is a useless waste of time (*śrama eva hi kevalam*).

Our Kṛṣṇa consciousness movement is being spread so that you do not forget your cultural life. We do not say that you stop your business and become a *sannyāsī* like me and give up everything. We do not say that. Nor did Kṛṣṇa say that. Kṛṣṇa never said, "Arjuna, give up your fighting business." No, He said, "Arjuna, you are a *kṣatriya.* You are declining to fight, saying, 'Oh, it is very abominable.' You should not say that. You *must* fight." That was Kṛṣṇa's instruction.

Similarly, we Kṛṣṇa conscious people are also advising everyone, "Don't give up your business. Go on with your business, but simply hear about Kṛṣṇa." Caitanya Mahāprabhu also said this, quoting from *Śrīmad-Bhāgavatam: sthāne sthitāḥ śruti-gatāṁ tanu-vāṅ-manobhiḥ.* Caitanya Mahāprabhu never said, "Give up your position." Giving up one's position is not very difficult. But to cultivate spiritual knowledge while one stays in his position – that is required. Among the animals there is no cultivation of spiritual life. That is not possible; the animals cannot cultivate this knowledge. Therefore, if human beings do not cultivate spiritual knowledge, they're exactly like animals (*dharmeṇa hīnāḥ paśubhiḥ samānāḥ*).

So we should be very conscious about our eternal existence. We, the spirit soul within the body, are eternal (*na hanyate hanyamāne śarīre*). We are not going to die after the annihilation of our body. This is the cultivation of knowledge, or *brahma-jijñāsā,* which means inquiry about one's self. Caitanya Mahāprabhu's first disciple, Sanātana Gosvāmī, was formerly finance minister in the government of Nawab Hussein Shah. Then he retired and approached Caitanya Mahāprabhu and humbly said, "My dear Lord, people call me *paṇḍita*." (Because he was a *brāhmaṇa* by caste, naturally he was called *paṇḍita,* meaning "a learned person.") "But I am such a *paṇḍita,*" he said, "that I do not even know who or what I am."

This is the position of everyone. You may be a businessman or you may be in another profession, but if you do not know what you are, wherefrom you have come, why you are under the tribulations of the laws of material nature, and where you are going in your next life – if you do not know these things, then whatever you are doing is useless. As stated in *Śrīmad-Bhāgavatam* [1.2.8],

dharmaḥ svanuṣṭhitaḥ puṁsāṁ
viṣvaksena-kathāsu yaḥ
notpādayed yadi ratiṁ
śrama eva hi kevalam

"The occupational activities a man performs according to his own position are only so much useless labor if they do not provoke attraction for the message of the Personality of Godhead." Therefore our request to everyone is that while you engage in your business, in whatever position Kṛṣṇa has posted you, do your duty nicely, but do not forget to cultivate Kṛṣṇa knowledge.

Kṛṣṇa knowledge means God consciousness. We must know that we are part and parcel of God (*mamaivāṁśo jīva-loke jīva-bhūtaḥ sanātanaḥ*). We are eternally part and parcel of Kṛṣṇa, or God, but we are now struggling with the mind and senses (*manaḥ ṣaṣṭhānīndriyāṇi prakṛti-sthāni karṣati*). Why this struggle for existence? We must inquire about our eternal life beyond this temporary life. Suppose in this temporary life I become a big businessman for, say, twenty years or fifty years or at the utmost one hundred years. There is no guarantee that in my next life I'm going to be a big businessman. No. There is no such guarantee. But this we do not care about. We are taking care of our present small span of life, but we are not taking care of our eternal life. That is our mistake.

In this life I may be a very great businessman, but in my next life, by my *karma*, I may become something else. There are 8,400,000 forms of life. *Jalajā nava-lakṣāṇi sthāvarā lakṣa-viṁśatiḥ:* There are 900,000 forms of life in the water, and 2,000,000 forms of trees and other plants. Then, *kṛmayo rudra-saṅkhyakāḥ pakṣiṇāṁ daśa-lakṣaṇam:* There are 1,100,000 species of insects and reptiles, and 1,000,000 species of birds. Finally, *triṁsāl-lakṣāni paśavaḥ catur-lakṣāni mānuṣaḥ:* There are 3,000,000 varieties of beasts and 400,000 human species. So we must pass through 8,000,000 different forms of life before we come to the human form of life.

Therefore Prahlāda Mahārāja says,

kaumāra ācaret prājño
dharmān bhāgavatān iha
durlabhaṁ mānuṣaṁ janma
tad apy adhruvam arthadam

"One who is sufficiently intelligent should use the human form of body from the very beginning of life – in other words, from the tender age of childhood – to practice the activities of devotional service, giving up all other engagements. The human body is most rarely achieved, and although temporary like other bodies, it is meaningful because in human life one can perform devotional service. Even a slight amount of sincere devotional service can give one complete perfection." [*Śrīmad-Bhāgavatam* 7.6.1] This human birth is very rare. We should not be satisfied simply with becoming a big businessman. We must know what our next life is, what we are going to be.

There are different kinds of men. Some are called *karmīs,* some are called *jñānīs,* some are called *yogīs,* and some are called *bhaktas.* The *karmīs* are after material happiness. They want the best material comforts in this life, and they want to be elevated to the heavenly planets after death. The *jñānīs* also want happiness, but being fed up with the materialistic way of life, they want to merge into the existence of Brahman, the Absolute. The *yogīs* want mystic power. And the *bhaktas,* the devotees, simply want the service of the Lord. But unless one understands who the Lord is, how can one render service to Him? So cultivating knowledge of God is the highest culture.

There are different kinds of culture: the culture of the *karmīs*, the culture of the *jñānīs*, the culture of the *yogīs*, and the culture of the *bhaktas*. Actually, all of these people are called *yogīs* if they are doing their duty sincerely. Then they are known as *karma-yogīs, jñāna-yogīs, dhyāna-yogīs*, and *bhakti-yogīs*. But in *Bhagavad-gītā* [6.47] Kṛṣṇa says,

yoginām api sarveṣāṁ
mad-gatenāntar-ātmanā
śraddhāvān bhajate yo māṁ
sa me yuktatamo mataḥ

Who is the first-class *yogī*? Kṛṣṇa answers, "He who is always thinking of Me." This means the Kṛṣṇa conscious person is the best *yogī*. As already mentioned, there are different kinds of *yogīs* (the *karma-yogī*, the *jñāna-yogī*, the *dhyāna-yogī*, and the *bhakti-yogī*), but the best *yogī* is he who always thinks of Kṛṣṇa within himself with faith and love. One who is rendering service to the Lord – he is the first-class *yogī*.

So we request everyone to try to know what he is, what Kṛṣṇa is, what his relationship with Kṛṣṇa is, what his real life is, and what the goal of his life is. Unless we cultivate all this knowledge, we are simply wasting our time, wasting our valuable human form of life. Although everyone will die – that's a fact – one who dies after knowing these things is benefited. His life is successful.

The cat will die, the dog will die – everyone will die. But one who dies knowing Kṛṣṇa – oh, that is a successful death. As Kṛṣṇa says in *Bhagavad-gītā* [4.9],

janma karma ca me divyam
evaṁ yo vetti tattvataḥ
tyaktvā dehaṁ punar janma
naiti mām eti so 'rjuna

"One who knows in truth the transcendental nature of My appearance and activities does not, upon leaving the body, take his birth again in this material world, but attains My eternal abode, O Arjuna."

So wherever we go all over the world, our only request is, "Please try to understand Kṛṣṇa. Then your life is successful." It doesn't matter what your business is. You have to do something to live. Kṛṣṇa says, *śarīra-yātrāpi ca te na prasiddhyed akarmaṇaḥ:* If you stop working, your life will be hampered. One has to do something for his livelihood, but at the same time he has to cultivate knowledge for the perfection of his life. The perfection of life is simple: try to understand Kṛṣṇa. This is what we are prescribing all over the world. It is not very difficult. If you read *Bhagavad-gītā As It Is,* you will come to understand Kṛṣṇa. Kṛṣṇa explains everything.

For the neophytes, Kṛṣṇa says, *raso 'ham apsu kaunteya prabhāsmi śaśi-sūryayoḥ:* "My dear Kaunteya, I am the taste of water, and I am the light of the sun and the moon." There is no need to say, "I cannot see God." Here is God: the taste of water is God. Everyone drinks water, and when one tastes it he is perceiving God. Then why do you say, "I cannot see God"? Think as God directs, and then gradually you'll see Him. Simply remember this one instruction from *Bhagavad-gītā – raso 'ham apsu kaunteya prabhāsmi śaśi-sūryayoḥ:* "I am the taste of water; I am the shining illumination of the sun and moon." Who has not seen the sunlight? Who has not seen the moonlight? Who has not tasted water? Then why do you say, "I have not seen God"? If you simply practice this *bhakti-yoga,* as soon as you taste water and feel satisfied you will think, "Oh, here is Kṛṣṇa." Immediately you will remember Kṛṣṇa. As soon as you see the sunshine, you will remember, "Oh, here is Kṛṣṇa." As soon as you see the moonshine, you will remember, "Oh, here is Kṛṣṇa." And *śabdaḥ khe:* As soon as you hear some sound in the sky, you will remember, "Here is Kṛṣṇa."

In this way, you will remember Kṛṣṇa at every step of your life. And if you remember Kṛṣṇa at every step of life, you become the topmost *yogī.* And above all, if you practice the chanting of Hare Kṛṣṇa, Hare Kṛṣṇa, Kṛṣṇa Kṛṣṇa, Hare Hare/ Hare Rāma, Hare Rāma, Rāma Rāma, Hare Hare, you will easily remember Kṛṣṇa. There is no tax. There is no loss to your business. If you chant the Hare Kṛṣṇa *mantra,* if you remember Kṛṣṇa while drinking water, what is your loss? Why don't you try it? This is the real culture of knowledge. If you cultivate this knowledge and at the same time go on doing your business, your life will be successful. Thank you very much.

Ancient Prophecies Fulfilled

A little-known fact is that a book written over five thousand years ago – Śrīmad-Bhāgavatam *– predicted many current trends and events with amazing accuracy. Śrīla Prabhupāda quotes profusely from this Sanskrit text in a lecture given at the Los Angeles Hare Kṛṣṇa temple during the summer of 1974. About present day society, the* Śrīmad-Bhāgavatam's *Twelfth Canto prophesies: "Religious principles will be determined by a show of strength [and] measured by a person's reputation for material accomplishments." And: "Those without money will be unable to get justice, and anyone who can cleverly juggle words will be considered a scholar."*

tataś cānu-dinaṁ dharmaḥ
satyaṁ śaucam kṣamā dayā
kālena balinā rājan
naṅkṣyaty āyur balaṁ smṛtiḥ

"My dear King, with each day religion, truthfulness, cleanliness, forgiveness, mercy, duration of life, bodily strength, and memory will all decrease more and more by the mighty force of time." [*Śrīmad-Bhāgavatam* 12.2.1]

This description of the Kali-yuga [the present age of quarrel and hypocrisy] is given in the Twelfth Canto of *Śrīmad-Bhāgavatam. Śrīmad-Bhāgavatam* was written five thousand years ago, when the Kali-yuga was about to begin, and many things that would happen in the future are spoken of there. Therefore we accept *Śrīmad-Bhāgavatam* as *śāstra* [revealed scripture]. The compiler of *śāstra* (the *śāstra-kāra*) must be a liberated person so that he can describe past, present, and future.

In *Śrīmad-Bhāgavatam* you will find many things which are foretold. There is mention of Lord Buddha's appearance and Lord Kalki's appearance. (Lord Kalki will appear at the end of the Kali-yuga.) There is also mention of Lord Caitanya's appearance. Although the *Bhāgavatam* was written five thousand years ago, the writer knew past, present, and future (*tri-kāla-jña*), and thus he could predict all these events with perfect accuracy.

So here Śukadeva Gosvāmī is describing the chief symptoms of this age. He says, *tataś cānu-dinam:* With the progress of this age [Kali-yuga], *dharma,* religious principles; *satyam,* truthfulness; *śaucam,* cleanliness; *kṣamā,* forgiveness; *dayā,* mercifulness; *āyuḥ,* duration of life; *balam,* bodily strength; *smṛti,* memory – these eight things will gradually decrease to nil or almost nil.

Of course, there are other *yugas* besides Kali-yuga. During the Satya-yuga, which lasted eighteen hundred thousand years, human beings lived for one hundred thousand years. The duration of the next age, the Tretā-yuga, was twelve hundred thousand years, and the people of that age used to live for ten thousand years. In other words, the duration of life was ten times reduced. In the next age, Dvāpara-yuga, the life span was again ten times reduced – people used to live for one thousand years – and the duration of the Dvāpara Age was eight hundred thousand years. Then, in the next age, this Kali-yuga, we can live up to one hundred years at the utmost. We are not living one hundred years, but still, the limit is one hundred years. So just see: from one hundred years the average duration of life has decreased to about seventy years. And it will eventually decrease to the point where if a man lives for twenty to thirty years, he will be considered a very old man.

Another symptom of the Kali-yuga predicted in the *Śrīmad-Bhāgavatam* is the decrease in memory (*smṛti*). We see nowadays that people do not have very sharp memories – they forget easily. They may hear something daily, yet still they forget it. Similarly, bodily strength (*balam*) is decreasing. You can all understand this, because you know that your father or grandfather was physically stronger than you are. So, bodily strength is decreasing, memory is decreasing, and the duration of life is decreasing – and all of this is predicted in *Śrīmad-Bhāgavatam.*

Another symptom of Kali-yuga is the decrease in religion. There is practically no question of religion in this age – it has almost decreased to nil. No one is interested in religion. The churches and temples are being closed, locked up. The building we are sitting in was once a church, but it was sold because no one was coming. Similarly, we are purchasing a very big church in Australia, and in London I have seen many hundreds of vacant churches – no one is going there. And not only churches: in India also, except for a few important temples, the ordinary, small temples are being closed. They have become the habitation of the dogs. So *dharma*, religion, is decreasing.

Truthfulness, cleanliness, and forgiveness are also decreasing. Formerly, if someone did something wrong, the other party would forgive him. For example, Arjuna was tortured by his enemies, yet still, on the Battlefield of Kurukṣetra he said, "Kṛṣṇa, let me leave. I don't want to kill them." This is forgiveness. But now, even for a small insult people will kill. This is going on. Also, there is now no mercifulness (*dayā*). Even if you see someone being killed in front of you, you will not take interest. These things are happening already. So, religion, truthfulness, cleanliness, forgiveness, mercifulness, duration of life, bodily strength, and memory – these eight things will decrease, decrease, decrease, decrease. When you see these symptoms, you should know the age of Kali is making progress.

Another symptom is *vittam eva kalau nṛṇāṁ janmācāra-guṇodayaḥ:* "In Kali-yuga, a man's qualities and social position will be calculated according to the extent of his wealth." [*Śrīmad-Bhāgavatam* 12.2.2] Formerly a man's position was calculated according to his spiritual understanding. For example, a *brāhmaṇa* was honored because he knew *brahma* – he was aware of the Supreme Spirit. But now in Kali-yuga there are actually no *brāhmaṇas,* because people are taking the title of *brāhmaṇa* simply by *janma,* or birthright. Previously there was also birthright, but one was actually known according to his behavior. If a man was born in a *brāhmaṇa* family or a *kṣatriya* [administrative or military] family, he had to behave like a *brāhmaṇa* or *kṣatriya.* And it was the king's duty to see that no one was falsely representing himself. In other words, respectability was awarded according to culture and education. But nowadays, *vittam eva kalau nṛṇām:* if you get money somehow or other, then everything is available. You may be a third-class or a fourth-class or a tenth-class man, but if you get money somehow or other, then you are very much respected. There is no question of your culture or education or knowledge. This is Kali-yuga.

Another symptom of Kali-yuga: *dharma-nyāya-vyavasthāyāṁ kāraṇaṁ balam eva hi.* "Religious principles and justice will be determined by a show of strength." [*Śrīmad-Bhāgavatam* 12.2.2] If you have some influence, then everything will be decided in your favor. You may be the most irreligious person, but if you can bribe a priest he will certify that you are religious. So character will be decided by money, not by actual qualification. Next is *dāmpatye 'bhirucir hetur māyaiva vyāvahārike:* "Marriages will be arranged according to temporary affection, and to be a successful businessman, one will have to cheat." [*Śrīmad-Bhāgavatam* 12.2.3] The relationship between husband and wife will depend on *abhiruci,* their liking each other. If a girl likes a boy and a boy likes a girl, then they think, "All right, now let the marriage take place." No one ever knows what the future of the girl and boy will be. Therefore everyone becomes unhappy. Six months after marriage – divorce. This is because the marriage took place simply on the basis of superficial liking, not deep understanding.

Formerly, at least in India during my time, marriages did not take place because the boy and girl liked each other. No. Marriages were decided by the parents. I married when I was a student, but I did not know who my wife would be; my parents arranged everything. Another example is Dr. Rajendra Prasada, the first president of India. In his biography he wrote that he married at the age of eight. Similarly, my father-in-law married when he was eleven years old, and my mother-in-law when she was seven. So the point is that formerly, in India, marriage took place only after an astrological calculation of past, present, and future had determined whether the couple would be happy in their life together. When marriage is thus sanctified, the man and the woman live peacefully and practice spiritual culture. Each one helps the other, so they live very happily and become advanced in spiritual life. And at last they go back home, back to Godhead. That is the system. Not that a grown-up girl and a grown-up boy mix together, and if he likes her and she likes him they get married, and then he leaves or she leaves . . . This kind of marriage was not sanctioned. But of this Kali-yuga it is said, *dāmpatye 'bhirucih:* Marriage will take place simply because of mutual liking, that's all. Liking one moment means disliking the next moment. That is a fact. So a marriage based on mutual liking has no value.

The next symptoms of this age are *strītve puṁstve ca hi ratir vipratve sūtram eva hi:* "A husband and wife will stay together only as long as there is sex attraction, and *brāhmaṇas* [saintly intellectuals] will be known only by their wearing a sacred thread." [*Śrīmad-Bhāgavatam* 12.2.3] *Brāhmanas* are offered a sacred thread. So now people are thinking, "Now I have a sacred thread, so I have become a *brāhmaṇa.* I may act like a *caṇḍāla* [dog-eater], but it doesn't matter." This is going on. One doesn't understand that as a *brāhmaṇa* he has so much responsibility. Simply because he has the two-cent sacred thread, he thinks he has become a *brāhmaṇa.* And *strītve puṁstve ca hi ratiḥ:* A husband and wife will remain together because they like each other, but as soon as there will be some sex difficulty, their affection will slacken.

Another symptom of Kali-yuga is *avṛttyā nyāya-daurbalyaṁ pāṇḍitye cāpalaṁ vacaḥ:* "Those without money will be unable to get justice, and anyone who can cleverly juggle words will be considered a scholar." [*Śrīmad-Bhāgavatam* 12.2.4] If you have no money, then you will never get justice in court. This is Kali-yuga. Nowadays even the high-court judges are taking bribes to give you a favorable judgment. But if you have no money, then don't go to court. And *pāṇḍitye cāpalaṁ vacaḥ.* If a man can talk expertly – it doesn't matter what he says, and nobody has to understand it – then he is a *paṇḍita.* He is a learned scholar. [*Imitating gibberish:*] "*Aban gulakslena bugavad tugalad kulela gundulas,* by the latricism of wife . . . " Like this, if you go on speaking, no one will understand you. [*Laughter.*] Yet people will say, "Ah, see how learned he is." [*Laughter.*] This is actually happening. There are so many rascals writing books, but if you ask one of them to explain what he has understood, he'll say, "Oh, it is inexplicable." These things are going on.

Next *Śrīmad-Bhāgavatam* says,

anāḍhyataivāsādhutve
sādhutve dambha eva tu
svīkāra eva codvāhe
snānam eva prasādhanam

"Poverty will be looked on as dishonorable, while a hypocrite who can put on a show will be thought pious. Marriage will be based on arbitrary agreement, and simply taking a bath will be considered proper cleansing and decoration of the body." [*Śrīmad-Bhāgavatam* 12.2.5]

First, *anāḍhyatā:* If you are a poor man, then you are dishonorable. People will think that a man is not honorable because he does not know how to earn money by hook or crook. And *svīkāra eva codvāhe:* Marriages will take place by agreement. This is being experienced in your country, and in my country also. The government appoints a marriage magistrate, and any boy and girl who want to can simply go to him and get married. Maybe there is some fee. "Yes, we agree to marry," they say, and he certifies that they are married. Formerly, the father and mother used to select the bride and bridegroom by consulting an astrologer who could see the future. Nowadays marriage is taking place according to *svīkāra,* agreement.

Another symptom is *dūre vāry-ayanaṁ tīrthaṁ lāvaṇyaṁ keśa-dhāraṇam:* "Just going to some faraway river will be considered a proper pilgrimage, and a man will think he is beautiful if he has long hair." [*Śrīmad-Bhāgavatam* 12.2.6] Just see how perfectly *Śrīmad-Bhāgavatam* predicts the future! "In Kali-yuga a man will think he has become very beautiful by keeping long hair." You have very good experience of this in your country. Who could have known that people would be interested in keeping long hair? Yet that is stated in the *Bhāgavatam: keśa-dhāraṇam. Keśa* means "long hair" and *dhāraṇam* means "keeping." Another symptom is *dūre vāry-ayanaṁ tīrtham:* People will think that a place of pilgrimage must be far away. For example, the Ganges flows through Calcutta, but no one cares to take a bath in the Calcutta Ganges; they'd rather go to Hardwar. It is the same Ganges. The Ganges is coming from Hardwar down to the Bay of Bengal. But people would rather suffer so much hardship to go to Hardwar and take a bath there, because that has become a *tīrtha,* a place of pilgrimage. Every religion has a *tīrtha.* The Muslims have Mecca and Medina, and the Christians have Golgotha. Similarly, the Hindus also think they must travel very far to find a *tīrtha.* But actually, *tīrthī-kurvanti tīrthāni:* a *tīrtha* is a place where there are saintly persons. That is a *tīrtha.* Not that one goes ten thousand miles and simply takes a dip in the water and then comes back.

The next symptoms are:

udaraṁ-bharatā svārthaḥ
satyatve dhārṣṭyam eva hi
dākṣyaṁ kuṭumba-bharaṇaṁ
yaśo 'rthe dharma-sevanam

"The purpose of life will consist simply of filling one's stomach, and audacity will become equivalent to conclusive truth. If a man can even maintain his own family members, he will be honored as very expert, and religiosity will be measured by a person's reputation for material accomplishments." [*Śrīmad-Bhāgavatam* 12.2.6] So, if somehow one can eat very sumptuously, then he will think all his interests are fulfilled. People will be very hungry, with nothing to eat, and therefore if they can eat very sumptuously on one day, that will be the fulfillment of all their desires. The next symptom is *satyatve dhārṣṭyam eva hi:* Anyone who is expert at word jugglery will be considered very truthful. Another symptom, *dākṣyaṁ kuṭumba-bharaṇam:* One shall be considered very expert if he can maintain his family – his wife and children. In other words, this will become very difficult. In fact, it has already become difficult. To maintain a wife and two children is now a great burden. Therefore no one wants to marry.

The next verse describes what will happen when all the people have been thus infected by the poison of Kali-yuga.

evaṁ prajābhir duṣṭābhir
ākīrṇe kṣiti-maṇḍale
brahma-viṭ-kṣatra-śūdrāṇāṁ
yo balī bhavitā nṛpaḥ

It won't matter whether one is a *brāhmaṇa* [a learned and pure intellectual] or a *kṣatriya* [an administrator or soldier] or a *vaiśya* [a merchant or farmer] or a *śūdra* [a laborer] or a *caṇḍāla* [a dog-eater]. If one is powerful in getting votes, he will occupy the presidential or royal post. Formerly the system was that only a *kṣatriya* could occupy the royal throne, not a *brāhmaṇa, vaiśya,* or *śūdra.* But now, in the Kali-yuga, there is no such thing as a *kṣatriya* or a *brāhmaṇa.* Now we have democracy.

Anyone who can get your votes by hook or crook can occupy the post of leader. He may be rascal number one, but he will be given the supreme, exalted presidential post. The *Bhāgavatam* describes these leaders in the next verse:

prajā hi lubdhai rājanyair
nirghṛṇair dasyu-dharmabhiḥ
ācchinna-dāra-draviṇā
yāsyanti giri-kānanam

"The citizens will be so oppressed by merciless rogues in the guise of rulers that they will give up their spouses and property and flee to the hills and forests." [*Śrīmad-Bhāgavatam* 12.2.8] So, the men who acquire a government post by vote are mostly *lubdhai rājanyaiḥ,* greedy government men. *Nirghṛṇair dasyu:* Their business is plundering the public. And we actually see that every year the government men are exacting heavy taxes, and whatever money is received they divide among themselves, while the citizens' condition remains the same. Every government is doing that. Gradually, all people will feel so much harassed that *ācchinna-dāra-draviṇāḥ:* They will want to give up their family life (their wife and their money) and go to the forest. This we have also seen.

So, *kaler doṣa-nidhe rājan:* The faults of this age are just like an ocean. If you were put into the Pacific Ocean, you would not know how to save your life. Even if you were a very expert swimmer, it would not be possible for you to cross the Pacific Ocean. Similarly, the Kali-yuga is described in the *Bhāgavatam* as an ocean of faults. It is infected with so many anomalies that there seems to be no way out. But there is one medicine: *kīrtanād eva kṛṣṇasya mukta-saṅgaḥ paraṁ vrajet.* The *Bhāgavatam* explains that if you chant the name of Kṛṣṇa – the Hare Kṛṣṇa *mantra* – you will be relieved from the infection of this Kali-yuga.

Thank you very much.

Slaughterhouse Civilization

In June of 1974, at the Hare Kṛṣṇa movement's community in Paris, France, Śrīla Prabhupāda talks to a group of intimate disciples. He points out that modern civilization's hunger for meat and its extensive system of vicious and barbaric slaughtering facilities bring karmic reactions in the form of world wars, which Śrīla Prabhupāda refers to as "slaughterhouses for humankind."

Puṣṭa Kṛṣṇa Swami: The other day, Śrīla Prabhupāda, you were saying that in India, at least until recently, it was forbidden to eat cows – that those who ate meat would eat only lower animals like dogs and goats.
Śrīla Prabhupāda: Yes. For meat-eaters, that is what the Vedic culture recommends: "Eat dogs." As in Korea they are eating dogs, so you also can eat dogs. But don't eat cows until after they have died a natural death. We don't say, "Don't eat." You are so very fond of eating cows. All right, you can eat them, because after their death we have to give them to somebody, some living entity. Generally, cow carcasses are given to the vultures. But then, why only to the vultures? Why not to the modern "civilized" people, who are as good as vultures? [*Laughter.*]

These so-called civilized people – what is the difference between these rascals and vultures? The vultures also enjoy killing and then eating the dead body. "Make it dead and then enjoy" – people have become vultures. And their civilization is a vulture civilization. Animal-eaters – they're like jackals, vultures, dogs. Flesh is not proper food for human beings. Here in the Vedic culture is civilized food, human food: milk, fruit, vegetables, nuts, grains. Let them learn it. Uncivilized rogues, vultures, *rākṣasas* [demons] – and they're *leaders.*

Therefore I say that today the leaders are all fourth-class men. And that is why the whole world is in a chaotic condition. We require learned spiritual teachers – first-class men – to lead. My disciples are training to become first-class men. If people will take our advice, then everything will be all right. What is the use of fourth-class men leading a confused and chaotic society?

If I speak so frankly, people will be very angry. But basically, their leaders are all fourth class. First-class men are great devotees of the Lord, who can guide the administrators and the citizens through their words and practical example. Second-class men are administrative, military men, who look after the smooth running of the government and the safety of the citizens. And third-class men are farmers, who grow crops and protect the cows. But today who is protecting the cows? That is the third-class men's business. So therefore everyone is fourth class or lower. *Śva-viḍ-varāhoṣṭra-kharaiḥ saṁstutaḥ puruṣaḥ paśuḥ* [*Śrīmad-Bhāgavatam* 2.3.19]: People are living just like animals – without regulative, spiritual principles – and from among themselves they are electing the biggest animals. Anyone can do whatever he likes, whatever he thinks – no regulative principles.

But human life is meant for regulative principles. We are insisting that our students follow regulative principles – no meat-eating, no illicit sex, no intoxication, no gambling – just to make them real human beings. Without regulative principles it is animal life. Animal life.

In the human form of life, after passing through millions of lives in the plant and animal species, the spirit soul gets the chance to take up the *yoga* system – and *yoga* means strict regulative principles. *Indriya-saṁyamaḥ* – controlling the senses. That is the real *yoga* system. But today most people, though they may say they are practicing *yoga*, are misusing it. Just like the animals, they cannot control their senses. As human beings, they have higher intelligence; they should learn how to control the senses. This is human life. *Na yat-karṇa-pathopetaḥ:* One who has not heard the message of Kṛṣṇa, the Supreme Personality of Godhead – even for a moment – he's an animal. The general mass of people, unless they are trained systematically for a higher standard of life in spiritual values, are no better than animals. They are on the level of dogs, hogs, camels, and asses.

Modern university education practically prepares one to acquire a doggish mentality for accepting the service of a greater master. Like

the dogs, after finishing their so-called education the so-called educated persons move from door to door with applications for some service. We have this experience in India. There are so many educated men who are unemployed – because they have been educated as dogs. They must find a master; otherwise they have no power to work independently. Just like a dog – unless he finds a master, he is a street dog, loitering in the street.
Bhagavān dāsa: So many Ph.D.'s are graduating from school now that there are not enough jobs for them. So they have to take jobs as truck drivers or taxi drivers.
Yogeśvara dāsa: They're supposed to be the educated class too – *brāhmaṇas.*
Śrīla Prabhupāda: No, they are not *brāhmaṇas.* Those who give education in exchange for money – they are not *brāhmaṇas.* For instance, we are lecturing, educating people. We don't say, "Give us a salary." We simply ask them, "Please come." That is why we are cooking food and holding so many free festivals. "We'll give you food. We'll give you a comfortable seat. Please come and hear about self-realization and God consciousness." We are not asking money – "First of all pay the fee; then you can come and learn *Bhagavad-gītā.*" We never say that. But these so-called teachers who first of all bargain for a salary – "What salary will you give me?" – that is a dog's concern. That is not a *brāhmaṇa's* concern. A *brāhmaṇa* will never ask about a salary. A *brāhmaṇa* is eager to see that people are educated. "Take free education and be educated; be a human being" – this is a *brāhmaṇa's* concern: You see? I came here not to ask for any money but to give instruction.
Bhagavān dāsa: Today the priests are afraid to speak too strongly – or else they'll be fired and get no salary. And the politicians – they're also afraid to say what they really believe. They're afraid that they'll be voted out or get no more money to support themselves.
Śrīla Prabhupāda: The priests are after money. They are not first class; they are low-class men. This is the reason that Christianity has fallen down. The priests cannot speak straightforwardly. There is a straightforward commandment – "Thou shalt not kill." But because people are already killing, the priests are afraid to present the commandment straightforwardly. Now they are even granting man-to-man marriage, what to speak of other things. The priests are sermonizing on this idea

of man-to-man marriage. Just see how degraded they have become! Previously was there any conception like this, at least outside America? Nobody thought that a man could be married to another man. What is this? And the priests are supporting it. Do you know that? So what is their standard?

Jyotirmayī-devī dāsī: That priest who visited was telling you that he was asking all his parishioners to follow God's law. So you asked him if he was going to get them to follow the fifth commandment, the law against killing – including animal-killing and especially cow-killing.

Śrīla Prabhupāda: Yes, this is our proposal: "Why should you kill the cow? Let the cow be protected." You can take the cow's milk and use this milk for making so many nutritious, delicious preparations. Aside from that, as far as meat-eating is concerned, every cow will die – so you just wait a while, and there will be so many dead cows. Then you can take all the dead cows and eat. So how is this a bad proposal? If you say, "You are restraining us from meat-eating" – no, we don't restrain you. We simply ask you, "Don't kill. When the cow is dead, you can eat it."

Yogeśvara dāsa: You've pointed out that the cow is just like a mother.

Śrīla Prabhupāda: Yes. She gives us her milk.

Yogeśvara dāsa: But in the West now, when their parents grow old the people generally send them away to old age homes. So if people have no compassion even toward their own parents, how can we educate them to protect the cow?

Śrīla Prabhupāda: They don't have to protect the cow. *We* shall protect the cow. Simply we ask them, "Don't purchase meat from the slaughterhouse. We shall supply you the cow after her death." Where is the difficulty?

Satsvarūpa dāsa Goswami: Not enough meat fast enough – they're eating so much meat.

Śrīla Prabhupāda: "Not enough"? By killing the cows, how will you get any more meat? The total number of cows will remain the same. Simply wait for their natural death. That is the only restriction. You have got a limited number of cows. Either you wait for their death or you kill them at once – the number of cows is the same. So we simply ask you, "Don't kill them. Wait for their natural death and then take the meat." What is the difficulty? And we simply ask you, "As long as they're alive, let us take the cow's milk and prepare delicious foods for the whole human society."

Yogeśvara dāsa: If people don't kill the cows they will have even more meat, because that way the cows will have more time to reproduce more cows. If they don't kill the cows right away, there will be even more cows.

Śrīla Prabhupāda: More cows, yes. They'll have more cows. We simply request, "Don't kill. Don't maintain slaughterhouses." That is very sinful. It brings down very severe karmic reactions upon society. Stop these slaughterhouses. We don't say, "Stop eating meat." You can eat meat, but don't take it from the slaughterhouse, by killing. Simply wait, and you'll get the carcasses.

After all, how long will the cows live? Their maximum age is twenty years, and there are many cows who live only eighteen, sixteen, or ten years. So wait that much time; then regularly get dead cows and eat. What is the difficulty?

For the first few years you may not get quite as much as now. During that time you can eat some dogs and cats. [*Laughter.*] Yes. In Korea they eat dogs. What is the difference between here and Korea? You can also eat dogs for the time being. Or hogs. Eat hogs. We don't prohibit the killing of these less important animals. We neither sanction nor prohibit. But especially we request cow protection, because it is ordered by Lord Kṛṣṇa. *Go-rakṣya:* "Protect the cows." That is our duty.

And economically, also, it is very useful. Kṛṣṇa has not recommended this for nothing; it is not like that. Kṛṣṇa's order has meaning. The cows on our Hare Kṛṣṇa farms are giving more milk than other cows – because they are confident, "We will not be killed here." It is not like these rascals, these so-called Christians, say: "They have no soul; they have no intelligence." They *have* intelligence. In other places they do not give so much milk. But on our farms they are very jolly. As soon as the devotees call, they'll come. Yes – just like friends. And they are confident, "We'll not be killed." So they are jubilant, and they are giving much milk. Yes.

In Europe and America the cows are very good, but the cow-killing system is also very good. So you stop this. You simply request them, "You'll get the cow's flesh. As soon as she is dead, we shall supply you free of charge. You haven't got to pay so much money. You can get the flesh free and eat it then. Why are you killing? Stop these slaughterhouses." What is wrong with this proposal?

We don't want to stop trade or the production of grains and vegetables and fruit. But we want to stop these killing houses. It is very, very sinful. That is why all over the world they have so many wars. Every ten or fifteen years there is a big war – a wholesale slaughterhouse for humankind. But these rascals – they do not see it, that by the law of *karma,* every action must have its reaction.

You are killing innocent cows and other animals – nature will take revenge. Just wait. As soon as the time is right, nature will gather all these rascals and slaughter them. Finished. They'll fight amongst themselves – Protestants and Catholics, Russia and America, this one and that one. It is going on. Why? That is nature's law. Tit for tat. "You have killed. Now you kill *yourselves.*"

They are sending animals to the slaughterhouse, and now they'll create their own slaughterhouse. [*Imitating gunfire:*] *Tung! Tung!* Kill! Kill! You see? Just take Belfast, for example. The Roman Catholics are killing the Protestants, and the Protestants are killing the Catholics. This is nature's law. It's not necessary that you be sent to the ordinary slaughterhouse. You'll make a slaughterhouse at home. You'll kill your own child – abortion. This is nature's law. Who are these children being killed? They are these meat-eaters. They enjoyed themselves when so many animals were killed, and now they're being killed by their mothers. People do not know how nature is working. *If you kill, you must be killed.* If you kill the cow, who is your mother, then in some future lifetime your mother will kill you. Yes. The mother becomes the child, and the child becomes the mother.

Māṁ sa khādatīti māṁsaḥ. The Sanskrit word is *māṁsa. Mām* means "me," and *sa* means "he." I am killing this animal; I am eating him. And in my next lifetime he'll kill me and eat *me.* When the animal is sacrificed, this *mantra* is recited into the ear of the animal – "You are giving your life, so in your next life you will get the opportunity of becoming a human being. And I who am now killing you will become an animal, and you will kill me." So after understanding this *mantra,* who will be ready to kill an animal?

Bhagavān dāsa: Many people today are discussing this topic of reincarnation, but they don't understand the significance of the effects—

Śrīla Prabhupāda: How will they understand? All dull-headed fools and rascals, dressed like gentlemen. That's all. *Tāvac ca śobhate mūrkho yāvat kiñcin na bhāṣate.* A rascal, a fool, is prestigious as long as he does not speak. As soon as he speaks, his nature will be revealed – what he really is. Therefore that priest who came did not stay long. He did not want to expose himself.

Bhagavān dāsa: Less intelligent.

Śrīla Prabhupāda: Now, we must take to agricultural work – produce food and give protection to the cows. And if we produce a surplus, we can trade. It is a simple thing that we must do. Our people should live peacefully in farming villages, produce grain and fruit and vegetables, protect the cows, and work hard. And if there is a surplus, we can start restaurants. Kṛṣṇa conscious people will never be losers by following the instructions of Kṛṣṇa. They will live comfortably, without any material want, and *tyaktvā dehaṁ punar janma naiti* [*Bhagavad-gītā* 4.90]: After leaving this body they will go directly to God. This is our way of life.

So open restaurants in any part of any city and make nice *kacaurīs, śrīkhaṇḍa, purīs, halavā,* and so many other delicacies. And people will purchase them. They will come and sit down. I have given the format: "Every preparation is ready – you can sit down. This is our standard charge for a meal. Now, as much as you like you take. You can take one helping or two, three, four – as much as you like. But don't waste. Don't waste." Suppose one man eats a single savory and another man eats four savories. That does not mean we shall charge more. Same charge. Same charge. "You can sit down, eat to your heart's content, and be satisfied." Let everyone be satisfied. "We will supply. Simply don't waste." This is our program. Not that each time – just as the hotel does – each time a plate is brought, immediately a bill. No. "You can sit down and eat to your satisfaction. The charge stays the same."

Bhagavān dāsa: I think people will leave the restaurant with their pockets full of savories. [*Laughter.*]

Śrīla Prabhupāda: That we shall not allow.

Bhagavān dāsa: You were telling us one time that in India, if a person has a mango orchard and you're hungry you can come in and eat, but you cannot take any away with you.

Śrīla Prabhupāda: Yes. If you have a garden and somebody says, "I want to eat some fruit," you'll say, "Yes, come on. Take as much fruit as you like." But he should not gather up more than he can eat and take it away. Any number of men can come and eat to their satisfaction. The farmers do not even prohibit the monkeys – "All right, let them come in. After all, it is God's property." This is the Kṛṣṇa conscious system: If an animal, say a monkey, comes to your garden to eat, don't prohibit him. He is also part and parcel of Kṛṣṇa. If you prohibit him, where will he eat?

I have another story; this one was told by my father. My father's elder brother was running a cloth shop. Before closing the shop my uncle would put out a basin filled with rice. Of course, as in any village, there were rats. But the rats would take the rice and not cut even a single cloth. Cloth is very costly. If even one cloth had been cut by a rat, then it would have been a great loss. So with a few pennies' worth of rice, he saved many dollars' worth of cloth. This Kṛṣṇa culture is practical. "They are also part and parcel of God. Give them food. They'll not create any disturbance. Give them food."

Everyone has an obligation to feed whoever is hungry – even if it is a tiger. Once a certain spiritual teacher was living in the jungle. His disciples knew, "The tigers will never come and disturb us, because our teacher keeps some milk a little distance from the *āśrama,* and the tigers come and drink and go away."

The teacher would call, "You! Tiger! You can come and take your milk here!" [*Laughter.*] And they would come and take the milk and go away. And they would never attack any members of the *āśrama*. The teacher would say, "They are my men – don't harm them."

I remember seeing at the World's Fair that a man had trained a lion. And the man was playing with that lion just like one plays with a dog. These animals can understand, "This man loves me. He gives me food; he is my friend." They also appreciate.

When Haridāsa Ṭhākura was living in a cave and chanting Hare Kṛṣṇa, a big snake who also lived there decided to go away. The snake knew – "He's a saintly person. He should not be disturbed. Let me go away." And from *Bhagavad-gītā* we understand, *īśvaraḥ sarva-bhūtānāṁ hṛd-deśe* – Kṛṣṇa is in everyone's heart, and He is dictating. So Kṛṣṇa can dictate peace and harmony to the animals, to the serpent, to everyone. [*Śrīla Prabhupāda pauses reflectively.*]

The Vedic culture offers so many nice, delicious foods, and mostly they are made with milk products. But these so-called civilized people – they do not know. They kill the cows and throw the milk away to the hogs, and they are proud of their civilization – like jackals and vultures. Actually, this Kṛṣṇa consciousness movement will transform the uncivilized people and bring the whole world to real civilization.

A Formula for Peace

This article by Śrīla Prabhupāda was first published in 1956 in New Delhi, India, in Back to Godhead, *the magazine he founded in 1944. Appealing to his Indian readers to "employ everything in transcendental service for the interest of the Lord," he concludes that "this alone can bring the desired peace."*

In the revealed scriptures the Supreme Lord is described as *sac-cid-ānanda-vigraha. Sat* means "eternal," *cit* means "fully cognizant," *ānanda* means "joyful," and *vigraha* means "a specific personality." Therefore the Lord, or the Supreme Godhead, who is one without a second, is an eternal, joyful personality with a full sense of His own identity. That is a concise description of the Supreme Lord, and no one is equal to or greater than Him.

The living entities, or *jīvas,* are minute samples of the Supreme Lord, and therefore we find in their activities the desire for eternal existence, the desire for knowledge of everything, and an urge for seeking happiness in diverse ways. These three qualities of the living being are minutely visible in human society, but they are increased and enjoyed one hundred times more by the beings who reside in the upper planets, which are called Bhūrloka, Svarloka, Janaloka, Tapoloka, Maharloka, Brahmaloka, and so forth.

But even the standard of enjoyment on the highest planet in the material world, which is thousands and thousands of times superior to what we enjoy on this earth, is also described as insignificant in comparison to the spiritual bliss enjoyed in the company of the Supreme Lord. His loving service in different mellows (relationships) makes even the enjoyment of merging with the impersonal spiritual effulgence as insignificant as a drop of water compared with the ocean.

Every living being is ambitious to have the topmost level of enjoyment in the material world, and yet one is always unhappy here. This unhappiness is present on all the above-mentioned planets, in spite of a long life span and high standards of comfort.

That is the law of material nature. One can increase the duration of life and standard of comfort to the highest capacity, and yet by the law of material nature one will be unhappy. The reason is that the quality of happiness suitable for our constitution is different from the happiness derived from material activities. The living entity is a minute particle of *sac-cid-ānanda-vigraha,* and therefore he necessarily has a propensity for joyfulness that is spiritual in quality. But he is vainly trying to derive his spiritual joyfulness from the foreign atmosphere of the material nature.

A fish that is taken out of the water cannot be happy by any arrangement for happiness on the land – it must have an aquatic habitation. In the same way, the minute *sac-cid-ānanda* living entity cannot be really happy through any amount of material planning conceived by his illusioned brain. Therefore, the living entity must be given a different type of happiness, a transcendental happiness, which is called spiritual bliss. Our ambitions should be aimed at enjoying spiritual bliss and not material happiness.

The ambition for spiritual bliss is good, but the method of attaining this standard is not merely to negate material happiness. Theoretical negation of material activities, as propounded by Śrīpāda Śaṅkarācārya, may be relevant for an insignificant section of men, but the devotional activities propounded by Śrī Caitanya Mahāprabhu are the best and surest way of attaining spiritual bliss. In fact, they change the very face of material nature.

Hankering after material happiness is called lust, and in the long run lustful activities are sure to meet with frustration. The body of a venomous snake is very cool. But if a man wants to enjoy the coolness of the snake's body and therefore garlands himself with the snake, then surely he will be killed by the snake's bite. The material senses are like snakes, and indulging in so-called material happiness surely kills one's spiritual self-awareness. Therefore a sane man should be ambitious to find the real source of happiness.

Once, a foolish man who had no experience of the taste of

sugarcane was told by a friend to taste its sweetness. When the man inquired about sugarcane's appearance, the friend imperfectly informed him that sugarcane resembles a bamboo stick. The foolish man thus began trying to extract sugarcane juice from a bamboo stick, but naturally he was baffled in his attempt.

That is the position of the illusioned living being in his search for eternal happiness within the material world, which is not only full of miseries but also transient and flickering. In the *Bhagavad-gītā,* the material world is described as full of miseries. The ambition for happiness is good, but the attempt to derive it from inert matter by so-called scientific arrangements is an illusion. Befooled persons cannot understand this. The *Gītā* [16.13] describes how a person driven by the lust for material happiness thinks, "So much wealth do I have today, and I will gain more according to my schemes. So much is mine now, and it will increase in the future."

The atheistic, or godless, civilization is a huge affair of sense gratification, and everyone is now mad after money to keep up an empty show. Everyone is seeking money because that is the medium of exchange for sense-gratificatory objects. To expect peace in such an atmosphere of gold-rush pandemonium is a utopian dream. As long as there is even a slight tinge of madness for sense gratification, peace will remain far, far away. The reason is that by nature everyone is an eternal servitor of the Supreme Lord, and therefore we cannot enjoy anything for our personal interest. We have to employ everything in transcendental service for the interest of the Lord. This alone can bring about the desired peace. A part of the body cannot make itself satisfied; it can only serve the whole body and derive satisfaction from that service. But now everyone is busy in self-interested business, and no one is prepared to serve the Lord. That is the basic cause of material existence.

From the highest executive administrator down to the lowest sweeper in the street, everyone is working with the thought of unlawful accumulation of wealth. But to work merely for one's self-interest is unlawful and destructive. Even the cultivation of spiritual realization merely for one's self-interest is unlawful and destructive.

As a result of all the unlawful money-making, there is no scarcity of money in the world. But there is a scarcity of peace. Since the whole of our human energy has been diverted to this money-making, the money-making capacity of the total population has certainly increased. But the result is that such an unrestricted and unlawful inflation of money has created a bad economy and has enabled us to manufacture huge, costly weapons that threaten to destroy the very result of such money-making.

Instead of enjoying peace, the leaders of big money-making countries are now making big plans how they can save themselves from the modern destructive weapons, and yet a huge sum of money is being thrown into the sea for experiments with such dreadful weapons. Such experiments are being carried out not only at huge monetary costs, but also at the cost of many poor lives, thereby binding such nations to the laws of *karma*. That is the illusion of material nature. As a result of the impulse for sense gratification, money is earned by spoiled energy, and it is then spent for the destruction of the human race. The energy of the human race is thus spoiled by the law of nature because that energy is diverted from the service of the Lord, who is actually the owner of all energies.

Wealth derives from mother Lakṣmī, or the goddess of fortune. As the Vedic literatures explain, the goddess of fortune is meant to serve Lord Nārāyaṇa, the source of all the *naras,* or living beings. The *naras* are also meant to serve Nārāyaṇa, the Supreme Lord, under the guidance of the goddess of fortune. The living being cannot enjoy the goddess of fortune without serving Nārāyaṇa, or Kṛṣṇa, and therefore whoever desires to enjoy her wrongly will be punished by the laws of nature, and the money itself will become the cause of destruction instead of being the cause of peace and prosperity.

Such unlawfully accumulated money is now being snatched away from the miserly citizens by various methods of state taxation for the various national and international war funds, which spend the money in a wasteful manner. The citizen is no longer satisfied with just enough money to maintain his family nicely and cultivate spiritual knowledge, both of which are essential in human life. He now wants money unlimitedly for satisfying insatiable desires, and in proportion to his unlawful desires his accumulated money is now being taken away by the agents of the illusory nature in the shape of medical practitioners, lawyers, tax collectors, societies, institutions, and so-called religionists, as well as by famines, earthquakes, and many other such calamities.

One miser who, under the dictation of the illusory nature, hesitated to purchase a copy of *Back to Godhead* spent twenty-five hundred dollars for a week's supply of medicine and then died. A similar thing happened when a man who refused to spend a cent for the service of the Lord wasted thirty-five hundred dollars in a legal suit between the members of his household. That is the law of nature. If money is not devoted to the service of the Lord, by the law of nature it must be spent as spoiled energy in the fight against legal problems, diseases, and so on. Foolish people have no eyes to see such facts, so necessarily the laws of the Supreme Lord befool them.

The laws of nature do not allow us to accept more money than is required for proper maintenance. There is ample arrangement by the law of nature to provide every living being with his due share of food and shelter, but the insatiable lust of the human being has disturbed the whole arrangement of the almighty father of all species of life.

By the arrangement of the Supreme Lord, there is an ocean of salt, because salt is necessary for the living being. In the same manner, God has arranged for sufficient air and light, which are also essential for the living being. One can collect any amount of salt from the storehouse, but one cannot take more salt than he needs. If he takes more salt he spoils the broth, and if he takes less salt his eatables become tasteless. On the other hand, if he takes only what he absolutely requires, the food is tasty, and he is healthy. So ambition for wealth, for more than we need, is harmful, just as eating more salt than we absolutely need is harmful. That is the law of nature.

7

Perspectives on Science and Philosophy

Plato: Goodness and Government

In 1972 and 1973, Śrīla Prabhupāda held a series of philosophical discussions with his personal secretary, Śyāmasundara, while traveling around the world. These sessions were recorded and published to provide an understanding of Western philosophy, psychology, and science from the viewpoint of the timeless teachings of India's Vedic literature. In the following conversation, the striking similarities between Plato's ideal state and that outlined in the Bhagavad-gīta *prompt one to ask, "Could Plato have gotten his ideas from India's ancient* Vedas?"

Śyāmasundara: Plato believed society can enjoy prosperity and harmony only if it places people in working categories or classes according to their natural abilities. He thought people should find out their natural abilities and use those abilities to their fullest capacity – as administrators, as military men, or as craftsmen. Most important, the head of state should not be an average or mediocre man. Instead, society should be led by a very wise and good man – a "philosopher king" – or a group of very wise and good men.

Śrīla Prabhupāda: This idea appears to be taken from the *Bhagavad-gītā*, where Kṛṣṇa says that the ideal society has four divisions: *brāhmaṇas* [intellectuals], *kṣatriyas* [warriors and administrators], *vaiśyas* [merchants and farmers], and *śūdras* [laborers]. These divisions come about by the influence of the modes of nature. Everyone, both in human society and in animal society, is influenced by the modes of material nature [*sattva-guṇa, rajo-guṇa,* and *tamo-guṇa,* or goodness, passion, and ignorance]. By scientifically classifying men according to these qualities, society can become perfect. But if we place a man in the mode of ignorance in a philosopher's post, or put a philosopher to work as an ordinary laborer, havoc will result.

In the *Bhagavad-gītā* Kṛṣṇa says that the *brāhmaṇas* – the most intelligent men, who are interested in transcendental knowledge and philosophy – should be given the topmost posts, and under their instructions the *kṣatriyas* [administrators] should work. The administrators should see that there is law and order and that everyone is doing his duty. The next section is the productive class, the *vaiśyas,* who engage in agriculture and cow protection. And finally there are the *śūdras,* common laborers who help the other sections. This is Vedic civilization – people living simply, on agriculture and cow protection. If you have enough milk, grains, fruits, and vegetables, you can live very nicely.

The *Śrīmad-Bhāgavatam* compares the four divisions of society to the different parts of the body – the head, the arms, the belly, and the legs. Just as all parts of the body cooperate to keep the body fit, in the ideal state all sections of society cooperate under the leadership of the *brāhmaṇas.* Comparatively, the head is the most important part of the body, for it gives directions to the other parts of the body. Similarly, the ideal state functions under the directions of the *brāhmaṇas,* who are not personally interested in political affairs or administration because they have a higher duty. At present this Kṛṣṇa consciousness movement is training *brāhmaṇas.* If the administrators take our advice and conduct the state in a Kṛṣṇa conscious way, there will be an ideal society throughout the world.

Śyāmasundara: How does modern society differ from the Vedic ideal?

Śrīla Prabhupāda: Now there is large-scale industrialization, which means exploitation of one man by another. Such industry was unknown in Vedic civilization – it was unnecessary. In addition, modern civilization has taken to slaughtering and eating animals, which is barbarous. It is not even human.

In Vedic civilization, when a person was unfit to rule he was deposed. For instance, King Vena proved to be an unfit king. He was simply interested in hunting. Of course, *kṣatriyas* are allowed to hunt, but not whimsically. They are not allowed to kill many birds and beasts unnecessarily, as King Vena was doing and as people do today. At that time the intelligent *brāhmaṇas* objected and immediately killed him with a curse.

Formerly, the *brāhmaṇas* had so much power that they could kill simply by cursing; weapons were unnecessary.

At present, however – because the head of the social body is missing – it is a dead body. The head is very important, and our Kṛṣṇa consciousness movement is attempting to create some *brāhmaṇas* who will form the head of society. Then the administrators will be able to rule very nicely under the instructions of the philosophers and theologians – that is, under the instructions of God conscious people. A God conscious *brāhmaṇa* would never advise opening slaughterhouses. But now, the many rascals heading the government allow animal slaughter. When Mahārāja Parīkṣit saw a degraded man trying to kill a cow, he immediately drew his sword and said, "Who are you? Why are you trying to kill this cow?" He was a real king. Nowadays, unqualified men have taken the presidential post. And although they may pose themselves as very religious, they are simply rascals. Why? Because under their noses thousands of cows are being killed, while they collect a good salary. Any leader who is at all religious should resign his post in protest if cow slaughter goes on under his rule. Since people do not know that these administrators are rascals, they are suffering. And the people are also rascals because they are voting for these bigger rascals. It is Plato's view that the government should be ideal, and this is the ideal: The saintly philosophers should be at the head of the state; according to their advice the politicians should rule; under the protection of the politicians, the productive class should provide the necessities of life; and the laborer class should help. This is the scientific division of society that Kṛṣṇa advocates in the *Bhagavad-gītā* [4.13]: *cātur-varṇyaṁ mayā sṛṣṭaṁ guṇa-karma-vibhāgaśaḥ*. "According to the three modes of material nature and the work ascribed to them, the four divisions of human society were created by Me."

Śyāmasundara: Plato also observed social divisions. However, he advocated three divisions. One class consisted of the guardians, men of wisdom who governed society. Another class consisted of the warriors, who were courageous and who protected the rest of society. And the third class consisted of the artisans, who performed their services obediently and worked only to satisfy their appetites.

Śrīla Prabhupāda: Yes, human society does have this threefold division, also. The first-class man is in the mode of goodness, the second-class man is in the mode of passion, and the third-class man is in the mode of ignorance.

Śyāmasundara: Plato's understanding of the social order was based on his observation that man has a threefold division of intelligence, courage, and appetite. He said that the soul has these three qualities.

Śrīla Prabhupāda: That is a mistake. The soul does not have any material qualities. The soul is pure, but because of his contact with the different qualities of material nature, he is "dressed" in various bodies. This Kṛṣṇa consciousness movement aims at removing this material dress. Our first instruction is "You are not this body." It appears that in his practical understanding Plato identified the soul with the bodily dress, and that does not show very good intelligence.

Śyāmasundara: Plato believed that man's position is marginal – between matter and spirit – and therefore he also stressed the development of the body. He thought that everyone should be educated from an early age, and that part of that education should be gymnastics – to keep the body fit.

Śrīla Prabhupāda: This means that in practice Plato very strongly identified the self as the body. What was Plato's idea of education?

Śyāmasundara: To awaken the student to his natural position – whatever his natural abilities or talents are.

Śrīla Prabhupāda: And what is that natural position?

Śyāmasundara: The position of moral goodness. In other words, Plato thought everyone should be educated to work in whatever way is best suited to awaken his natural moral goodness.

Śrīla Prabhupāda: But moral goodness is not enough, because simple morality will not satisfy the soul. One has to go above morality – to Kṛṣṇa consciousness. Of course, in this material world morality is taken as the highest principle, but there is another platform, which is called the transcendental (*vasudeva*) platform. Man's highest perfection is on that platform, and this is confirmed in *Śrīmad-Bhāgavatam*. However, because Western philosophers have no information of the *vasudeva* platform, they consider the material mode of goodness to be the highest perfection and the end of morality. But in this world even moral goodness is infected by the lower modes of ignorance and passion. You cannot find pure goodness (*śuddha-sattva*) in this material world, for pure goodness is the transcendental platform. To come to the platform of pure goodness, which is the ideal, one has to undergo austerities (*tapasā brahmacaryeṇa śamena ca damena ca*). One has to practice celibacy and control the mind and senses. If he has money, he should distribute it in charity. Also, one should always be very clean. In this way one can rise to the platform of pure goodness.

There is another process for coming to the platform of pure goodness – and that is Kṛṣṇa consciousness. If one becomes Kṛṣṇa conscious, all the good qualities automatically develop in him. Automatically he leads a life of celibacy, controls his mind and senses, and has a charitable disposition. In this age of Kali, people cannot possibly be trained to engage in austerity. Formerly, a *brahmacārī* [celibate student] would undergo austere training. Even though he might be from a royal or learned family, a *brahmacārī* would humble himself and serve the spiritual master as a menial servant. He would immediately do whatever the spiritual master ordered. The *brahmacārī* would beg alms from door to door and bring them to the spiritual master, claiming nothing for himself. Whatever he earned he would give to the spiritual master, because the spiritual master would not spoil the money by spending it for sense gratification – he would use it for Kṛṣṇa. This is austerity. The *brahmacārī* would also observe celibacy, and because he followed the directions of the spiritual master, his mind and senses were controlled.

Today, however, this austerity is very difficult to follow, so Śrī Caitanya Mahāprabhu has given the process of taking to Kṛṣṇa consciousness directly. In this case, one need simply chant Hare Kṛṣṇa, Hare Kṛṣṇa, Kṛṣṇa Kṛṣṇa, Hare Hare/ Hare Rāma, Hare Rāma, Rāma Rāma, Hare Hare and follow the regulative principles given by the spiritual master. Then one immediately rises to the platform of pure goodness.

Śyāmasundara: Plato thought the state should train citizens to be virtuous. His system of education went like this: For the first three years of life, the child should play and strengthen his body. From three to six, the child should learn religious stories. From seven to ten, he should learn gymnastics; from ten to thirteen, reading and writing; from fourteen to sixteen, poetry and music; from sixteen to eighteen, mathematics. And from eighteen to twenty, he should undergo military drill. From twenty to thirty-five, those who are scientific and philosophical should remain in school and continue learning, and the warriors should engage in military exercises.

Śrīla Prabhupāda: Is this educational program for all men, or are there different types of education for different men?

Śyāmasundara: No, this is for everyone.

Śrīla Prabhupāda: This is not very good. If a boy is intelligent and inclined to philosophy and theology, why should he be forced to undergo military training?

Śyāmasundara: Well, Plato said that everyone should undergo two years of military drill.

Śrīla Prabhupāda: But why should someone waste two years? No one should waste even two days. This is nonsense – imperfect ideas.

Śyāmasundara: Plato said this type of education reveals what category a person belongs to. He did have the right idea that one belongs to a particular class according to his qualification.

Śrīla Prabhupāda: Yes, that we also say, but we disagree that everyone should go through the same training. The spiritual master should judge the tendency or disposition of the student at the start of his education. He should be able to see whether a boy is fit for military training, administration, or philosophy, and then he should fully train the boy according to his particular tendency. If one is naturally inclined to philosophical study, why should he waste his time in the military? And if one is naturally inclined to military training, why should he waste his time with other things? Arjuna belonged to a *kṣatriya* [warrior] family. He and his brothers were never trained as philosophers. Droṇācārya was their master and teacher, and although he was a *brāhmaṇa,* he taught them *Dhanur Veda* [military science], not *brahma-vidyā. Brahma-vidyā* is theistic philosophy. No one should be trained in everything; that is a waste of time. If one is inclined toward production, business, or agriculture, he should be trained in those fields. If one is philosophical, he should be trained as a philosopher. If one is militaristic, he should be trained as a warrior. And if one has ordinary ability, he should remain a *śūdra,* or laborer. This is stated by Nārada Muni in *Śrīmad-Bhāgavatam: yasya yal-lakṣaṇaṁ proktam.* The four classes of society are recognized by their symptoms and qualifications. Nārada Muni also says that one should be selected for training according to his qualifications. Even if one is born in a *brāhmaṇa* family, he should be considered a *śūdra* if his qualifications are those of a *śūdra*. And if one is born in a *śūdra* family, he should be taken as a *brāhmaṇa* if his symptoms are brahminical. The spiritual master should be expert enough to recognize the tendencies of the student and immediately train him in that line. This is perfect education.

Śyāmasundara: Plato believed that the student's natural tendency wouldn't come out unless he practiced everything.

Śrīla Prabhupāda: No, that is wrong – because the soul is continuous, and therefore everyone has some tendency from his previous birth. I think Plato didn't realize this continuity of the soul from body to body. According to the Vedic culture, immediately after a boy's birth astrologers should calculate what category he belongs to. Astrology can help if there is a first-class astrologer. Such an astrologer can tell what line a boy is coming from and how he should be trained. Plato's method of education was imperfect because it was based on speculation.

Śyāmasundara: Plato observed that a particular combination of the three modes of nature is acting in each individual.

Śrīla Prabhupāda: Then why did he say that everyone should be trained in the same way?

Śyāmasundara: Because he claimed that the person's natural abilities will not manifest unless he is given a chance to try everything. He saw that some people listen primarily to their intelligence, and he said they are governed by the head. He saw that some people have an aggressive disposition, and he said such courageous types are governed by the heart – by passion. And he saw that some people, who are inferior, simply want to feed their appetites. He said these people are animalistic, and he believed they are governed by the liver.

Śrīla Prabhupāda: That is not a perfect description. Everyone has a liver, a heart, and all the bodily limbs. Whether one is in the mode of goodness, passion, or ignorance depends on one's training and on the qualities he acquired during his previous life. According to the Vedic process, at birth one is immediately given a classification. Psychological and physical symptoms are considered, and generally it is ascertained from birth that a child has a particular tendency. However, this tendency may change according to circumstances, and if one does not fulfill his assigned role, he can be transferred to another class. One may have had brahminical training in a previous life, and he may exhibit brahminical symptoms in this life, but one should not think that because he has taken birth in a *brāhmaṇa* family he is automatically a *brāhmaṇa*. A person may be born in a *brāhmaṇa* family and be a *śūdra*. It is a question not of birth but of qualification.

Śyāmasundara: Plato also believed that one must qualify for his post. His system of government was very democratic. He thought everyone should be given a chance to occupy the different posts.

Śrīla Prabhupāda: Actually, we are the most democratic because we are giving everyone a chance to become a first-class *brāhmaṇa*. The Kṛṣṇa consciousness movement is giving even the lowest member of society a chance to become a *brāhmaṇa* by becoming Kṛṣṇa conscious. *Caṇḍālo 'pi dvija-śreṣṭho hari-bhakti-parāyaṇaḥ:* Although one may be born in a family of *caṇḍālas* [dog-eaters], as soon as he becomes God conscious, Kṛṣṇa conscious, he can be elevated to the highest position. Kṛṣṇa says that everyone can go back home, back to Godhead. *Samo 'haṁ sarva-bhūteṣu:* "I am equal to everyone. Everyone can come to Me. There is no hindrance."

Śyāmasundara: What is the purpose of the social orders and the state government?

Śrīla Prabhupāda: The ultimate purpose is to make everyone Kṛṣṇa conscious. That is the perfection of life, and the entire social structure should be molded with this aim in view. Of course, not everyone can become fully Kṛṣṇa conscious in one lifetime, just as not all students in a university can attain the Ph.D. degree in one attempt. But the idea of perfection is to pass the Ph.D. examination, and therefore the Ph.D. courses should be maintained. Similarly, an institution like this Kṛṣṇa consciousness movement should be maintained so that at least some people can attain and everyone can approach the ultimate goal – Kṛṣṇa consciousness.

Śyāmasundara: So the goal of the state government is to help everyone become Kṛṣṇa conscious?

Śrīla Prabhupāda: Yes, Kṛṣṇa consciousness is the highest goal. Therefore, everyone should help this movement and take advantage of it. Regardless of his work, everyone can come to the temple. The instructions are for everyone, and *prasādam* is distributed to everyone. Therefore, there is no difficulty. Everyone can contribute to this Kṛṣṇa consciousness movement. The *brāhmaṇas* can contribute their intelligence; the *kṣatriyas* their charity; the *vaiśyas* their grain, milk, fruits, and flowers; and the *śūdras* their bodily service. By such joint effort, everyone can reach the same goal – Kṛṣṇa consciousness, the perfection of life.

Shortcomings of Marxism

Twenty years before the fall of the Berlin Wall, Śrīla Prabhupāda explains why communism must fail and predicts the end of the Soviet Union. "A classless society is possible only when Kṛṣṇa is in the center," says Śrīla Prabhupāda. "The real change occurs when we say, 'Nothing belongs to me, everything belongs to God.' . . . So Kṛṣṇa consciousness is the final revolution."

Śyāmasundara: Karl Marx contended that philosophers have only interpreted the world; the point is to change it. His philosophy is often called "dialectical materialism" because it comes from the dialectic of George Hegel – thesis, antithesis, and synthesis. When applied to society, his philosophy is known as communism. His idea is that for many generations, the bourgeoisie [the property owners] have competed with the proletariat [the working class], and that this conflict will terminate in the communist society. In other words, the workers will overthrow the capitalistic class and establish a so-called dictatorship of the proletariat, which will finally become a classless society.

Śrīla Prabhupāda: But how is a classless society possible? Men naturally fall into different classes. Your nature is different from mine, so how can we artificially be brought to the same level?

Śyāmasundara: His idea is that human nature, or ideas, are molded by the means of production. Therefore everyone can be trained to participate in the classless society.

Śrīla Prabhupāda: Then training is required?

Śyāmasundara: Yes.

Śrīla Prabhupāda: And what will be the center of training for this classless society? What will be the motto?

Śyāmasundara: The motto is "From each according to his ability, to

each according to his need." The idea is that everyone would contribute something, and everyone would get what he needed.
Śrīla Prabhupāda: But everyone's contribution is different. A scientific man contributes something, and a philosopher contributes something else. The cow contributes milk, and the dog contributes service as a watchdog. Even the trees, the birds, the beasts – everyone is contributing something. So, by nature a reciprocal arrangement is already there among social classes. How can there be a classless society?
Śyāmasundara: Well, Marx's idea is that the means of production will be owned in common. No one would have an advantage over anyone else, and thus one person could not exploit another. Marx is thinking in terms of profit.
Śrīla Prabhupāda: First we must know what profit actually is. For example, the American hippies already had "profit." They were from the best homes, their fathers were rich – they had everything. Yet they were not satisfied; they rejected it. No, this idea of a classless society based on profit-sharing is imperfect. Besides, the communists have not created a classless society. We have seen in Moscow how a poor woman will wash the streets while her boss sits comfortably in his car. So where is the classless society? As long as society is maintained, there must be some higher and lower classification. But if the central point of society is one, then whether one works in a lower or a higher position, he doesn't care. For example, our body has different parts – the head, the legs, the hands – but everything works for the stomach.
Śyāmasundara: Actually, the Russians supposedly have the same idea: they claim the common worker is just as glorious as the top scientist or manager.
Śrīla Prabhupāda: But in Moscow we have seen that not everyone is satisfied. One boy who came to us was very unhappy because in Russia young boys are not allowed to go out at night.
Śyāmasundara: The Russian authorities would say that he has an improper understanding of Marxist philosophy.
Śrīla Prabhupāda: That "improper understanding" is inevitable. They will never be able to create a classless society because, as I have already explained, everyone's mentality is different.
Śyāmasundara: Marx says that if everyone is engaged according to his

abilities in a certain type of production, and everyone works for the central interest, then everyone's ideas will become uniform.

Śrīla Prabhupāda: Therefore we must find out the real central interest. In our International Society for Krishna Consciousness, everyone has a central interest in Kṛṣṇa. Therefore one person is speaking, another person is typing, another is going to the press or washing the dishes, and no one is grudging, because they are all convinced they are serving Kṛṣṇa.

Śyāmasundara: Marx's idea is that the center is the state.

Śrīla Prabhupāda: But the state cannot be perfect. If the Russian state is perfect, then why was Khrushchev driven from power? He was elected premier. Why was he driven from power?

Śyāmasundara: Because he was not fulfilling the aims of the people.

Śrīla Prabhupāda: Well, then, what is the guarantee the next premier will do that? There is no guarantee. The same thing will happen again and again. Because the center, Khrushchev, was imperfect, people begrudged their labor. The same thing is going on in noncommunist countries as well. The government is changed, the prime minister is deposed, the president is impeached. So what is the real difference between Russian communism and other political systems? What is happening in other countries is also happening in Russia, only they call it by a different name. When we talked with Professor Kotovsky of Moscow University, we told him he had to surrender: either he must surrender to Kṛṣṇa or to Lenin, but he must surrender. He was taken aback at this.

Śyāmasundara: From studying history, Marx concluded that the characteristics of culture, the social structure, and even the thoughts of the people are determined by the means of economic production.

Śrīla Prabhupāda: How does he account for all the social disruption in countries like America, which is so advanced in economic production?

Śyāmasundara: He says that capitalism is a decadent form of economic production because it relies on the exploitation of one class by another.

Śrīla Prabhupāda: But there is exploitation in the communist countries also. Khrushchev was driven out of power because he was exploiting his position. He was giving big government posts to his son and son-in-law.

Śyāmasundara: He was deviating from the doctrine.

Śrīla Prabhupāda: But since any leader can deviate, how will perfection come? First the person in the center must be perfect, then his dictations will be correct. Otherwise, if the leaders are all imperfect men, what is the use of changing this or that? The corruption will continue.

Śyāmasundara: Presumably the perfect leader would be the one who practiced Marx's philosophy without deviation.

Śrīla Prabhupāda: But Marx's philosophy is also imperfect! His proposal for a classless society is unworkable. There must be one class of men to administer the government and one class of men to sweep the streets. How can there be a classless society? Why should a sweeper be satisfied seeing someone else in the administrative post? He will think, "He is forcing me to work as a sweeper in the street while he sits comfortably in a chair." In our International Society, I am also holding the superior post: I am sitting in a chair, and you are offering me garlands and the best food. Why? *Because you see a perfect man whom you can follow.* That mentality must be there. Everyone in the society must be able to say, "Yes, here is a perfect man. Let him sit in a chair, and let us all bow down and work like menials." Where is that perfect man in the communist countries?

Śyāmasundara: The Russians claim that Lenin is a perfect man.

Śrīla Prabhupāda: Lenin? But no one is following Lenin. Lenin's only perfection was that he overthrew the czar's government. What other perfection has he shown? The people are not happy simply reading Lenin's books. I studied the people in Moscow. They are unhappy. The government cannot force them to be happy artificially. Unless there is a perfect, ideal man in the center, there cannot possibly be a classless society.

Śyāmasundara: Perhaps they see the workers and the managers in the same way that we do – in the absolute sense. Since everyone is serving the state, the sweeper is as good as the administrator.

Śrīla Prabhupāda: But unless the state gives perfect satisfaction to the people, there will always be distinctions between higher and lower classes. In the Russian state, that sense of perfection in the center is lacking.

Śyāmasundara: Their goal is the production of material goods for the enhancement of human well-being.

Śrīla Prabhupāda: That is useless! Economic production in America has no comparison in the world, yet still people are dissatisfied. The young men are confused. It is nonsensical to think that simply by increasing production everyone will become satisfied. No one will be satisfied. Man is not meant simply for eating. He has mental necessities, intellectual necessities, spiritual necessities. In India many people sit alone silently in the jungle and practice *yoga*. They do not require anything. How will increased production satisfy them? If someone were to say to them, "If you give up this *yoga* practice, I will give you two hundred bags of rice," they would laugh at the proposal. It is animalistic to think that simply by increasing production everyone will become satisfied. Real happiness does not depend on either production or starvation, but upon peace of mind. For example, if a child is crying but the mother does not know why, the child will not stop simply by giving him some milk. Sometimes this actually happens: the mother cannot understand why her child is crying, and though she is giving him her breast, he continues to cry. Similarly, dissatisfaction in human society is not caused solely by low economic production. That is nonsense. There are many causes of dissatisfaction. The practical example is America, where there is sufficient production of everything, yet the young men are becoming hippies. They are dissatisfied, confused. No, simply by increasing economic production people will not become satisfied. Marx's knowledge is insufficient. Perhaps because he came from a country where people were starving, he had that idea.

Śyāmasundara: Yes, now we've seen that production of material goods alone will not make people happy.

Śrīla Prabhupāda: Because they do not know that real happiness comes from spiritual understanding. That understanding is given in the *Bhagavad-gītā:* God is the supreme enjoyer, and He is the proprietor of everything. We are not actually enjoyers; we are all workers. These two things must be there: an enjoyer and a worker. For example, in our body the stomach is the enjoyer and all other parts of the body are workers. So this system is natural: there must always be someone who is the enjoyer and someone who is the worker. It is present in the capitalist system also. In Russia there is always conflict between the managers and the workers. The workers say, "If this is a classless society, why is that man sitting comfortably and ordering us to work?" The Russians have not been able to avoid this dilemma, and it cannot be avoided. There *must* be one class of men who are the directors or enjoyers and another class of men who are the workers. Therefore the only way to have a truly classless society is to find that method by which both the managers and the workers will feel equal happiness. For example, if the stomach is hungry and the eyes see some food, immediately the brain will say, "O legs, please go there!" and "Hand, pick it up," and "Now please put it into the mouth." Immediately the food goes into the stomach, and as soon as the stomach is satisfied, the eyes are satisfied, the legs are satisfied, and the hand is satisfied.

Śyāmasundara: But Marx would use this as a perfect example of communism.

Śrīla Prabhupāda: But he has neglected to find out the real stomach.

Śyāmasundara: His is the material stomach.

Śrīla Prabhupāda: But the material stomach is always hungry again; it can never be satisfied. In the Kṛṣṇa consciousness movement we have the substance for feeding our brains, our minds, and our souls. *Yasya prasādād bhagavat-prasādaḥ.* If the spiritual master is satisfied, then Kṛṣṇa is satisfied, and if Kṛṣṇa is satisfied, then everyone is satisfied. Therefore you are all trying to satisfy your spiritual master. Similarly, if the communist countries can come up with a dictator who, if satisfied, automatically gives satisfaction to all the people, then we will accept such a classless society. But this is impossible. A classless society is only possible when Kṛṣṇa is in the center. For the satisfaction of Kṛṣṇa, the intellectual can work in his own way, the administrator can work in his way, the merchant can work in his way, and the laborer can work in his way. This is truly a classless society.

Śyāmasundara: How is this different from the communist country, where all sorts of men contribute for the same central purpose, which is the state?

Śrīla Prabhupāda: The difference is that if the state is not perfect, no one will willingly contribute to it. They may be forced to contribute, but they will not voluntarily contribute unless there is a perfect state in the center. For example, the hands, legs, and brain are working in perfect harmony for the satisfaction of the stomach. Why? Because they know without a doubt that by satisfying the stomach they will all share the energy and also be satisfied. Therefore, unless the people have this kind of perfect faith in the leader of the country, there is no possibility of a classless society.

Śyāmasundara: The communists theorize that if the worker contributes to the central fund, he will get satisfaction in return.

Śrīla Prabhupāda: Yes, but if he sees imperfection in the center, he will not work enthusiastically because he will have no faith that he will get full satisfaction. That perfection of the state will never be there, and therefore the workers will always remain dissatisfied.

Śyāmasundara: The propagandists play upon this dissatisfaction and tell the people that foreigners are causing it.

Śrīla Prabhupāda: But if the people were truly satisfied, they could not be influenced by outsiders. If you are satisfied that your spiritual master is perfect – that he is guiding you nicely – will you be influenced by outsiders?

Śyāmasundara: No.

Śrīla Prabhupāda: Because the communist state will never be perfect, there is no possibility of a classless society.

Śyāmasundara: Marx examines history and sees that in Greek times, in Roman times, and in the Middle Ages slaves were always required for production.

Śrīla Prabhupāda: The Russians are also creating slaves – the working class. Joseph Stalin stayed in power simply by killing all his enemies. He killed so many men that he is recorded in history as the greatest criminal. He was certainly imperfect, yet he held the position of dictator, and the people were forced to obey him.

Śyāmasundara: His followers have denounced him.

Śrīla Prabhupāda: That's all well and good, but his followers should also be denounced. The point is that in any society there must be a leader, there must be directors, and there must be workers, but everyone should be so satisfied that they forget the difference.

Śyāmasundara: No envy.

Śrīla Prabhupāda: Ah, no envy. But that perfection is not possible in the material world. Therefore Marx's theories are useless.
Śyāmasundara: But on the other hand, the capitalists also make slaves of their workers.
Śrīla Prabhupāda: Wherever there is materialistic activity, there must be imperfection. But if they make Kṛṣṇa the center, then all problems will be resolved.
Śyāmasundara: Are you saying that any system of organizing the means of production is bound to be full of exploitation?
Śrīla Prabhupāda: Yes, certainly, certainly! The materialistic mentality *means* exploitation.
Śyāmasundara: Then what is the solution?
Śrīla Prabhupāda: Kṛṣṇa consciousness!
Śyāmasundara: How is that?
Śrīla Prabhupāda: Just make Kṛṣṇa the center and work for Him. Then everyone will be satisfied. As it is stated in the *Śrīmad-Bhāgavatam* [4.31.14]:

yathā taror mūla-niṣecanena
tṛpyanti tat-skandha-bhujopaśākhāḥ
prāṇopahārāc ca yathendriyāṇāṁ
tathaiva sarvārhaṇam acyutejyā

If you simply pour water on the root of a tree, all the branches, twigs, leaves, and flowers will be nourished. Similarly, everyone can be satisfied simply by *acyutejyā*. *Acyuta* means Kṛṣṇa, and *ijyā* means worship. So this is the formula for a classless society: Make Kṛṣṇa [God] the center and do everything for Him. There are no classes in our International Society for Krishna Consciousness. Now you are writing philosophy, but if I want you to wash dishes, you will do so immediately because you know that whatever you do, you are working for Kṛṣṇa and for your spiritual master. In the material world different kinds of work have different values, but in Kṛṣṇa consciousness everything is done on the absolute platform. Whether you wash dishes or write books or worship the Deity, the value is the same because you are serving Kṛṣṇa. That is a classless society. Actually, the perfect classless society is Vṛndāvana. In Vṛndāvana, some are cowherd boys, some are cows, some are trees, some are fathers, some are mothers, but the center is Kṛṣṇa, and everyone is satisfied simply by loving Him. When all people become Kṛṣṇa conscious and understand how to love Him, then there will be a classless society. Otherwise it is not possible.

Śyāmasundara: Marx's definition of communism is "The common or public ownership of the means of production, and the abolition of private property." In our International Society for Krishna Consciousness, don't we have the same idea? We also say, "Nothing is mine." We have also abolished private property.

Śrīla Prabhupāda: While the communist says, "Nothing is mine," he thinks everything belongs to the state. The state, however, is simply an extended "mine." For example, if I am the head of a family, I might say, "I do not want anything for myself, but I want many things for my children." Mahatma Gandhi, who sacrificed so much to drive the English out of India, was at the same time thinking, "I am a very good man; I am doing national work." Therefore, this so-called nationalism or so-called communism is simply extended selfishness. The quality remains the same. The real change occurs when we say, "Nothing belongs to me; everything belongs to God, Kṛṣṇa, and therefore I should use everything in His service." That is factual.

Śyāmasundara: Marx says that the capitalists are parasites living at the cost of the workers.

Śrīla Prabhupāda: But the communists are also living at the cost of the workers: the managers are drawing big salaries, and the common workers are dissatisfied. Indeed, their godless society is becoming more and more troublesome. Unless everyone accepts God as the only enjoyer and himself simply as His servant, there will always be conflict. In the broad sense, there is no difference between the communists and the capitalists because God is not accepted as the supreme enjoyer and proprietor in either system. Actually, no property belongs to either the communists or the capitalists. Everything belongs to God.

Śyāmasundara: Marx condemns the capitalists for making a profit. He says that profit-making is exploitation and that the capitalists are unnecessary for the production of commodities.

Śrīla Prabhupāda: Profit-making may be wrong, but that exploitative tendency is always there, whether it is a communist or a capitalist system. In Bengal it is said that during the winter season the bugs cannot come out because of the severe cold. So they become dried up, being unable to suck any blood. But as soon as the summer season comes, the bugs get the opportunity to come out, so they immediately bite someone and suck his blood to their full satisfaction. Our mentality in this material world is the same: to exploit others and become wealthy. Whether you are a communist in the winter season or a capitalist in the summer season, your tendency is to exploit others. Unless there is a change of heart, this exploitation will go on.

I once knew a mill worker who acquired some money. Then he became the proprietor of the mill and took advantage of his good fortune to become a capitalist. Henry Ford is another example. He was an errand boy, but he got the opportunity to become a capitalist. There are many such instances. So, to a greater or lesser degree, the propensity is always there in human nature to exploit others and become wealthy. Unless this mentality is changed, there is no point in changing from a capitalist to a communist society. Material life means that everyone is seeking some profit, some adoration, and some position. By threats the state can force people to curb this tendency, but for how long? Can they change everyone's mind by force? No, it is impossible. Therefore, Marx's proposition is nonsense.

Śyāmasundara: Marx thinks the minds of people can be changed by forced conditioning.

Śrīla Prabhupāda: That is not possible. Even a child cannot be convinced by force, what to speak of a mature, educated man. We have the real process for changing people's minds: chanting the Hare Kṛṣṇa *mantra. Ceto-darpaṇa-mārjanam:* This process cleanses the heart of material desires. We have seen that people in Moscow are not happy. They are simply waiting for another revolution. We talked to one working-class boy who was very unhappy. When a pot of rice is boiling, you can take one grain and press it between your fingers, and if it is hot you can understand all the rice is boiling. Thus we can understand the position of the Russian people from the sample of that boy. We could also get further ideas by talking with Professor Kotovsky from the India

Department of Moscow University. How foolish he was! He said that after death everything is finished. If this is his knowledge, and if that young boy is a sample of the citizenry, then the situation in Russia is very bleak. They may theorize about so many things, but we could not even purchase sufficient groceries in Moscow. There were no vegetables, fruits, or rice, and the milk was of poor quality. If that Madrasi gentleman had not contributed some dahl and rice, then practically speaking we would have starved. The Russians' diet seemed to consist of only meat and liquor.

Śyāmasundara: The communists play upon this universal profit motive. The worker who produces the most units at his factory is glorified by the state or receives a small bonus.

Śrīla Prabhupāda: Why should he get a bonus?

Śyāmasundara: To give him some incentive to work hard.

Śrīla Prabhupāda: Just to satisfy his tendency to lord it over others and make a profit, his superiors bribe him. This Russian communist idea is very good, provided the citizens do not want any profit. But that is impossible, because everyone wants profit. The state cannot destroy this tendency either by law or by force.

Śyāmasundara: The communists try to centralize everything – money, communications, and transport – in the hands of the state.

Śrīla Prabhupāda: But what benefit will there be in that? As soon as all the wealth is centralized, the members of the central government will appropriate it, just as Khrushchev did. These are all useless ideas as long as the tendency for exploitation is not reformed. The Russians have organized their country according to Marx's theories, yet all their leaders have turned out to be cheaters. Where is their program for reforming this cheating propensity?

Śyāmasundara: Their program is to first change the social condition, and then, they believe, the corrupt mentality will change automatically.

Śrīla Prabhupāda: Impossible. Such repression will simply cause a reaction in the form of another revolution.

Śyāmasundara: Are you implying that the people's mentality must first be changed, and then a change in the social structure will naturally follow?

Śrīla Prabhupāda: Yes. But the leaders will never be able to train all the people to think that everything belongs to the state. This idea is simply utopian nonsense.

Śyāmasundara: Marx has another slogan: "Human nature has no reality." He says that man's nature changes through history according to material conditions.

Śrīla Prabhupāda: He does not know the real human nature. It is certainly true that everything in this cosmic creation, or *jagat,* is changing. Your body changes daily. Everything is changing, just like waves in the ocean. This is not a very advanced philosophy. Marx's theory is also being changed; it cannot last. But man does have a fundamental nature that never changes: his spiritual nature. We are teaching people to come to the standard of acting according to their spiritual nature, which will never change. Acting spiritually means serving Kṛṣṇa. If we try to serve Kṛṣṇa now, we will continue to serve Kṛṣṇa when we go to Vaikuṇṭha, the spiritual world. Therefore, loving service to Lord Kṛṣṇa is called *nitya,* or eternal. As Kṛṣṇa says in the *Bhagavad-gītā, nitya-yuktā upāsate:* "My pure devotees perpetually worship Me with devotion."

The communists give up Kṛṣṇa and replace Him with the state. Then they expect to get the people to think, "Nothing in my favor; everything in favor of the state." But people will never accept this idea. It is impossible; let the rascals try it! All they can do is simply force the people to work, as Stalin did. As soon as he found someone opposed to him, he immediately cut his throat. The same disease is still there today, so how will their program be successful?

Śyāmasundara: Their idea is that human nature has no reality of its own. It is simply a product of the material environment. Thus, by putting a man in the factory and making him identify with the state and something like scientific achievement, they think they can transform him into a selfless person.

Śrīla Prabhupāda: But because he has the basic disease, envy, he will remain selfish. When he sees that he is working so hard but that the profit is not coming to him, his enthusiasm will immediately slacken. In Bengal there is a proverb: "As a proprietor I can turn sand into gold, but as soon as I am no longer the proprietor, the gold becomes sand." The Russian people are in this position. They are not as rich as the Europeans or the Americans, and because of this they are unhappy.

Śyāmasundara: One of the methods the authorities in Russia use is to constantly whip the people into believing there may be a war at any moment. Then they think, "To protect our country, we must work hard."
Śrīla Prabhupāda: If the people cannot make any profit on their work, however, they will eventually lose all interest in the country. The average man will think, "Whether I work or not, I get the same result. I cannot adequately feed and clothe my family." Then he will begin to lose his incentive to work. A scientist will see that despite his high position, his wife and children are dressed just like the common laborer.
Śyāmasundara: Marx says that industrial and scientific work is the highest kind of activity.
Śrīla Prabhupāda: But unless the scientists and the industrialists receive sufficient profit, they will be reluctant to work for the state.
Śyāmasundara: The Russian goal is the production of material goods for the enhancement of human well-being.
Śrīla Prabhupāda: Their "human well-being" actually means, "If you don't agree with me, I'll cut your throat." This is their "well-being." Stalin had his idea of "human well-being," but anyone who disagreed with his version of it was killed or imprisoned. They may say that a few must suffer for the sake of many, but we have personally seen that Russia has achieved neither general happiness nor prosperity. For example, in Moscow none of the big buildings have been recently built. They are old and ravaged, or poorly renovated. Also, at the stores the people had to stand in long lines to make purchases. These are indications that economic conditions are unsound.
Śyāmasundara: Marx considered religion an illusion that must be condemned.
Śrīla Prabhupāda: The divisions between different religious faiths may be an illusion, but Marx's philosophy is also an illusion.
Śyāmasundara: Do you mean that it's not being practiced?
Śrīla Prabhupāda: In the sixty years since the Russian Revolution, his philosophy has become distorted. On the other hand, Lord Brahmā began the Vedic religion countless years ago, and though foreigners have been trying to devastate it for the last two thousand years, it is still intact. Vedic religion is not an illusion, at least not for India.
Śyāmasundara: Here is Marx's famous statement about religion. He

says, "Religion is the sigh of the oppressed creature, the heart of the heartless world, just as it is the spirit of the spiritless situation. It is the opium of the people."

Śrīla Prabhupāda: He does not know what religion is. His definition is false. The *Vedas* state that religion is the course of action given by God. God is a fact, and His law is also a fact. It is not an illusion. Kṛṣṇa gives the definition of religion in *Bhagavad-gītā* [18.66]: *sarva-dharmān parityajya mām ekaṁ śaraṇaṁ vraja.* To surrender unto God – this is religion.

Śyāmasundara: Marx believes everything is produced from economic struggle and that religion is a technique invented by the bourgeoisie or the capitalists to dissuade the masses from revolution by promising them a better existence after death.

Śrīla Prabhupāda: He himself has created a philosophy that is presently being enforced by coercion and killing.

Śyāmasundara: And he promised that in the future things will be better. So he is guilty of the very thing that he condemns religion for.

Śrīla Prabhupāda: As we have often explained, religion is that part of our nature which is permanent, which we cannot give up. No one can give up his religion. And what is that religion? Service. Marx desires to serve humanity by putting forward his philosophy. Therefore that is his religion. Everyone is trying to render some service. The father is trying to serve his family, the statesman is trying to serve his country, and the philanthropist is trying to serve all humanity. Whether you are Karl Marx or Stalin or Mahatma Gandhi, a Hindu, a Muslim, or a Christian, you must serve. Because we are presently rendering service to so many people and so many things, we are becoming confused. Therefore, Kṛṣṇa advises us to give up all this service and serve Him alone:

sarva-dharmān parityajya
mām ekaṁ śaraṇaṁ vraja
ahaṁ tvāṁ sarva-pāpebhyo
mokṣayiṣyāmi mā śucaḥ

"Abandon all varieties of service and just surrender unto Me. I shall deliver you from all sinful reactions. Do not fear." [*Bhagavad-gītā* 18.66]

Śyāmasundara: The communists – and even to a certain extent the capitalists – believe that service for the production of goods is the only real service. Therefore they condemn us because we are not producing anything tangible.

Śrīla Prabhupāda: How can they condemn us? We are giving service to humanity by teaching the highest knowledge. A high court judge does not produce any grains in the field. He sits in a chair and gets $25,000 or $30,000. Does that mean he is not rendering any service? Of course he is. The theory that unless one performs manual labor in the factory or the fields he is not doing service would simply give credit to the peasant and the worker. It is a peasant philosophy.

There is a story about a king and his prime minister. Once the king's salaried workers complained, "We are actually working, and this minister is doing nothing, yet you are paying him such a large salary. Why is that?" The king then called his minister in and also had someone bring in an elephant. "Please take this elephant and weigh it," the king said to his workers. The workers took the elephant to all the markets, but they could not find a scale large enough to weigh the animal. When they returned to the palace the king asked, "What happened?" One of the workers answered, "Sir, we could not find a scale large enough to weigh the elephant." Then the king addressed his prime minister, "Will you please weigh this elephant?" "Yes, sir," said the prime minister, and he took the elephant away. He returned within a few minutes and said, "It weighs 11,650 pounds." All the workers were astonished. "How did you weigh the elephant so quickly?" one of them asked. "Did you find some very large scale?" The minister replied, "No. It is impossible to weigh an elephant on a scale. I went to the river, took the elephant on a boat, and noted the watermark. After taking the elephant off the boat, I put weights in the boat until the same watermark was reached. Then I had the elephant's weight." The king said to his workers, "Now do you see the difference?" One who has intelligence has strength, not the fools and the rascals. Marx and his followers are simply fools and rascals. We don't take advice from them; we take advice from Kṛṣṇa or His representative.

Śyāmasundara: So religion is not simply a police force to keep people in illusion?

Śrīla Prabhupāda: No. Religion means to serve the spirit. That is religion. Everyone is rendering service, but no one knows where his service will be most successful. Therefore Kṛṣṇa says, "Serve Me, and you will serve the spiritual society." This is real religion. The Marxists want to build a so-called perfect society without religion, yet even up to this day, because India's foundation is religion, people all over the world adore India.

Śyāmasundara: Marx says that God does not create man; rather, man creates God.

Śrīla Prabhupāda: That is more nonsense. From what he says, I can tell he is a nonsensical rascal and a fool. One cannot understand that someone is a fool unless he talks. A fool may dress very nicely and sit like a gentleman amongst gentlemen, but we can tell the fools from the learned men by their speech.

Śyāmasundara: Marx's follower was Nikolai Lenin. He reinforced all of Marx's ideas and added a few of his own. He believed that revolution is a fundamental fact of history. He said that history moves in leaps, and that it progresses toward the communist leap. He wanted Russia to leap into the dictatorship of the proletariat, which he called the final stage of historical development.

Śrīla Prabhupāda: No. We can say with confidence – and they may note it carefully – that after the Bolshevik Revolution there will be many other revolutions, because as long as people live on the mental plane there will be only revolution. Our proposition is to give up all these mental concoctions and come to the spiritual platform. If one comes to the spiritual platform, there will be no more revolution. As Dhruva Mahārāja said, *nātaḥ paraṁ parama vedmi na yatra vādaḥ:* "Now that I am seeing God, I am completely satisfied. Now all kinds of theorizing processes are finished." So God consciousness is the final revolution. There will be repeated revolutions in this material world unless people come to Kṛṣṇa consciousness.

Śyāmasundara: The Hare Kṛṣṇa revolution.

Śrīla Prabhupāda: The Vedic injunction is that people are searching after knowledge, and that when one understands the Absolute Truth, he understands everything. *Yasmin vijñāte sarvam evaṁ vijñātaṁ bhavati.* People are trying to approach an objective, but they do not know that the final objective is Kṛṣṇa. They are simply trying to make adjustments with so many materialistic revolutions. They have no knowledge that they are spiritual beings and that unless they go back to the spiritual world and associate with the Supreme Spirit, God, there is no question of happiness. We are like fish out of water. Just as a fish cannot be happy unless he is in the water, we cannot be happy apart from the spiritual world. We are part and parcel of the Supreme Spirit, Kṛṣṇa, but we have left His association and fallen from the spiritual world because of our desire to enjoy this material world. So unless we reawaken the understanding of our spiritual position and go back home to the spiritual world, we can never be happy. We can go on theorizing for many lifetimes, but we will only see one revolution after another. The old order changes, yielding its place to the new. Or in other words, history repeats itself.

Śyāmasundara: Marx says that there are always two conflicting properties in material nature, and that the inner pulsation of opposite forces causes history to take leaps from one revolution to another. He claims that the communist revolution is the final revolution because it is the perfect resolution of all social and political contradictions.

Śrīla Prabhupāda: If the communist idea is spiritualized, then it will become perfect. As long as the communist idea remains materialistic, it cannot be the final revolution. They believe that the state is the owner of everything. But the state is not the owner; the real owner is God. When they come to this conclusion, then the communist idea will be perfect. We also have a communistic philosophy. They say that everything must be done for the state, but in our International Society for Krishna Consciousness we are actually practicing perfect communism by doing everything for Kṛṣṇa. We know Kṛṣṇa is the supreme enjoyer of the result of all work (*bhoktāraṁ yajña-tapasām*). The communist philosophy as it is now practiced is vague, but it can become perfect if they accept the conclusion of the *Bhagavad-gītā* – that Kṛṣṇa is the supreme proprietor, the supreme enjoyer, and the supreme friend of everyone. Then people will be happy. Now they mistrust the state, but if the people accept Kṛṣṇa as their friend, they will have perfect confidence in Him, just as Arjuna was perfectly confident in Kṛṣṇa on the Battlefield of Kurukṣetra. The great victory of Arjuna and his associates on the Battlefield of Kurukṣetra showed that his confidence in Kṛṣṇa was justified:

yatra yogeśvaraḥ kṛṣṇo
yatra pārtho dhanur-dharaḥ
tatra śrīr vijayo bhūtir
dhruvā nītir matir mama

"Wherever there is Kṛṣṇa, the master of all mystics, and wherever there is Arjuna, the supreme archer, there will also certainly be opulence, victory, extraordinary power, and morality. That is my opinion." [*Bhagavad-gītā* 18.78] So if Kṛṣṇa is at the center of society, then the people will be perfectly secure and prosperous. The communist idea is welcome, provided they are prepared to replace the so-called state with God. That is religion.

Psychoanalysis and the Soul

Presenting a Vedic perspective on psychology, Śrīla Prabhupāda discusses the subject with his disciple Śyāmasundara in the following conversation, recorded in Calcutta on October 5, 1971. Śrīla Prabhupāda says, "By speculating on some shock that may or may not have occurred in childhood, one will never discover the root disease. . . . He [Freud] did not know the basic principle of spiritual understanding, which is that we are not this body. . . . We are different from this body, and we are transmigrating from one body to another."

Śyāmasundara: Sigmund Freud's idea was that many psychological problems originate with traumatic experiences in childhood or infancy. His method of cure was to have the patient try to recall these painful events and analyze them.

Śrīla Prabhupāda: But he did not know that one must again become an infant. After this life, one will be put into another womb, and the same traumatic experiences will happen again. Therefore it is the duty of the spiritual master and the parents to save the child from taking another birth. The opportunity of this human form of life is that we can understand the horrible experiences of birth, death, old age, and disease and act so that we shall not be forced to go through the same things again. Otherwise, after death we shall have to take birth in a womb and suffer repeated miseries.

Śyāmasundara: Freud treated many people suffering from neuroses. For instance, suppose a man is sexually impotent. By recalling his childhood, he may remember some harmful experience with his father or mother that caused him to be repelled by women. In this way he can resolve the conflict and lead a normal sex life.

Śrīla Prabhupāda: However, even in the so-called normal condition, the pleasure derived from sexual intercourse is simply frustrating and insignificant. For ordinary men attached to the materialistic way of life, their only pleasure is sexual intercourse. But the *śāstras* [Vedic scriptures] say, *yan maithunādi-gṛhamedhi-sukhaṁ hi tuccham:* the pleasure derived from sexual intercourse is tenth class at best. Because they have no idea of the pleasure of Kṛṣṇa consciousness, the materialists regard sex as the highest pleasure. And how is it actually experienced? We have an itch, and when we scratch it, we feel some pleasure. But the aftereffects of sexual pleasure are abominable. The mother has to undergo labor pains, and the father has to take responsibility for raising the children nicely and giving them an education. Of course, if one is irresponsible like cats and dogs, that is another thing. But for those who are actually gentlemen, is it not painful to bear and raise children? Certainly. Therefore everyone is avoiding children by contraceptive methods. But much better is to follow the injunction of the *śāstras:* Simply try to tolerate the itching sensation and avoid so much pain. This is real psychology. That itching sensation can be tolerated if one practices Kṛṣṇa consciousness. Then one will not be very attracted by sex life.

Śyāmasundara: Freud's philosophy is that people have neuroses or disorders of their total personality – various conflicts and anxieties – and that all these originate with the sexual impulse.

Śrīla Prabhupāda: That we admit. An embodied living being must have hunger, and he must have the sex impulse. We find that even in the animals these impulses are there.

Śyāmasundara: Freud believed that the ego tries to restrain these primitive drives, and that all anxieties arise from this conflict.

Śrīla Prabhupāda: Our explanation is as follows: Materialistic life is no doubt very painful. As soon as one acquires a material body, he must always suffer three kinds of miseries: miseries caused by other living beings, miseries caused by the elements, and miseries caused by his own body and mind. So the whole problem is how to stop these miseries and attain permanent happiness. Unless one stops his materialistic way of life, with its threefold miseries and repeated birth and death, there is no question of happiness. The whole Vedic civilization is based on how one can cure this materialistic disease. If we can cure this disease, its symptoms will automatically vanish. Freud is simply dealing with the symptoms of the basic disease. When you have a disease, sometimes you have headaches, sometimes your leg aches, sometimes you have a pain in your stomach, and so on. But if your disease is cured, then all your symptoms disappear. That is our program.

Śyāmasundara: In his theory of psychoanalysis, Freud states that by remembering and reevaluating emotional shocks from our childhood, we can release the tension we are feeling now.

Śrīla Prabhupāda: But what is the guarantee that one will not get shocked again? He may cure the results of one shock, but there is no guarantee that the patient will not receive another shock. Therefore Freud's treatment is useless. Our program is total cure – no more shocks of any kind. If one is situated in real Kṛṣṇa consciousness, he can face the most severe type of adversity and remain completely undisturbed. In our Kṛṣṇa consciousness movement, we are giving people this ability. Freud tries to cure the reactions of one kind of shock, but other shocks will come, one after another. This is how material nature works. If you solve one problem, another problem arises immediately. And if you solve that one, another one comes. As long as you are under the control of material nature, these repeated shocks will come. But if you become Kṛṣṇa conscious, there are no more shocks.

Śyāmasundara: Freud's idea is that the basic instinct in the human personality is the sexual drive, or libido, and that if the expressions of a child's sexuality are inhibited, then his personality becomes disordered.

Śrīla Prabhupāda: Everyone has the sex appetite: this tendency is innate. But our *brahmacarya* system restricts a child's sex life from the earliest stages of his development and diverts his attention to Kṛṣṇa consciousness. As a result there is very little chance that he will suffer such personality disorders. In the Vedic age the leaders of society knew that if a person engaged in unrestricted sex indulgence, then the duration of his materialistic life would increase. He would have to accept a material body birth after birth. Therefore the *śāstras* enjoin that one may have sexual intercourse only if married. Otherwise it is illicit. In our Kṛṣṇa consciousness society, we prohibit illicit sex, but not legal sex. In the *Bhagavad-gītā* [7.11] Kṛṣṇa says, *dharmāviruddho bhūteṣu kamo 'smi bharatarṣabha:* "I am sexual intercourse that is not against religious principles." This means that sex must be regulated. Everyone has a tendency to have sex unrestrictedly – and in Western countries they are actually doing this – but according to the Vedic system, there must be restrictions. And not only must sex be restricted, but meat-eating, gambling, and drinking as well. So in our Society we have eliminated all these things, and our Western students are becoming pure devotees of Kṛṣṇa. The people at large, however, must at least restrict these sinful activities, as explained in the Vedic *śāstras.*

The Vedic system of *varṇāśrama-dharma* [four social orders and four spiritual orders] is so scientific that everything is automatically adjusted. Life becomes very peaceful, and everyone can make progress in Kṛṣṇa consciousness. If the Vedic system is followed by human society, there will be no more of these mental disturbances.

Śyāmasundara: Freud says that sexual energy is not only expressed in sexual intercourse, but is associated with a wide variety of pleasurable bodily sensations such as pleasures of the mouth, like eating and sucking.

Śrīla Prabhupāda: That is confirmed in the *śāstras: yan maithunādi-gṛhamedhi-sukham.* The only pleasure in this material world is sex. The word *ādi* indicates that the basic principle is *maithuna,* sexual intercourse. The whole system of materialistic life revolves around this sexual pleasure. But this pleasure is like one drop of water in the desert. The desert requires an ocean of water. If you find one drop of water in a desert, you can certainly say, "Here is some water." But what is its value? Similarly, there is certainly some pleasure in sex life, but what is the value of that pleasure? Compared to the unlimited pleasure of Kṛṣṇa consciousness, it is like one drop of water in the desert. Everyone is seeking unlimited pleasure, but no one is becoming satisfied. They are having sex in so many different ways, and the young girls walking on the street are almost naked. The whole society has become degraded. Now the female population has increased everywhere, and every woman and girl is trying to attract a man. The men take advantage of the situation. There is a saying in Bengal: "When milk is available in the marketplace, what is the use of keeping a cow?" So men are declining to keep a wife because sex is so cheap. They are deserting their families. And the more that men become attached to women, the more the female population of the world will increase.

Śyāmasundara: How does that result in more women?

Śrīla Prabhupāda: When men have more sex, they lose the power to beget a male child. If the woman is sexually more powerful, a girl is born, and when the man is more powerful, a boy is born. This is Āyurvedic science. For instance, in the Punjab State of India, there are fewer women because the men are very stout and strong. So when women are very easily available, the men become weak and beget female children. Sometimes they become impotent. If sex life is not restricted, there are so many disasters. And now we are actually seeing them: impotency, no marriage, increased female population. But no one knows why these things are happening or how human psychology can be controlled to avoid them. For this they must look to the perfect system of Vedic civilization.

Śyāmasundara: Freud says that as the child grows up, he begins to learn that by giving up immediate sensual satisfaction, he can gain a greater benefit later on.

Śrīla Prabhupāda: But even this so-called greater benefit is illusory, because it is still based on the principle of material pleasure. The only way to entirely give up these lower pleasures is to take to Kṛṣṇa consciousness. As Kṛṣṇa states in the *Bhagavad-gītā* [2.59], *paraṁ dṛṣṭvā nivartate:* "By experiencing a higher taste, he is fixed in consciousness." And as Yāmunācārya said, "Since I have been engaged in the transcendental loving service of Kṛṣṇa, realizing ever-new pleasure in Him, whenever I think of sex pleasure I spit at the thought, and my lips curl in distaste." That is Kṛṣṇa consciousness. Our prescription is that in the beginning of life the child should be taught self-restraint (*brahmacarya*) and when he is past twenty he can marry. In the beginning he should learn how to restrain his senses. If a child is taught to become saintly, his semen rises to his brain, and he is able to understand spiritual values. Wasting semen decreases intelligence. So from the beginning, if he is a *brahmacārī* and does not misuse his semen, then he will become intelligent and strong and fully grown.

For want of this education, everyone's brain and bodily growth are being stunted. After the boy has been trained as a *brahmacārī,* if he still wants to enjoy sex he may get married. But because he then has full strength of body and brain, he will immediately beget a male child. And because he has been trained from childhood to renounce materialistic enjoyment, when he is fifty years old he can retire from household life. At that time naturally his firstborn child will be twenty-five years old, and he can take responsibility for maintaining the household. Household life is simply a license for sex life – that's all. Sex is not required, but one who cannot restrain himself is given a license to get married and have sex. This is the real program that will save society. By speculating on some shock that may or may not have occurred in childhood, one will never discover the root disease. The sex impulse, as well as the impulse to become intoxicated and to eat meat, is present from the very beginning of life. Therefore one must restrain himself. Otherwise he will be implicated.

Śyāmasundara: So the Western system of bringing up children seems artificial because the parents either repress the child too severely or don't restrict him at all.

Śrīla Prabhupāda: That is not good. The Vedic system is to give the child direction for becoming Kṛṣṇa conscious. There must be some repression, but our use of repression is different. We say the child must rise early in the morning, worship the Deity in the temple, and chant Hare Kṛṣṇa. In the beginning, force may be necessary. Otherwise the child will not become habituated. But the idea is to divert his attention to Kṛṣṇa conscious activities. Then, when he realizes he is not his body, all difficulties will disappear. As one increases his Kṛṣṇa consciousness, he becomes neglectful of all these material things. So Kṛṣṇa consciousness is the prime remedy – the panacea for all diseases.

Śyāmasundara: Freud divided the personality into three departments: the ego, the superego, and the id. The id is the irrational instinct for enjoyment. The ego is one's image of his own body, and is the instinct for self-preservation. The superego represents the moral restrictions of parents and other authorities.

Śrīla Prabhupāda: It is certainly true that everyone has some false egoism, or *ahaṅkāra.* For example, Freud thought he was Austrian. That is false ego, or identifying oneself with one's place of birth. We are giving everyone the information that this identification with a material body is ignorance. It is due to ignorance only that I think I am Indian, American, Hindu, or Muslim. This is egoism of the inferior quality. The superior egoism is, "I am Brahman. I am an eternal servant of Kṛṣṇa." If a child is taught this superior egoism from the beginning, then automatically his false egoism is stopped.

Śyāmasundara: Freud says that the ego tries to preserve the individual by organizing and controlling the irrational demands of the id. In other words, if the id sees something, like food, it automatically demands to eat it, and the ego controls that desire in order to preserve the individual. The superego reinforces this control. So these three systems are always conflicting in the personality.

Śrīla Prabhupāda: But the basic principle is false, since Freud has no conception of the soul existing beyond the body. He is considering the body only. Therefore he is a great fool. According to *bhāgavata* philosophy, anyone in the bodily concept of life – anyone who identifies this body, composed of mucus, bile, and air, as his self – is no better than an ass.

Śyāmasundara: Then these interactions of the id, the ego, and the superego are all bodily interactions?

Śrīla Prabhupāda: Yes, they are all subtle bodily interactions. The mind is the first element of the subtle body. The gross senses are controlled by the mind, which in turn is controlled by the intelligence. And the intelligence is controlled by the ego. So if the ego is false, then everything is false. If I falsely identify with this body because of false ego, then anything based on this false idea is also false. This is called *māyā*, or illusion. The whole of Vedic education aims at getting off this false platform and coming to the real platform of spiritual knowledge, called *brahma-jñāna*. When one comes to the knowledge that he is spirit soul, he immediately becomes happy. All his troubles are due to the false ego, and as soon as the individual realizes his true ego, the blazing fire of material existence is immediately extinguished. These philosophers are simply describing the blazing fire, but we are trying to get him out of the burning prison house of the material world altogether. They may attempt to make him happy within the fire, but how can they be successful? He must be saved from the fire. Then he will be happy. That is the message of Caitanya Mahāprabhu, and that is Lord Kṛṣṇa's message in the *Bhagavad-gītā.* Freud identifies the body with the soul. He does not know the basic principle of spiritual understanding, which is that we are not this body. We are different from this body and are transmigrating from one body to another. Without this knowledge, all his theories are based on a misunderstanding.

Not only Freud, but everyone in this material world is under illusion. In Bengal, a psychiatrist in the civil service was once called to give evidence in a case where the murderer was pleading insanity. The civil servant examined him to discover whether he actually was insane or whether he was simply under intense stress. In the courtroom he said, "I have tested many persons, and I have concluded that everyone is insane to some degree. In the present case, if the defendant is pleading insanity, then you may acquit him if you like, but as far as I know, everyone is more or less insane." And that is our conclusion as well. Anyone who identifies with his material body must be crazy, for his life is based on a misconception.

Śyāmasundara: Freud also investigated the problem of anxiety, which he said was produced when the impulses of the id threaten to overpower the rational ego and the moral superego.

Śrīla Prabhupāda: Anxiety will continue as long as one is in the material condition. No one can be free from anxiety in conditioned life.

Śyāmasundara: Is it because our desires are always frustrated?

Śrīla Prabhupāda: Yes. Your desires must be frustrated because you desire something that is not permanent. Suppose I wish to live forever, but since I have accepted a material body, there is no question of living forever. Therefore I am always anxious that death will come. I am afraid of death, when the body will be destroyed. This is the cause of all anxiety: acceptance of something impermanent as permanent.

Śyāmasundara: Freud says that anxiety develops when the superego represses the primitive desires of the id to protect the ego. Is such repression of basic instincts very healthy?

Śrīla Prabhupāda: Yes. For us repression means restraining oneself from doing something which, in the long run, is against one's welfare. For example, suppose you are suffering from diabetes and the doctor says, "Don't eat any sweet food." If you desire to eat sweets, you must repress that desire. Similarly, in our system of *brahmacarya* there is also repression. A *brahmacārī* should not sit down with a young woman, or even see one. He may desire to see a young woman, but he must repress the desire. This is called *tapasya,* or voluntary repression.

Śyāmasundara: But aren't these desires given outlet in other ways? For instance, instead of looking at a beautiful woman, we look at the beautiful form of Kṛṣṇa.

Śrīla Prabhupāda: Yes, that is our process: *paraṁ dṛṣṭvā nivartate.* If you have a better engagement, you can give up an inferior engagement. When you are captivated by seeing the beautiful form of Kṛṣṇa, naturally you have no more desire to see the beautiful form of a young woman.

Śyāmasundara: What's the effect of childhood experiences on one's later development?

Śrīla Prabhupāda: Children imitate whoever they associate with. You all know the movie *Tarzan.* He was brought up by monkeys, and he took on the habits of monkeys. If you keep children in good association, their psychological development will be very good – they will become like demigods. But if you keep them in bad association, they will turn out to be demons. Children are a blank slate. You can mold them as you like, and they are eager to learn.

Śyāmasundara: So a child's personality doesn't develop according to a fixed pattern?

Śrīla Prabhupāda: No. You can mold them in any way, like soft dough. However you put them into the mold, they will come out – like *bharats, capātīs,* or *kacaurīs* [types of Indian pastries]. Therefore if you give children good association, they will develop nicely, and if you put them in bad association, they will develop poorly. They have no independent psychology.

Śyāmasundara: Actually, Freud had a rather pessimistic view of human nature: he believed that we are all beset with irrational and chaotic impulses that cannot be eliminated.

Śrīla Prabhupāda: This is not only pessimism, but evidence of his poor fund of knowledge. He did not have perfect knowledge, nor was he trained by a perfect man. Therefore his theories are all nonsense.

Śyāmasundara: He concluded that it was impossible to be happy in this material world, but that one can alleviate some of the conflicts through psychoanalysis. He thought one can try to make the path as smooth as possible, but it will always be troublesome.

Śrīla Prabhupāda: It is true that one cannot be happy in this material world. But if one becomes spiritually elevated – if his consciousness is changed to Kṛṣṇa consciousness – then he will be happy.

Evolution in Fact and Fantasy

Los Angeles, June 1972: Śrīla Prabhupāda asserts that Darwin's theory of evolution is inconclusive and illogical. But Darwin's is not the only theory of evolution. The Vedas *explain that an evolutionary process governs the progress of the soul. "We accept evolution," Śrīla Prabhupāda says, "but not that the forms of the species are changing. The bodies are all already there, but the soul is evolving by changing bodies and by transmigrating from one body to another. . . . The defect of the evolutionists is that they have no information of the soul."*

Devotee: Darwin tried to show how the origin of living species could be fully explained by the purely mechanical, unplanned action of natural forces. By the process he called "natural selection," all the higher, complex forms of life gradually evolved from more primitive and rudimentary ones. In a given animal population, for example, some individuals will have traits that make them adapt better to their environment; these more fit individuals will survive to pass on their favorable traits to their offspring. The unfit will gradually be weeded out naturally. Thus a cold climate will favor those who have, say, long hair or fatty tissue, and the species will then gradually evolve in that direction.

Śrīla Prabhupāda: The question is that in the development of the body, is there any plan that a particular kind of body – with, as you say, long hair or fatty tissue – should exist under certain natural conditions? Who has made these arrangements? That is the question.

Devotee: No one. Modern evolutionists ultimately base their theory on the existence of chance variations.

Śrīla Prabhupāda: That is nonsense. There is no such thing as chance. If they say "chance," then they are nonsense. Our question remains. Who has created the different circumstances for the existence of different kinds of animals?

Devotee: For example, a frog may lay thousands of eggs, but out of all of them only a few may survive to adulthood. Those who do are more fit than the others. If the environment did not favorably select the fittest, then too many frogs—

Śrīla Prabhupāda: Yes, frogs and many other animals lay eggs by the hundreds. A snake gives birth to scores of snakes at a time, and if all were allowed to exist, there would be a great disturbance. Therefore, big snakes devour the small snakes. That is nature's law. But behind nature's law is a brain. That is our proposition. Nature's law is not blind, for behind it there is a brain, and that brain is God. We learn this from the *Bhagavad-gītā* [9.10]: *mayādhyakṣeṇa prakṛtiḥ sūyate sa-carācaram.* Whatever is taking place in material nature is being directed by the Supreme Lord, who maintains everything in order. So the snake lays eggs by the score, and if many were not killed, the world would be overwhelmed by snakes. Similarly, male tigers kill the cubs. The economic theory of Malthus states that whenever there is overpopulation, there must be an outbreak of war, epidemic, famine, or the like to curb it. These natural activities do not take place by chance but are planned. Anyone who says they are a matter of chance has insufficient knowledge.

Devotee: But Darwin has a huge amount of evidence—

Śrīla Prabhupāda: Evidence? That is all right. We also have got evidence. Evidence must be there. But as soon as there is evidence, there should be no talk of "chance."

Devotee: For example, out of millions of frogs, one may happen to be better adapted to living in the water.

Śrīla Prabhupāda: But that is not by chance! That is by plan! He doesn't know that. As soon as one says "chance," it means his knowledge is imperfect. A man says "chance" when he cannot explain. It is evasive. So the conclusion is that he is without perfect knowledge and therefore unfit for giving *any* knowledge. He is cheating, that's all.

Devotee: Well, Darwin sees a "plan" or "design" in a sense, but—

Śrīla Prabhupāda: If he sees a plan or design, then whose design?

As soon as you recognize a design, you must acknowledge a designer. If you see a plan, then you must accept a planner. That he does not know.

Devotee: But the "plan" is only the involuntary working of nature.

Śrīla Prabhupāda: Nonsense. There *is* a plan. The sun rises daily according to exact calculation. It does not follow *our* calculation; rather, we calculate according to the sun. Experiencing that in such-and-such season the sun rises at such-and-such time, we learn that according to the season the sun rises exactly on the minute, the second. It is not by whimsy or chance but by minute plan.

Devotee: But can't you say it's just mechanical?

Śrīla Prabhupāda: Then who made it mechanical? If something is mechanical, then there must be a mechanic, a brain, who made the machine. Here is something mechanical [*Śrīla Prabhupāda points to a Telex machine*]: Who made it? This machine has not come out by itself. It is made of iron, and the iron did not mold itself into a machine; there is a brain who made the machine possible. So everything in nature has a plan or design, and behind that plan or design is a brain, a very big brain.

Devotee: Darwin tried to make the appearance and disappearance of living forms seem so natural and involuntary that God is removed from the picture. Evolutionary theory makes it appear as if combinations of material ingredients created life, and then various species evolved one from another naturally.

Śrīla Prabhupāda: That is foolishness. Combination means God. God is combining. Combination does not take place automatically. Suppose I am cooking. There are many ingredients gathered for cooking, but they do not combine together by themselves. I am the cooker, and in cooking I combine together ghee, spices, rice, *dāl,* and so on; and in this way, nice dishes are produced. Similarly, the combination of ingredients in nature requires God. Otherwise how does the moment arise in which the combination takes place? Do you place all the ingredients in the kitchen and in an hour come back and say, "Oh, where is my meal?" Nonsense! Who will cook your meal? You'll starve. But take help of a living being, and then we'll cook and we can eat. This is our experience. So if there is combination, then who is combining? They are fools not to know how combination takes place.

Devotee: Scientists now say life arose out of four basic elements: carbon, hydrogen, nitrogen, oxygen.

Śrīla Prabhupāda: If the basic principle is chemicals, who made the chemicals? That question should be asked.

Devotee: Isn't it possible that one day science will discover the source of these chemicals?

Śrīla Prabhupāda: There is no question of discovering: the answer is already known, although it may not be known to *you*. We know. The *Vedānta* says, *janmādy asya yataḥ:* the original source of everything is Brahman, Kṛṣṇa. Kṛṣṇa says, *ahaṁ sarvasya prabhavo mattaḥ sarvaṁ pravartate:* "I am the origin of everything." [*Bhagavad-gītā* 10.8] So we know that there is a big brain who is doing everything. We know. The scientists may not know; that is their foolishness.

Devotee: They might say the same thing about us.

Śrīla Prabhupāda: No, they cannot say the same thing about us. We accept Kṛṣṇa, but not blindly. Our predecessors, the great *ācāryas* and learned scholars, have accepted Kṛṣṇa as the origin of everything, so we are not following blindly. We claim that Kṛṣṇa is the origin, but what claim can the scientist make? As soon as he says "chance," it means that he has no knowledge. We don't say "chance." We have an original cause; but he says chance. Therefore he has no knowledge.

Devotee: They try to trace back the origin by means of excavation. And they have found that gradually through the years the animal forms are evolving toward increasingly more complex and specialized forms, from invertebrates to fishes, then to amphibians, then to reptiles and insects, to mammals and birds, and finally to humans. In that process many species, like the dinosaurs, appeared, flourished, and then disappeared forever, became extinct. Eventually, primitive apelike creatures appeared, and from them man gradually developed.

Śrīla Prabhupāda: Is the theory that the human body comes from the monkeys?

Devotee: Humans and monkeys are related. They come from the same—

Śrīla Prabhupāda: Related? Everything is related; that is another thing. But if the monkey body is developing into a human body, then why, after the human body is developed, doesn't the monkey species cease to exist?

Devotee: The humans and the monkeys are branches of the same tree.

Śrīla Prabhupāda: Yes, and both are now existing. Similarly, we say that at the time the evolutionists say life began, there were human beings existing.

Devotee: They find no evidence for that.

Śrīla Prabhupāda: Why no evidence?

Devotee: In the ground. By excavation. They find no evidence in the ground.

Śrīla Prabhupāda: Is the ground the only evidence? Is there no other evidence?

Devotee: The only evidence they accept is the testimony of their senses.

Śrīla Prabhupāda: But they still cannot prove that there was no human being at the time they say life originated. They cannot prove that.

Devotee: It appears that in certain layers of earth there are remains of apelike men—

Śrīla Prabhupāda: Apelike men or manlike apes are still existing now, alongside human beings. If one thing has been developed by the transformation of another thing, then that original thing should no longer be in existence. When in this way a cause has produced its effect, the cause ceases to exist. But in this case we see that the cause is still present, that there are still monkeys and apes.

Devotee: But monkeys did not cause men; both came from the same common ancestor. That is their account.

Śrīla Prabhupāda: We say that we *all* come from God, the same ancestor, the same father. The original father is Kṛṣṇa. As Kṛṣṇa says in the *Bhagavad-gītā* [14.4], *sarva-yoniṣu kaunteya:* "Of as many forms as there are, . . ." *ahaṁ bīja-pradaḥ pitā:* "I am the seed-giving father." So what is your objection to this?

Devotee: Well, if I examine the layers of earth, I find in the deepest layers no evidence—

Śrīla Prabhupāda: You are packed up with layers of earth, that's all. That is the boundary of your knowledge. But that is not knowledge; there are many other evidences.

Devotee: But surely if men were living millions of years ago, they would have left evidence, tangible evidence, behind them. I could see their remains.

Śrīla Prabhupāda: So I say that in human society bodies are burned after death, cremated. So where does your excavator get his bones?

Devotee: Well, that's possible, but—

Śrīla Prabhupāda: According to our Vedic system, the body is burned to ashes after death. Where, therefore, would the rascal get the bones? Animals are not burned; their bones remain. But human beings are burned, and therefore they cannot find their bones.

Devotee: I'm just saying that it appears, through layer after layer of deposits in the earth, that biological forms tend to progress from simple and primitive forms to more and more complex and specialized ones, until finally civilized man appears.

Śrīla Prabhupāda: But at the present moment both simple and complex forms are existing. One did not develop into the other. For example, my childhood body has developed into my adult body, and the child's body is no longer there. So if the higher, complex species developed from the simpler, lower species, then we should see no simple species. But all species are now existing simultaneously.

When I see all 8,400,000 species of life existing, what is the question of development? Each species exists now, and it existed long ago. You might not have seen it, but you have no proper source of knowledge. You might have missed it. That is another thing.

Devotee: But all the evidence shows otherwise. Five hundred million years ago there were no land animals; there were only aquatics.

Śrīla Prabhupāda: That is nonsense. You cannot give a history of five hundred million years! Where is the history of five hundred million years? You are simply imagining. You say "historical evidence," but where is your evidence? You cannot give a history for more than three thousand years, and you are speaking about five hundred million. This is all nonsense.

Devotee: If I dig far into the ground, layer by layer—

Śrīla Prabhupāda: By dirt you are calculating five hundred million years? It could be *ten* years. You cannot give the history of human society past three thousand years, so how can you speak of four hundred or five hundred million years ago? Where were you then? Were you there, so you can say that all these species were not there? This is imagination. In this way everyone can imagine and say some nonsense.

We accept evolution, but not that the forms of the species are changing. The bodies are all already there, but the soul is evolving by changing bodies and by transmigrating from one body to another. I have evolved from my childhood body to my adult body, and now my childhood body is extinct. But there are many other children. Similarly, all the species are now existing simultaneously, and they were all there in the past.

For example, if you are traveling in a train, you find first class, second class, third class; they are all existing. If you pay a higher fare and enter the first-class carriage, you cannot say, "Now the first class is created." It was always existing. So the defect of the evolutionists is that they have no information of the soul. The soul is evolving, transmigrating, from one compartment to another compartment, simply changing place. The *Padma Purāṇa* says that there are 8,400,000 species of life, and the soul evolves through them. This evolutionary process we accept: the soul evolves from aquatics to plants, to insects, to birds, to animals, and then to the human forms. But all these forms are already there. They do not change. One does not become extinct and another survive. All of them are existing simultaneously.

Devotee: But Darwin says there are many species, like dinosaurs, that are seen to be extinct.

Śrīla Prabhupāda: What has he seen? He is not so powerful that he can see everywhere or everything. His power to see is limited, and by that limited power he cannot conclude that one species is extinct. That is not possible. No scientist will accept that. After all, all the senses by which you gather knowledge are limited, so how can you say this is finished or that is extinct? You cannot see. You cannot search out. The earth's circumference is twenty-five thousand miles; have you searched through all the layers of rock and soil over the whole earth? Have you excavated all those places?

Devotee: No.

Śrīla Prabhupāda: Therefore our first charge against Darwin is this: He says there were no human beings millions of years ago. That is not a fact. We now see human beings existing along with all other species, and it should be concluded that this situation always existed. Human life has always been there. Darwin cannot say there was no human life.

Devotee: We don't see any dinosaurs existing.

Śrīla Prabhupāda: *You* do not see because you have no power to see. Your senses are very limited, so what you see or don't see cannot be authoritative. So many people – the majority of people – say, "I don't see God." Shall we accept, then, that there is no God? Are we crazy for being devotees of God?

Devotee: No, but dinosaurs—

Śrīla Prabhupāda: But simply by dinosaurs being missing you cannot make your case. What about all the other species?

Devotee: Many, many others are also extinct.

Śrīla Prabhupāda: Say I accept that many are extinct – because the evolutionary process means that as an earlier species gradually changes into a later species, the earlier vanishes, becomes extinct. But we see that many monkeys are still here. Man evolved from the simians, but simians have not disappeared. Monkeys are here, and men are here.

Devotee: But still I'm not convinced. If we make geological investigations all over the world, not just here and there, but in many parts of the world, and in every case we find the same thing—

Śrīla Prabhupāda: But I say you have not studied all over the world. Has Darwin studied all the continents on this planet? Has he gone down into the depths of the seas and there excavated all the layers of the earth? No. So his knowledge is imperfect. This is the relative world, and here everyone speaks with relative knowledge. Therefore we should accept knowledge from a person who is not within this relativity.

Devotee: Actually, Darwin hit upon his theory because of what he observed on his voyage in 1835 to the Galapagos Islands, off the coast of South America. He found there species that exist nowhere else.

Śrīla Prabhupāda: That means he has not seen all the species. He has not traveled all over the universe. He has seen one island, but he has not seen the whole creation. So how can he determine what species exist and don't exist? He has studied one part of this earth, but there are many millions of planets. He has not seen all of them; he has not excavated the depths of all the planets. So how can he conclude, "This is nature"?

He has not seen everything, nor is it possible for any human being to see everything.

Devotee: Let's just confine ourselves to this planet.

Śrīla Prabhupāda: No, why should we? Nature is not only on this planet.

Devotee: Because you said that on this planet there were complex forms of living beings millions and millions of years ago.

Śrīla Prabhupāda: We are not talking about this planet, but about anywhere. You are referring to nature. Nature is not limited or confined to this planet. You cannot say that. Nature, material nature, includes millions of universes, and in each and every universe there are millions of planets. If you have studied only this planet, your knowledge is insufficient.

Devotee: But you said before that millions of years ago on this planet there were horses, elephants, civilized men—

Śrīla Prabhupāda: Yes, yes.

Devotee: But from hundreds of different sources there is no evidence.

Śrīla Prabhupāda: I say they are existing now – men, horses, snakes, insects, trees. So why not millions of years ago?

Devotee: Because there is no evidence.

Śrīla Prabhupāda: That doesn't mean . . . ! You limit your study to one planet. That is not full knowledge.

Devotee: I just want to find out for the time being about—

Śrīla Prabhupāda: Why the time being? If you are not perfect in your knowledge, then why should I accept your theory? That is my point.

Devotee: Well, if you claim that millions of years ago there were complex forms of life on this planet—

Śrīla Prabhupāda: Whether on this planet or on another planet, that is not the point. The point is that all species exist and keep on existing by the arrangement of nature. We learn from the Vedic texts that there are 8,400,000 species established. They may be in your neighborhood or they may be in my neighborhood – the number and types are fixed. But if you simply study your neighborhood, it is not perfect knowledge. Evolution we admit. But your evolutionary theory is not perfect. Our theory of evolution is perfect. From the *Vedas* we know that there are 8,400,000 forms of bodies provided by nature, but the soul is the same in all, in spite of the different types of body. There is no change in the soul, and therefore the *Bhagavad-gītā* [5.18] says that one who is wise, a *paṇḍita,* does not see the species or the class; he sees oneness, equality. *Paṇḍitāḥ sama-darśinaḥ.* One who sees to the bottom sees the soul, and he does not find there any difference between all these species.

Devotee: So Darwin and other material scientists who have no information about the soul—

Śrīla Prabhupāda: They're missing the whole point.

Devotee: They say that all living things tend to evolve from lower to higher. In the history of the earth—

Śrīla Prabhupāda: That may be accepted. For example, in an apartment building there are different kinds of apartments: first-class apartments, second-class apartments, third-class apartments. According to your desire and qualification, as you are fit to pay the rent, you are allowed to move up to the better apartments. But the different apartments are already there. *They* are not evolving. The residents are evolving by moving to new apartments as they desire.

Devotee: As they desire.

Śrīla Prabhupāda: Yes. According to our mentality at the time of death, we get another "apartment," another body. But the "apartment" is already there, not that I'm creating the "apartment."

And the classes of "apartments" are fixed at 8,400,000. Just like the hotel-keeper: he has experience of his customers coming and wanting different kinds of facilities. So he has made all sorts of accommodations to oblige all kinds of customers. Similarly, this is God's creation. He knows how far a living entity can think, so He has made all these different species accordingly. When God thinks, "Come on, come here," nature obliges. *Prakṛteḥ kriyamāṇāni guṇaiḥ karmāṇi* [*Bhagavad-gītā* 3.27]: Nature is offering facility. God, Kṛṣṇa, is sitting in the heart of the living entity as Paramātmā, and He knows, "He wants this." So the Lord orders nature, "Give him this apartment," and nature obliges: "Yes, come on; here is your apartment." This is the real explanation.

Devotee: I understand and accept that. But I'm still puzzled as to why there is no geological evidence that in former times on this planet there were more complex forms.

Śrīla Prabhupāda: Why are you taking geological evidence as final? Is it final? Science is progressing. You cannot say it is final.
Devotee: But I have excavated all parts of the world, and every time—
Śrīla Prabhupāda: No. You have not excavated all parts of the world.
Devotee: Well, on seven continents.
Śrīla Prabhupāda: Seven continents is not the whole world. You say you have excavated the whole world, but we say no, not even an insignificant portion. So your knowledge is limited. Dr. Frog has examined his three-foot-wide well, and now he claims to know the ocean.

Experimental knowledge is always imperfect, because one experiments with imperfect senses. Therefore, scientific knowledge *must* be imperfect. Our source of knowledge is different. We do not depend on experimental knowledge.

Now you see no dinosaurs, nor have I seen all the 8,400,000 different forms of life. But my source of knowledge is different. You are an experimenter with imperfect senses. I have taken knowledge from the perfect person, who has seen everything, who knows everything. Therefore, my knowledge is perfect.

Say, for example, that I receive knowledge from my mother: "Here is your father." But you are trying to search out your father on your own. You don't go to your mother and ask; you just search and search. Therefore, no matter how much you search, your knowledge will always remain imperfect.
Devotee: And your knowledge says that millions of years ago there were higher forms of life on this planet.
Śrīla Prabhupāda: Oh, yes, because our Vedic information is that the first created being is the *most* intelligent, the most intellectual person within the universe – Lord Brahmā, the cosmic engineer. So how can we accept your theory that intellect develops by evolution? We have received our Vedic knowledge from Brahmā, who is so perfect.

Dr. Frog has studied his three-foot well, his little reservoir of water. The Atlantic Ocean is also a reservoir of water, but there is a vast difference. Dr. Frog cannot inform us about the Atlantic Ocean. But we take knowledge from the one who has made the Atlantic Ocean. So our knowledge is perfect.
Devotee: But wouldn't there be evidence in the earth, some remains?

Śrīla Prabhupāda: Our evidence is intelligence, not stones and bones. Our evidence is intelligence. We get Vedic information by disciplic succession from the most intelligent. It is coming down by *śruti,* hearing. Vyāsadeva heard from Nārada, Nārada heard from Brahmā – millions and millions of years ago. Millions and millions of our years pass, and it is not even one day for Brahmā. So millions and billions and trillions of years are not very astonishing to us, for that is not even one day of Brahmā. But Brahmā was born of Kṛṣṇa, and intelligent philosophy has been existing in our universe from the date of Brahmā's birth. Brahmā was first educated by God, and His knowledge has been passed down to us in the Vedic literature. So we get such intelligent information in the *Vedas.*

But those so-called scientists and philosophers who do not follow this system of descending knowledge, who do not accept knowledge thus received from higher authorities – they can't have any perfect knowledge, no matter what research work they carry out with their blunt senses. So whatever they say, we take it as imperfect.

Our method is different from theirs. They are searching after dead bones, and we are searching after living brains. This point should be stressed. They are dealing with dead bones and we are dealing with living brains. So which should be considered better?

Appendixes

The Author

His Divine Grace A.C. Bhaktivedanta Swami Prabhupāda appeared in this world in 1896 in Calcutta, India. He first met his spiritual master, Śrīla Bhaktisiddhānta Sarasvatī Gosvāmī, in Calcutta in 1922. Bhaktisiddhānta Sarasvatī, a prominent religious scholar and the founder of sixty-four Gauḍīya Maṭhas (Vedic institutes), liked this educated young man and convinced him to dedicate his life to teaching Vedic knowledge. Śrīla Prabhupāda became his student and, in 1933, his formally initiated disciple.

At their first meeting, in 1922, Śrīla Bhaktisiddhānta Sarasvatī requested Śrīla Prabhupāda to broadcast Vedic knowledge in English. In the years that followed, Śrīla Prabhupāda wrote a commentary on the *Bhagavad-gītā,* assisted the Gauḍīya Maṭha in its work, and, in 1944, started *Back to Godhead,* an English fortnightly magazine. Singlehandedly, Śrīla Prabhupāda edited it, typed the manuscripts, checked the galley proofs, and even distributed the individual copies. The magazine is now being continued by his disciples.

In 1950 Śrīla Prabhupāda retired from married life, adopting the *vānaprastha* (retired) order to devote more time to his studies and writing. He traveled to the holy city of Vṛndāvana, where he lived in humble circumstances in the historic temple of Rādhā-Dāmodara. There he engaged for several years in deep study and writing. He accepted the renounced order of life (*sannyāsa*) in 1959. At Rādhā-Dāmodara, Śrīla Prabhupāda began work on his life's masterpiece: a multivolume commentated translation of the eighteen-thousand-verse *Śrīmad-Bhāgavatam (Bhāgavata Purāṇa*). He also wrote *Easy Journey to Other Planets.*

After publishing three volumes of the *Bhāgavatam,* Śrīla Prabhupāda came to the United States, in September 1965, to fulfill the mission of his spiritual master. Subsequently, His Divine Grace wrote more than fifty volumes of authoritative commentated translations and summary studies of the philosophical and religious classics of India.

When he first arrived by freighter in New York City, Śrīla Prabhupāda was practically penniless. Only after almost a year of great difficulty did he establish the International Society for Krishna Consciousness, in July of 1966. Before he passed away on November 14, 1977, he had guided the Society and seen it grow to a worldwide confederation of more than one hundred *āśramas,* schools, temples, institutes, and farm communities.

In 1972 His Divine Grace introduced the Vedic system of primary and secondary education in the West by founding the *gurukula* school in Dallas, Texas. Since then his disciples have established similar schools throughout the United States and the rest of the world.

Śrīla Prabhupāda also inspired the construction of several large international cultural centers in India. At Śrīdhāma Māyāpur, in West Bengal, devotees are building a spiritual city centered on a magnificent temple – an ambitious project for which construction will extend over many years to come. In Vṛndāvana are the Kṛṣṇa-Balarāma Temple and International Guesthouse, *gurukula* school, and Śrīla Prabhupāda Memorial and Museum. There are also major temples and cultural centers in Mumbai, New Delhi, Ahmedabad, Siliguri, and Ujjain. Other centers are planned in many important locations on the Indian subcontinent.

Śrīla Prabhupāda's most significant contribution, however, is his books. Highly respected by scholars for their authority, depth, and clarity, they are used as textbooks in numerous college courses. His writings have been translated into over fifty languages. The Bhaktivedanta Book Trust, established in 1972 to publish the works of His Divine Grace, has thus become the world's largest publisher of books in the field of Indian religion and philosophy.

In just twelve years, despite his advanced age, Śrīla Prabhupāda circled the globe fourteen times on lecture tours that took him to six continents. In spite of such a vigorous schedule, Śrīla Prabhupāda continued to write prolifically. His writings constitute a veritable library of Vedic philosophy, religion, literature, and culture.

Guide to Sanskrit Pronunciation

The system of transliteration used in this book conforms to a system that scholars have accepted to indicate the pronunciation of each sound in the Sanskrit language.

The short vowel **a** is pronounced like the **u** in b**u**t, long **ā** like the **a** in f**a**r. Short **i** is pronounced as **i** in pin, long **ī** as in pique, short **u** as in p**u**ll, and long **ū** as in r**u**le. The vowel **ṛ** is pronounced like **ri** in **ri**m, **e** like the **ey** in th**ey**, **o** like the **o** in g**o**, **ai** like the **ai** in **ai**sle, and **au** like the **ow** in h**ow**. The *anusvara* (**ṁ**) is pronounced like the **n** in the French word *bo***n**, and *visarga* (**ḥ**) is pronounced as a final **h** sound. At the end of a couplet, **aḥ** is pronounced **aha**, and **iḥ** is pronounced **ihi**.

The guttural consonants – **k, kh, g, gh,** and **ṅ** – are pronounced from the throat in much the same manner as in English. **K** is pronounced as in **k**ite, **kh** as in Ec**kh**art, **g** as in **g**ive, **gh** as in di**g-h**ard and **ṅ** as in si**ng**.

The palatal consonants – **c, ch, j, jh,** and **ñ** – are pronounced with the tongue touching the firm ridge behind the teeth. **C** is pronounced as in **ch**air, **ch** as in staun**ch-h**eart, **j** as in **j**oy, **jh** as in he**dgeh**og, and **ñ** as in ca**n**yon.

The cerebral consonants – **ṭ, ṭh, ḍ, ḍh,** and **ṇ** – are pronounced with the tip of the tongue turned up and drawn back against the dome of the palate. **Ṭ** is pronounced as in **t**ub, **ṭh** as in ligh**t-h**eart, **ḍ** as in **d**ove, **ḍh** as in re**d-h**ot, and **ṇ** as in **n**ut.

The dental consonants – **t, th, d, dh,** and **n** – are pronounced in the same manner as the cerebrals, but with the forepart of the tongue against the teeth.

The labial consonants – **p, ph, b, bh,** and **m** – are pronounced with the lips. **P** is pronounced as in **p**ine, **ph** as in u**ph**ill, **b** as in **b**ird, **bh** as in ru**b-h**ard, and **m** as in **m**other.

The semivowels – **y, r, l,** and **v** – are pronounced as in **y**es, **r**un, **l**ight, and **v**ine respectively. The sibilants – **ś, ṣ,** and **s** – are pronounced, respectively, as in the German word **s***prechen* and the English words **sh**ine and **s**un. The letter **h** is pronounced as in **h**ome.

Centers of the International Society for Krishna Consciousness

Founder-*Ācārya:* His Divine Grace A.C. Bhaktivedanta Swami Prabhupāda

For further information on classes, programs, festivals, residential courses, and local meetings, please contact the center nearest you.

✦ *Temples with restaurants or dining.*

EUROPE

UNITED KINGDOM AND IRELAND

Belfast, Northern Ireland — 140 Upper Dunmurray Lane, Belfast BT17 OHE; Tel. +44-28-90620530; belfast@iskcon.org.uk; www.iskcon.org.uk/belfast

Cardiff, Wales — The Soul Centre, 116 Cowbridge Road East, Canton, Cardiff, CF11 9DX; Tel. +44-2920-390391; the.soul.centre@pamho.net; www.thesoulcentre.net

✦ **Dublin, Ireland** — 83 Middle Abbey Street, Dublin 1; Tel. +353-1-8729775; dublin@krishna.ie; www.krishna.ie; restaurant: www.govindas.ie

Lanarkshire, Scotland (Karuna Bhavan) — Bankhouse Road, Lesmahagow, Lanarkshire, ML11 0ES; Tel. +44-1555-894790; Fax +44-1555-894526; karunabhavan@aol.com; www.iskcon.org.uk/scotland

Leicester, England — 21 Thoresby Street, North Evington, Leicester LE5 4GU; Tel. +44-116-2762587; leicester@iskcon.org.uk; www.iskconleicester.org

✦ **London, England** (city) — 10 Soho Street, London W1D 3DL; Tel. +44-20-74373662; shop: 72870269; Govinda's Restaurant: 74374928; Fax +44-20-74391127; london@pamho.net; www.iskcon-london.org

✦ **London, England** (country) — Bhaktivedanta Manor, Dharam Marg, Hilfield Lane, Aldenham, near Watford, Herts WD25 8EZ; Tel. +44-1923-857244; Fax +44-1923-852896; bhaktivedanta.manor@pamho.net; for accommodations: accommodations.requests@pamho.net; www.krishnatemple.com

London, England (south) — 42 Enmore Road, South Norwood, London SE25 5NG; Tel. +44-20-86564296; www.iskcon.org.uk/snorwood

Manchester, England — 20 Mayfield Road, Whalley Range, Manchester M16 8FT; Tel. +44-161-2264416; manchester@iskcon.org.uk; www.iskcon.org.uk/manchester

Newcastle, England — 304 Westgate Road, Newcastle-upon-Tyne, Tyne & Wear NE4 6AR; Tel. +44-191-2721911; newcastle@iskcon.org.uk; www.iskcon.org.uk/newcastle

✦ **Swansea, Wales** — 8 Craddock Street, Swansea SA1 3EN; Tel. +44-1792-468469; iskcon.swansea@pamho.net; restaurant: govindas.swansea@pamho.net; www.iskconwales.org

RURAL COMMUNITIES

London, England — (contact Bhaktivedanta Manor)

Upper Lough Erne, Northern Ireland (Govindadwipa) — Inisrath Island, Derrylin, Co. Fermanagh BT92 9GN; Tel. +44-28-67721512; bbt@krishnaisland.com; www.krishnaisland.com

ADDITIONAL RESTAURANTS

Dublin, Ireland — Govinda's, 4 Aungier Street, Dublin 2; Tel. +353-1-4750309; info@govindas.ie; www.govindas.ie

Dublin, Ireland — Govinda's, 18 Merrion Row, Dublin 2; Tel. +353-1-6615095; info@govindas.ie; www.govindas.ie

Hare Krishna meetings are held regularly in more than 40 centers in the UK and Ireland. For more information, contact the temple nearest you or go to www.iskcon.org.uk.

OTHER COUNTRIES

Abentheuer, Germany — Böckingstrasse 4a, 55767 Abentheuer; Tel. +49-6782-2214; Fax +49-6782-980437; www.goloka-dhama.de

Amsterdam, Netherlands — Van Hilligaertstraat 17, Amsterdam 1072 JX; Tel. +31-20-6751404; Fax +31-20-6751405; amsterdam@pamho.net

Barcelona, Spain — Plaza Reial 12, Entlo 2, 08002 Barcelona; Tel. +34-93-3025194; emplobcn@hotmail.com

Bergamo, Italy — Villaggio Hare Krishna (da Medolago strada per Terno d'Isola), 24040 Chignolo d'Isola (BG); Tel. +39-035-4940706

Berlin, Germany — Kastanienallee 3, 10435 Berlin Pankow, Prenzlauer Berg; Tel. +49-30-44357296; Fax +49-30-48494074; harekrishna-berlin@pamho.net; www.krsna-is-cool.de

Budapest, Hungary — Lehel u. 15-17, 1039 Budapest; Tel. +36-1-3910435; Fax +36-1-2423233; budapest@pamho.net; www.haribol.hu

Copenhagen, Denmark — Skjulhøj allé 44, 2720 Vanløse; Tel. +45-48-286446; Fax +45-48-287331; iskcon.denmark@pamho.net

✦ **Durbuy, Belgium** (Radhadesh) — Chateau de Petite Somme, 6940 Septon-Durbuy; Tel. +32-86-322926; radhadesh@pamho.net; www.radhadesh.com

Helsinki, Finland — Ruoholahdenkatu 24 D (III krs) 00180 Helsinki; Tel. +358-9-6949879; Fax +358-9-6949837; harekrishna@harekrishna.fi; www. harekrishna.fi

Kaunas, Lithuania — 37, Savanoriu pr., 3000 Kaunas; Tel. +370-7-222574; Fax +370-7-706642

Kokosovce, Slovak Republic — Abranovce 60, 08252 Kokosovce; Tel. +421-51-7798482

✦ **Lisbon, Portugal** — Rua Dona Estefânia, 91 r/c 1000 Lisboa; Tel./ Fax +351-1-3140314; iskcon.lisbon@pamho.net

Ljubljana, Slovenia — Zibertova 27, 1000 Ljubljana; Tel. +386-1-4312319; Fax +386-61-310815; ananta.rns@pamho.net

Málaga, Spain — Ctra. Alora 3, Int., 29140 Churriana; Tel. +34-95-2621038; malaga@pamho.net

Paris, France — 35 Rue Docteur Jean Vaquier, 93160 Noisy le Grand; Tel./ Fax +33-1-4303 0951; paramgati.swami@pamho.net

Prague, Czech Republic — Jilova 290, Prague 5-Zlicin 15521; Tel. +42-2-57950391; info@vedavision.cz

✦ **Riga, Latvia** — 56, K. Baron St., 1011 Riga; Tel. +371-2-272490; Fax +371-2-274120

✦ **Rome**, Italy— Govinda Centro Hare Krsna, via Santa Maria del Pianto 16, 00186 Roma; Tel. +39-06-68891540; govinda.roma@harekrsna.it

Sofia, Bulgaria — 119 Kliment Ohridski Street, kv. Malinova Dolina; Tel. +359-2-9616050; oks_sofia@abv.bg

✦ **Stockholm, Sweden** (city)— Fridhemsgatan 22, 11240 Stockholm; Tel. +46-8-6549002; Fax +46-8-6508813; tapasa.rns@pamho.net

Stockholm, Sweden (country) — Radha-Krishna Temple, Korsnäs Gård, 14792 Grödinge; Tel. +46-8-53029800; Fax +46-8-53025062; info@pamho.net; www.krishna.se

Timisoara, Romania — Porumbescu 92, 1900 Timisoara; Tel./ Fax +40-56-154776

Warsaw, Poland — Mysiadlo k. Warszawy, 05-500 Piaseczno, ul. Zakret 11; Tel. +48-22-7507797; Fax +48-22-7508249; kryszna@post.pl

Zagreb, Croatia — Centar Za Vedske Studije, II Bizet 36, 10000 Zagreb (mail: P.O. Box 68, 10001); Tel./ Fax +385-1-3772643; ripuha@pamho.net

Zürich, Switzerland — Bergstrasse 54, 8030 Zürich; Tel. +41-1-2623388; Fax +41-1-2623114; kgs@pamho.net; www.krishna.ch

RURAL COMMUNITIES

Brihuega, Spain (New Vraja Mandala) — (Santa Clara) 19411 Brihuega; Tel. +34-949-280436

✦ **Florence, Italy** (Villa Vrindavan) — via Scopeti 108, 50026 San Casciano in Val di Pesa (FI); Tel. +39-055-820054; Fax +39-055-828470; isvaripriya@libero.it

Jandelsbrunn, Germany (Simhachalam) — Zielberg 20, 94118 Jandelsbrunn; Tel. +49-8583-316; Fax +49-8583-1671; simhachalam@pamho.net

Järna, Sweden — Almviks Gård, 15395 Järna; Tel. +46-8-55152050; Fax +46-8-55152060; almviks.gard@pamho.net

Krisna-völgy, Hungary (New Vraja-dhama) — Fö út. 38., 8699 Somogyvámos; Tel./ Fax +36-85-340185; krisna-volgy@pamho.net; www.krisna-volgy.hu

Postupice, Czech Republic — Krišnuv Dvur, 25701 Postupice; Tel. +420-317-796008

RESTAURANTS

Barcelona, Spain — Restaurante Govinda, Plaza de la Villa de Madrid 4-5, 08002 Barcelona; Tel. +34-93-3187729
Budapest, Hungary — Govinda Restaurant, Vigyázó Ferenc utca 4., 1051 Budapest; Tel. +36-1-2691625; govinda@invitel.hu
Copenhagen, Denmark — Govinda's, Nørre Farimagsgade 82, DK-1364 Kbh K; Tel. +45-33337444
Milan, Italy — Govinda's, via Valpetrosa 5, 20123 Milano; Tel. +39-02-862417
Prague, Czech Republic — Govinda's, Soukenicka 27, 11000 Prague-1; Tel. +420-2-24816631; info@vedavision.cz
Tallinn, Estonia — Damodara, Lauteri St. 1, 10114 Tallinn; Tel. +372-6442650
Zürich, Switzerland — Govinda's Veda-Kultur, Preyergasse 16, 8001 Zürich; Tel./ Fax +41-1-2518859; info@govinda-shop.ch

ASIA

Colombo, Sri Lanka — 188 New Chetty St., Colombo 13; Tel. +94 (1) 433325; iskcon@slt.lk
Jakarta, Indonesia — Yayasan Radha-Govinda, P.O. Box 2694, Jakarta Pusat 10001; Tel. +62 (21) 489 9646; matsyads@bogor.wasantara.net.id
✦ **Mayapur, WB, India** — ISKCON, Shree Mayapur Chandrodaya Mandir, Shree Mayapur Dham, Dist. Nadia, 741 313; Tel. +91 (3472) 245239, 245240, or 245233; Fax +91 (3472) 245238; mayapur.chandrodaya@pamho.net
✦ **New Delhi, UP, India** — Hare Krishna Hill, Sant Nagar Main Road, East of Kailash, 110 065; Tel. +91(11) 2623 5133, 4, 5, 6, 7; Fax +91 (11) 2621 5421; delhi@pamho.net, Guesthouse: neel.sunder@pamho.net
✦ **Vrindavan, UP, India** — Krishna-Balaram Mandir, Bhaktivedanta Swami Marg, Raman Reti, Mathura Dist., 281 124; Tel. +91 (565) 254 0021; Fax +91 (565) 254 0053; vrindavan@pamho.net; (Guesthouse:) Tel. +91 (565) 254 0022; ramamani@sancharnet.in

RURAL COMMUNITIES

Puri, Orissa, India — ISKCON, Bhaktivedanta Asram, Sipasirubuli, 752 001; Tel. +91 (6752) 230494
Vrindavan, UP, India — Vrinda Kund, Nandagaon, Dist. Mathura, UP; vrinda@aol.com

RESTAURANT

Kolkata, WB, India — Govinda's, ISKCON House, 22 Gurusaday Road, 700019; Tel. (33) 24756922, 24749009

NORTH AMERICA

Boston, Massachusetts, USA — 72 Commonwealth Ave.,02116; Tel. +1 (617) 247-8611
✦ **Los Angeles, California, USA** — 3764 Watseka Ave., 90034; Tel. +1 (310) 836-2676; Fax +1 (310) 839-2715; nirantara@juno.com; restaurant: arcita@webcom.com
Montreal, Quebec, Canada — 1626 Pie IX Boulevard, H1V 2C5; Tel./ Fax +1 (514) 521-1301; iskconmontreal@bellnet.ca
✦ **New York, New York, USA** — 305 Schermerhorn St., Brooklyn 11217; Tel. +1 (718) 855-6714; Fax +1 (718) 875-6127; ramabhadra@aol.com
✦ **Toronto, Ontario, Canada** — 243 Avenue Road, M5R 2J6; Tel. +1 (416) 922-5415; Fax +1 (416) 922-1021; toronto@iskcon.net

RURAL COMMUNITIES

Alachua, Florida, USA (New Raman Reti) — 17306 N.W., 112th Blvd., 32615 (mail: P.O. Box 819, 32616); Tel. +1 (386) 462-2017; Fax +1 (386) 462-3468; alachuatemple@alltel.net
✦ **Moundsville, West Virginia, USA** (New Vrindaban) — R.D. No. 1, Box 319, Hare Krishna Ridge, 26041; Tel. +1 (304) 843-1600; Guest House, +1 (304) 854-5905; Fax +1 (304) 854-0023; mail@newvrindaban.com

RESTAURANTS

Seattle, Washington, USA — My Sweet Lord, 5521 University Way, 98105; Tel. +1 (425) 643-4664
Tallahassee, Florida — Higher Taste, 411 St. Francis St., 32301; Tel. (850) 894-4296

AUSTRALIA

Brisbane — 95 Bank Road, Graceville (mail: P.O. Box 83, Indooroopilly), QLD 4068; Tel. +61-7-33795455; Fax +61-7-33795880; brisbane@pamho.net
Melbourne — 197 Danks Street (mail: P.O. Box 125), Albert Park , VIC 3206; Tel. +61-3-96995122; Fax +61-3-96904093; melbourne@pamho.net
Sydney — 180 Falcon Street, North Sydney, NSW 2060 (mail: P.O. Box 459, Cammeray, NSW 2062); Tel. +61-2-99594558; Fax +61-2-99571893; info@iskcon.com.au

RESTAURANTS

Brisbane — Govinda's, 99 Elizabeth Street, 1st floor, QLD 4000; Tel. +61 7 32100255
Perth — Hare Krishna Food for Life, 200 William Street, Northbridge, WA 6003; Tel. +61 8 92271684; perth@pamho.net

AFRICA

✦ **Durban, South Africa** — 50 Bhaktivedanta Swami Circle, Unit 5 (mail: P.O. Box 56003), Chatsworth, 4030; Tel. +27 (31) 403 3328; Fax +27 (31) 403 4429; iskcon.durban@pamho.net
Nairobi, Kenya — Muhuroni Close, off West Nagara Road (mail: P.O. Box 28946); Tel. +254 (2) 744365; Fax +254 (2) 740957
✦ **Phoenix, Mauritius** — Hare Krishna Land, Pont Fer (mail: P. O. Box 108, Quartre Bornes); Tel. +230 696 5804; Fax +230 696 8576; iskcon.hkl@intnet.mu

RURAL COMMUNITIES

Mauritus (ISKCON Vedic Farm) — Hare Krishna Road, Vrindaban; Tel. +230 418 3185 or 418 3955
Uganda (Hare Krishna Farm) — Seeta Town, Kampala

CIS

Ekaterinburg, Russia — 23, Murzinskaya st., 620033, Tel. +7 (950) 208 70 15, +7 (343) 26 93 108
Kiev, Ukraine — 21V, Dmitrievskaya ap.13, 01054; Tel. +380 (44) 4844042; Tel./ Fax +380 (44) 4840934
Krasnodar, Russia — 418, Stepnaya st., selo Elizavetinskoye, Krsnodarski krai; Tel. +7 (861) 229 16 94
Minsk, Belarus — 11, Pavlova st., 220053; Tel. +375 (17) 288 06 29 or +375 (17) 233 14 94
Perm, Russia — 76, Chernyakhovskogo st., 614104; Tel. +7 (342) 275 50 02; ffl@pi.ccl.ru
Rostov-Na-Donu, Russia — 26, Belorusskaya st., 346888; Tel. +7 (863) 272 30 29
Samara, Russia — 122, Aeroportovskoye sh.; Tel. +7 (846) 931 37 45
Sochi, Russia — 64 Leselidze st., Nizhnyaya Plastunka; Tel. +7 9189173760
Tashkent, Uzbekistan — 54, Ul. Cervyakova, 700005

RURAL COMMUNITY

Kurjinovo, Russia — 8, Shosseinaya st., pos. Ershovo, Urupski region, Karachayevo-Cherkessia

LATIN AMERICA

Buenos Aires, Argentina — Centro Bhaktivedanta, Andonaegui 2054, Villa Urquiza, CP 1431; Tel. +54 (1) 5234232; Fax +54 (1) 5238085; iskcon-ba@gopalnet.com
✦ **Lima, Peru** — Pasaje Solea 101, Santa Maria-Chosica; Tel. +51 (511) 360 3381
Mexico City, Mexico — Tiburcio Montiel 45, Colonia San Miguel, Chapultepec D.F., 11850; Tel. +52 (55) 273 1953
Rio de Janeiro, RJ, Brazil — Rua Vilhena de Morais, 309, Barra da Tijuca, 22793-140; Tel. +55 (21) 2491 1887; sergio.carvalho@pobox.com

RESTAURANTS

Buenos Aires, Argentina — Jagannath Prasadam, Triunvirato 4266 (1431); Tel. +54 (1) 5213396
Rio de Janeiro, RJ, Brazil — Sabor Saber, Rua das Laranjeiras, 430-A, Sobreloja, Laranjeiras, 22240-006; Tel. +55 (21) 9169 3192
Sao Paulo, SP, Brazil — Gopala Prasada, Rua Antonio Carlos, 413, 01309-011; Tel. +55 (11) 3283 3867; gopalaprasada@bol.com.br